About Island Press

Since 1984, the nonprofit Island Press has been stimulating, shaping, and communicating the ideas that are essential for solving environmental problems worldwide. With more than 800 titles in print and some 40 new releases each year, we are the nation's leading publisher on environmental issues. We identify innovative thinkers and emerging trends in the environmental field. We work with world-renowned experts and authors to develop cross-disciplinary solutions to environmental challenges.

Island Press designs and implements coordinated book publication campaigns in order to communicate our critical messages in print, in person, and online using the latest technologies, programs, and the media. Our goal: to reach targeted audiences—scientists, policymakers, environmental advocates, the media, and concerned citizens—who can and will take action to protect the plants and animals that enrich our world, the ecosystems we need to survive, the water we drink, and the air we breathe.

Island Press gratefully acknowledges the support of its work by the Agua Fund, Inc., Annenberg Foundation, The Christensen Fund, The Nathan Cummings Foundation, The Geraldine R. Dodge Foundation, Doris Duke Charitable Foundation, The Educational Foundation of America, Betsy and Jesse Fink Foundation, The William and Flora Hewlett Foundation, The Kendeda Fund, The Andrew W. Mellon Foundation, The Curtis and Edith Munson Foundation, Oak Foundation, The Overbrook Foundation, the David and Lucile Packard Foundation, The Summit Fund of Washington, Trust for Architectural Easements, Wallace Global Fund, The Winslow Foundation, and other generous donors.

The opinions expressed in this book are those of the author(s) and do not necessarily reflect the views of our donors.

BUILDING AN EMERALD CITY

LUCIA ATHENS

BUILDING AN

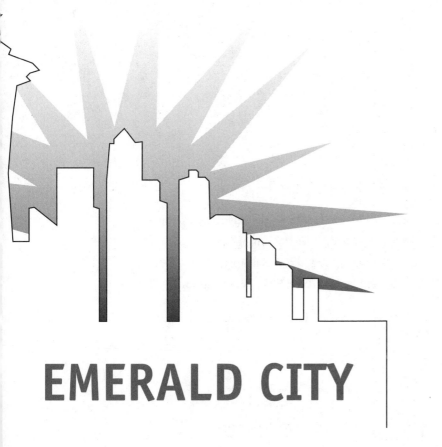

EMERALD CITY

A Guide to Creating

Green Building

Policies and Programs

Lucia Athens

ISLANDPRESS
WASHINGTON | COVELO | LONDON

Library of Congress Cataloging-in-Publication Data

Athens, Lucia, 1960–
 Building an emerald city : a guide to creating green building policies
and programs / Lucia Athens.
    p. cm.
 Includes bibliographical references and index.
 ISBN-13: 978-1-59726-583-6 (cloth : alk. paper)
 ISBN-10: 1-59726-583-7 (cloth : alk. paper)
 ISBN-13: 978-1-59726-584-3 (pbk. : alk. paper)
 ISBN-10: 1-59726-584-5 (pbk. : alk. paper)
 1. Urban ecology (Sociology)-United States. 2. City planning-Envi-
ronmental aspects-United States. 3. Sustainable buildings-United
States. I. Title.
 HT243.U6A84 2009 2010
 307.1'2160973—dc22

                                                    2009010657

Printed on recycled, acid-free paper ♽

Design by Joan Wolbier

Manufactured in the United States of America

10 9 8 7 6 5 4 3 2 1

*This book is dedicated to my parents:
to my father, Tony, who taught me
to fight to protect our urban quality of life,
and to my mother, Carol, who taught me
to love all living things.
Together, they instilled a deep regard
for this amazing planet we live on
and for all of the species who call it home.*

*It is also dedicated to the memories of
Greg Franta and Gail Lindsay, FAIA,
two amazing champions and pioneers of
green building who have recently passed on.
Their enthusiasm and inspiration are sorely missed.*

CONTENTS

FOREWORD

Pliny Fisk III and Gail Vittori

One of the most gratifying experiences in life is to witness the success of a dream: the green building movement taking off and making a tangible difference. But to see close friends and associates—with whom you have shared your deepest thoughts over many years—extending original concepts and becoming leaders in their own right is the best dream of all. To say that Lucia is one of our favorite people on a personal level is an understatement; all who know her think first of the person she is and then of what she is actually doing in the world. Even those who think they know both Lucia the person and her work will still be quite astonished, as we are, with this book. We could not have hoped for anything better.

Our Center for Maximum Building Potential has always benefited from a close relationship with young people and students. Our almost constant connection with the academic community since the founding of the center in 1975 has enabled this, as has our intern program. Lucia was one of those effervescent people who became rooted in the center's early years as intellectual partner, board member, and generous volunteer. Our board of directors and advisory board members were asked to join not because they had money and connections but because they had sparkle in their eyes—an urgency that one could tell was going to make things happen.

It is easy to take for granted green building programs today—indeed, they have proliferated at a pace and scale that we never thought possible just twenty short years ago. It was, in fact, in 1989 that we introduced the original concept of what is now the Austin Green Building Program to City of Austin staffers Michael Myers and Doug Seiter. We were stumbling onto a concept and movement that hadn't even been birthed yet, though the idea of recognizing that buildings should be measured based on multiple flows—for example, energy, water, waste, and materials—had already become intrinsic to the way we approached projects at the center. The "simple" idea of extending Austin's successful energy conservation program to these other indicators was the breakthrough. None of us at that time had the benefit of a facile vocabulary, best practices, legal requirements, magazines, case studies, or a sense of what we were creating. But that is the gift of creation— the path of discovery that is equally exhilarating and tentative as the exploration ensues. It is also a given that the act of creation—and the creative process—is rife with discomfort and isolation and requires an internal resolve to keep forging ahead despite the frequent challenges and questions, such as "What are you talking about?"

Indeed, the road is often rocky during times of change. We remember when Lucia was donating her time, entering competitions, and going through her thesis period at a school that, at the time, did not quite understand what she was doing in this emerging area of design. Lucia always came through brilliantly.

We remember our work together designing and constructing a large Texas ranch facility for an international gathering of indigenous elders, with virtually no time or money to pull it off. But pull it off we did, resulting in a teaching lodge sporting design details handcrafted by our team and a powerful sense of connectedness to the land it inhabited. We collaborated on the American Institute of Architects' first green poster competition, for which we were all going delightfully crazy about storytelling using icon sequences and about their future as artistic electronic bridges that became infectious in beauty and meaning. Then there was the landscape around the first state-funded green building—the Max's Pot's offices. It wasn't just any landscape but a landscape that represented six of the ten ecoregions of Texas because, after all, Austin is positioned at the crossroads and we need to authentically represent where we are in the world.

We didn't need to convince Lucia of the value of these endeavors. Instead, we experienced the wonderful serendipity of convincing each other—of course, let's do it! It didn't matter if there were no precedents or if we couldn't precisely define the deliverable, budget, or schedule. These early brain-nourishing opportunities set the spirit of what we are all doing today: an ongoing love of the maximum potential view of one's critical role in getting things going, getting them used, working, succeeding in a world that is in such need—and always being ready to have others come along to "kick the tires." After all, learning and feedback become intrinsic to the process. Who is it who has all the answers?

We will never forget following a wedding in Seattle hearing Lucia slyly say amid many big, personal happenings all around her, "You know, I think it would be a good idea that, before you go to the airport, you visit our city offices for a few minutes just to introduce yourself and let them know what you are doing—I think there might be some interest." Within an hour—after a scant, thirty-minute presentation to key City of Seattle staff, including, notably, Tony Gale, then city architect—we were stunned by the immediate sense of connection and buy-in as we presented ideas and concepts that we had never presented even in our own emerald city of Austin, Texas. This near-total synergy with City of Seattle officials yielded the makings of a contract before we got back on the transit to the airport.

It is moments like these when we realize Lucia's intrinsic, trusting, and honest leadership, and her ability to consistently surround herself with the people it takes to raise the bar with daring and unwavering tenacity.

So here we are, almost thirty years after those first, almost spiritual encounters from student times. We realize that Lucia has become not only a contributor but a force with unique experience like few others in her position in the world. She is a new kind of leader in a new kind of time—a time when we humbly realize that people are our most precious resource and when we look to those who "get" how the natural world is a part of every and any endeavor we pursue.

We share these stories because we love to share them and, in this case, because we believe this rich tapestry of experiences is an essential part of shaping Lucia's vision and resolve to forge the path of tangible accomplishments that this book so clearly shares. We hope others who read this are able to expand their worldview by stretching and challenging assumptions and conventions as Lucia has.

Steven Spielberg says, "I dream for a living." This quote is the inspirational coda that Lucia chooses to close her e-mail messages. It could just as easily be substituted with one of our favorite quotes from Goethe: "Whatever you can do, or dream you can, begin it. Boldness has genius, power, and magic in it."

As we approach the end of the first decade of the twenty-first century, the majority of the global community lives in cities. The U.S. Green Building Council has positioned "Sustainable Cities and Communities" as the first goal of its 2009–2013 Strategic Plan. The Clinton Climate Initiative is focusing on dramatic resets of forty of the world's most strategically positioned cities relative to reversing climate change. Providing an overview and nuts-and-bolts guidance of how cities can set the pace for putting this planet on a sustainable path is powerful and necessary. Doing it in a way that brilliantly embraces the ethos of the landscape—nature's *living* pattern book—extends this thinking to create *bureaucracies with a mission*, grounded in nature, in systems, in patterns, and in the collective human experience. As a landscape architect, Lucia is uniquely and intimately suited to do this work. This passionate quest that "dreams" of civic service setting the collective rhythms of supporting the global public good is exactly right and exactly needed at this time. It is, indeed, the imperative of our time.

Pliny Fisk III, *Co-Director*, Center for Maximum Potential Building Systems. *Signature Faculty*, Texas A&M University, Architecture, Landscape Architecture

and

Gail Vittori, *Co-Director*, Center for Maximum Potential Building Systems. *Chair*, U.S. Green-Building Council Board of Directors

He not busy being born is busy dying.
—BOB DYLAN

When the forms of an old culture are dying,
the new culture is created by a few people
who are not afraid to be insecure.
—RUDOLF BAHRO

The best way to subvert the dominant paradigm
is to have more fun than they are,
and make sure they know it.
—DAVID EISENBERG

Setting the Stage

During the ten years I served as manager of Seattle's City Green Building program, I received countless inquiries via telephone and e-mail. The questions were usually the same. How did you do it? How did you create the first LEED™ public policy and, along with it, one of the largest LEED public capital project portfolios in the world?[1] What did you learn, and what would you do differently if you had the opportunity to do it again? This book is an attempt to answer those questions.

I was inspired to write this book by the many creative and talented people who are striving to make green building happen in their particular corner of the planet. I have attempted to share what I have learned from my own experiences as well as what I am continuing to learn from other green building programs, including some examples from other leading green building cities. I have also left out many stories, as this is not intended to be a comprehensive review of public green building. I have primarily shared personal insights and lessons gleaned from my own experiences as well as selected stories from others' experiences.

My own experiences include my work with the City of Austin's Green Building Program, the first such program in the nation. Austin's initiative was the brainchild of Pliny Fisk III and Gail Vittori, who thought that some of the green building vision represented by their nonprofit work could be furthered more broadly if taken on by government leaders. Not only did the idea catch on in Austin, but it spawned a movement that has captured the imagination of tens of thousands of people in the building industry.

Austin's program started out with a focus on residential builders. I joined the program in 1991 as a research intern doing my postgraduate work with the University of Texas at Austin. I gravitated toward Pliny and Gail's nonprofit Center for Maximum Potential Building Systems for its hands-on approach and integrative approach to problem solving that includes regional and systemic thinking (see figure P.1). Laurence Doxsey and Doug Seiter led the City of Austin's Green Building Program development, and together we crafted Austin's *Green Building Sourcebook*, still published today in an updated version. The Austin program won a United Nations award at the Rio Earth Summit in 1992. It was becoming apparent that we were onto something important. Austin's environmentally progressive community latched on to the city's Green Building Program in a big way. Over time, the program evolved to include a focus on commercial buildings and city-funded public construction projects.

FIGURE P.1 Center for Maximum Potential Building Systems, Austin, Texas
This nonprofit center headquarters is a prototype for regionally appropriate design.
Credit: Photo courtesy of Pliny Fisk

THE CONTEXT FOR MY STORY

Many local government programs of all shapes and sizes, from cities large and small, now exist in all areas of North America. Each has its own story. Many have been enabled by some of the early pioneers in green building and are now part of a significant trend. The U.S. Green Building Council's Web site lists twelve federal, twelve state/provincial, and twenty-six local government green building programs. Each locale has its own geographic, cultural, economic, and political conditions that influence the timing and flavor of its own green building program. The specifics of such conditions are certainly not prerequisites for a program to succeed, as evidenced by the wide variety of programs that have evolved in various communities and municipalities. Why was Seattle an early leader in green building? Unique conditions within Seattle may have helped it take on its pioneering role in green building. These are mentioned here only to provide human interest to this story.

Seattle is characterized by its unique ecological splendor and an entrepreneurial, pioneering spirit. Water and mountains form the backdrop for daily life. The city stretches along the inland saltwater bay of Puget Sound, separated from the Pacific Ocean by two peninsulas. To the southeast, Mount Rainier rises up as the city's spiritual symbol, a perpetually snow-capped, extinct volcano surrounded by old-growth forest. Native salmon and local populations of Orca whales are much-loved animal symbols of the region. Seattle is one of only a few major urban areas with an endangered species (salmon) migratory habitat running directly through the city. When asked in one survey what makes the

Northwest different from the rest of the country, Seattle residents gave "the land" and "the environment" as the top answers, and 40 percent of those surveyed agreed that the Northwest is an important part of who they are. About 60 percent of people in the Northwest say they wouldn't move if offered a better-paying job elsewhere.[2]

Seattle has a reputation for inventiveness and is an economic and innovations gateway for such companies as Boeing, Microsoft, Starbucks, REI, and Amazon.com, to name only a few. But compared to much of the rest of the United States, Seattle is still a child in terms of its maturity as a European settlement. It was just over one hundred and fifty years ago, in 1851, that the first white settlers arrived at Alki Point in West Seattle. Westward expansion was brought to a halt by the Pacific Ocean, so the energy and drive that brought the early settlers to this place remain here and draw others with a pioneering spirit to settle here today.

It wasn't so long ago that Seattle was still a rough-and-tumble town, full of saloons and trading posts serving fortune seekers and followers of the Klondike gold rush. Ecological wealth in the form of timber forests has made enormous fortunes for the likes of Weyerhaeuser, but the visible legacy that clear-cutting leaves behind has also made northwesterners very aware of the environmental havoc that unsustainable practices can wreak.

Seattle's unique history has been one of change and reinvention. The infamous Seattle Fire of 1889 was the result of a hot glue pot overturned in a woodworker's shop. This catastrophic event destroyed most of the city's downtown. After the fire, a massive city rebuilding effort occurred, much of which can be seen today in the historic buildings of the Pioneer Square neighborhood. That rebuilding comprised twenty-five city blocks, 120 acres, and 465 buildings.[3]

A POLICY ADOPTION TALE

So how did Seattle adopt the first LEED-based green building policy? I started work in Seattle's government sector feeling very strongly that Seattle should be "walking the talk" of green building before it focused on trying to change the private sector. If we weren't doing it ourselves, how could we ask others to? Government must lead by example. Green building program development should first focus on an organization's own building assets, whether in new construction or in upgrades to existing buildings. Adoption by government for its own building projects sends a clear signal of commitment. If public authorities mandate or encourage change by others but do not take similar steps themselves, they will not be taken seriously and, at the very least, will be a prime target for criticism. Their role as a client for architectural design and construction services will eventually create living green building models and foster a building industry that has gained experience in an emerging field.

Although not prompted by a disaster this time, another history-making rebuilding effort was set to begin in 1998. The City of Seattle was poised to undertake the largest public building program since that great fire, which had occurred just a hundred years earlier. This time, the redevelopment was less vast in overall scale but no less vast in its ability to reshape the city. The sheer scale of this construction program stirred excitement among elected officials and capital projects staff, an excitement that helped enable the creation of a visionary green building policy. On the one hand, this was a major opportunity to make a mark on the city. On the other hand, there was no guarantee that any of these facilities would be built according to a green building standard that would ensure that the long-term legacy would be any better than the worst buildings allowed by code.

Soon after I started my employment with the City, I obtained a document called the "Environmental Management Program" from our Office of Sustainability and Environment. It contained policies that guide city operations in areas ranging from how much paper we used to what kinds of vehicles were in our fleet. The table of contents told me I'd find the City's sustainable building policy. I eagerly turned to the page but was dismayed to find the page was blank except for the words "to be added." This was one of those moments that appear pivotal only in the rearview mirror. What seemed at first blush to be a glaring omission turned out to be a well-timed opportunity to shape the future of green building in Seattle.

I picked up the phone and called a few people at the City whose expertise was well known. They included Kim Drury from the Office of Sustainability and Environment, Michael Aoki-Kramer from our building permitting department, and Barbara Erwine and Peter Hurley, who worked for our electric utility. I knew I would need help from a stakeholder group that represented multiple departments. One missing piece at first was the department that actually managed most of the city's own capital construction. Before long, however, we had the city architect, Tony Gale, on the team. The group had expertise in energy efficiency, lighting design, landscape design, code and policy development, sustainability, and city politics. This self-organized, cross-departmental staff team, dubbed the "green building team," immediately set to work to draft a policy.

It was 1999. The idea of green building in mainstream architecture was still relatively new. With the clear mandate that we needed a policy, we next needed to define green building and set the bar for just what shade of green our policy needed to be. We would need to be able to tie the policy to something we could measure, but we were within a large bureaucracy, where figuring things out could be slow. We had the expertise to cover most of the bases, but not a lot of time to research and develop standards. More than forty major capital projects were already in planning, and we knew that if we took too long to develop our policy, the opportunity to affect these projects would be lost. You could say we were in a hurry. After just a few weeks of meetings, the perfect answer landed right in our laps as the green building stars began to align. A new tool that no one had ever heard of before arrived in my mailbox. It was called LEED Pilot 1.0, and it was just what we needed. Of course, we wanted to know more about where it came from and who was behind it.

A few years previously, in 1993, a few visionary people, led by David Gottfried and Mike Italiano, got together to form a new organization called the U.S. Green Building Council (USGBC). They had previously been involved in the American Institute of Architects Committee on the Environment (COTE), but one of their primary goals was to create a more cross-disciplinary dialogue about what green building should be and to rigorously lead the charge. One of their early projects was creating the LEED tool, in the hope that such a tool might measure different levels of building green and might eventually transform the building industry.

Our Seattle green building team concluded that LEED was the work product of an impressive group of national experts from a broad range of fields. Since it was developed by USGBC, a national, industry-based member organization, it had certain credibility. Using a national standard would help us measure how we were doing with green building compared to other jurisdictions and to other parts of the nation, assuming that others started using the tool as well. We quickly reached a unanimous decision to adopt LEED as our policy benchmark.

LEED offered measurable achievement based on a point system, with clear requirements and benchmarking targets within four levels of performance. It provided a framework to utilize for both the design process and the construction process. It provided not only a referenced standard but also independent third-party verification, following the trend in many other sustainability endeavors, such as organic foods. This meant an independent third party would be responsible for verifying performance. With our limited staff resources, this was good news. Our team could focus more on political support, organizational change, and building design. Most importantly, LEED was off the shelf and ready to go on the day we needed it. Of course, it was only an untested pilot tool, but that was a risk we were willing to take.

The new system had four levels of performance available—at the time named Bronze (later changed to Certified), Silver, Gold, and Platinum. The LEED tool was designed for new construction and major renovation projects that were commercial, institutional, or high-rise residential. This would fit most of our upcoming forty projects well enough. We knew that we would also have many later opportunities for other projects, such as pass-through publicly funded housing, infrastructure projects, or small-scale building repairs and tenant improvements. However, with the large number of new major building projects coming up, that is where we decided to put our initial attention. We knew that we could focus on the other project types eventually, especially if we succeeded at our first attempts at green building.

Next we needed to set the threshold for the size of project that would activate the policy as well as what level of performance to establish. Initially, twenty thousand square feet was proposed as the policy threshold. We quickly realized, however, that many of our upcoming projects—such as renovations to libraries and community centers—would not trigger the policy because of their smaller size. So the minimum threshold was adjusted downward to five thousand square feet of occupied space, attempting to also specifically capture the human benefits of green building.

We then picked Silver LEED as the required performance level. This would clearly tell our capital projects managers and design teams what target to aim at, when they had met it, and when they could stop.

With no LEED track record, and no quantitative cost or performance data with which to make a decision, we went with our gut in selecting the Silver level, at the lower middle range. If we had picked the lowest level, there would have been nowhere to fall back to if it proved too aggressive. Additionally, if Silver proved too low, we could advance the policy to the next highest level, or LEED Gold. I learned that policy making can sometimes be a combination of analytical thinking and a healthy dose of intuition.

Even though the city council had not formally adopted any of the other policies within the City's Environmental Management System, they wanted to do so this time. They requested that the green building team draft a resolution that could be used to adopt the policy formally. Discussion with our mayor revealed that he was in full support. Council realized that, given a potentially controversial policy, those working to implement it would be a in a stronger position if clear, formal support was in place.

We quickly crafted Resolution Number 30121 to formally adopt the policy, which was passed in a matter of weeks by a unanimous 7-0 Council vote on February 14, 2000. Green building and LEED were now a Council-mandated part of the City's Environmental Management System.

The city council and mayor, Paul Schell, supported the green building policy rapidly and wholeheartedly because it matched their values and the values of their constituents, and because "they knew it was the right thing to do." They took a leap of faith. Most importantly, they knew that a significant legacy might be created with the forty projects under way. This was not just their political legacy, but a legacy they would be leaving to the children of Seattle's citizens, who would inherit our city.

Some refer to Seattle as the "Emerald City" based on the mild climate, which affords lush year-round vegetation. For others, the term *Emerald City* may denote the shimmering metropolis in the film *The Wizard of Oz*, an imaginary place that is the repository of dreams and longing. Here, I use the term *emerald* to suggest a deep and singularly transparent shade of green. Many of us are on the path of transforming our cities to become deeply green and sustainable urban environments. How can we learn from others? The variety of approaches we can take to create this change are as multifaceted as a polished gemstone. The Seattle and Austin programs have provided me diverse insight into how to create green building policies and programs. In addition, over years of participation in the USGBC's national and local committees, I have encountered many amazing people from both the governmental and private sectors who have been involved in the transformational change of their communities. From this breadth of experience and wealth of shared knowledge, I have drawn the lessons to be learned in this book. I hope they will help you to create your own emerald city.

Lucia Athens can be contacted at
http://www.buildinganemeraldcity.com/.

CHAPTER 1

Introduction
The Promise of Green Building

Sustainability at its heart addresses the challenge of balancing the needs of people with the needs of nature. In many fields—from fisheries management to green business practice, for example—applying sustainable thinking has helped us to understand the limitations of natural systems and the dangerous demands that human systems are imposing on natural resources.

The lens of sustainability presents sobering news, telling us we must find alternatives to our Western, resource-gobbling ways. It would require six planets' worth of resources to sustain the U.S. lifestyle at a global scale.

The media tend to focus on doom-and-gloom news, such as species loss, decreasing biological productivity of oceans, global climate change, and increasing pollution levels. While we cannot turn our back on negative trending of environmental indicators, what is needed is a more positive approach to the possibility of solving our ecological mess. As a society, we need a sense of hope and empowerment to energize people toward actions that make a difference. Sustainable building offers that hope—for design professionals, building officials, and the myriad of human beings that live and work inside buildings.

CLIMATE CHANGE AND GREEN BUILDING

On the global scale, green building has been identified as a key strategy for addressing climate change. As written in the U.S. Conference of Mayors Climate Protection Agreement, the goal of the agreement is to "meet or beat the target of reducing global warming pollution levels to 7 percent below 1990 levels by 2012."[1] One of the twelve key strategies in the statement says that these cities will "practice and promote sustainable building practices using the U.S. Green Building Council's LEED program or a similar system."[2]

This latter statement acknowledges the significant portion of greenhouse gas emissions represented by the building sector. Using U.S. Energy Information Administration statistics, architect Ed Mazria has calculated that buildings account for a whopping 76 percent of the total U.S. electricity consumption. Mazria has thrown down the gauntlet by creating the 2030 Challenge, which sets a goal for all buildings to be greenhouse

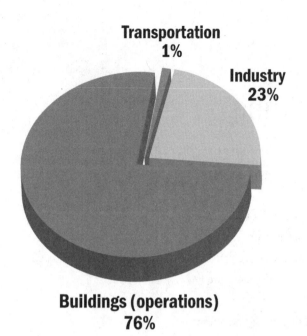

**Transportation
1%**

**Industry
23%**

**Buildings (operations)
76%**

FIGURE 1.1 U.S. Electricity Consumption
When the full impacts of buildings are included, they account for 76 percent of U.S. electricity use.
Credit: Image courtesy of http://www.architecture2030.org

gas–neutral by the year 2030 (see figure 1.1). The U.S. Conference of Mayors unanimously adopted a 2030 Challenge resolution in 2006. In addition, as of mid-2009, more than 944 cities had signed on to the U.S. Mayors Climate Protection Agreement, representing over 83 million citizens.[3] Such public declarations by elected officials provide a clear mandate for support of green building programs. When discussing with your elected officials why they should support green building, be sure to refer to such policy agreements.

A MOVEMENT WHOSE TIME HAS COME

The world of sustainable, or green, building is rapidly evolving. Until fairly recently, the modern-day built environment provided us with just a handful of grassroots examples of environmentally friendly buildings, and some of these may have been considered anomalies or, at the least, rather odd looking. Today, hundreds of more mainstream examples exist, ranging from college facilities to corporate headquarters to affordable housing. Just ten years ago, few firms, products, and sources of information were available. Today, the availability of information is expanding rapidly. In 2005, a Google search for "green building" resulted in more than six hundred thousand hits. In 2008, the same search results expanded to more than 5 million hits, and in 2009, to 7.3 million hits. Needless to say, there is a lot of information out there, but how do we make sense of it all to create green buildings that are both relevant and successful?

One goal of this book is to provide a mentoring tool for those endeavoring to create green building projects or programs in the public sector or within their organizations. While my experience is largely from ten years as the director of the Seattle green building program and from early work with the Austin green building program (see box 1.1), the tips and lessons provided in this book can be applied to other public jurisdictional authorities, such as at the county, state, or regional government level. In addition, some of the targeting strategies could be utilized by large corporations that develop, own, or manage a sizable building portfolio.

It is my hope that this book will provide valuable lessons and insights regarding the process of moving toward more sustainable buildings, cities, and organizations, with a particular focus on the public sector but with insights that can benefit many types of organizations. It should be instructive to the corporate sustainability officer, public policy maker, public or private building owner, project manager, architect, and student of green architecture.

Doug Seiter, codeveloper of the City of Austin Green Building Program, former state coordinator for Built Green Colorado

In the mid-1980s, the City of Austin was engaged in building an aggressive energy-efficiency portfolio that included financial incentives (rebates), low-income residential assistance, and low-interest loans for energy retrofits. One entrée on that menu of programs was the New Residential Construction Program, which developed a nonregulatory relationship with Austin home builders. Austin Energy Star encouraged voluntary energy improvements with a three-star rating system and local promotion. This market-based approach became a vehicle for continual energy improvement through educating builders and consumers and stimulating competition within the industry. It also became a core strategy for introducing a broader approach to environmental building a few years later.

In 1989, I had reconnected with a nationally known local sustainability think tank, the Center for Maximum Potential Building Systems, codirected by Pliny Fisk III and Gail Vittori. Coincidentally, I was asked by my division manager, Mike Myers, to come up with ideas for a potential grant opportunity from the Energy Task Force of Public Technology Incorporated (PTI). I called the Center to bounce around some ideas, and it was during that exchange that Gail proposed to expand Austin's successful Energy Star program to include other resource areas: water, materials, and waste. This built on a systems-based resource flow model that the Center had evolved over the prior decade. This more comprehensive method essentially laid the groundwork for a transformational approach to buildings and the environment, since energy was the principal focus of most building-related environmental initiatives at the time. With Austin Energy Star as a springboard for changing standard practices of mainstream builders and developers, Gail, Pliny, and I took this kernel of an idea and expanded it into a grant proposal to PTI. With a public-private partnership (the City of Austin and the Center for Maximum

Potential Building Systems) as the driver, the proposal was accepted. We were off and running.

The Center was contracted to develop a framework for an environmentally based rating system with an initial focus on single-family residential construction. The resulting icon-based rating system, while comprehensive and based on the Center's extensive systems and life cycle–oriented research, was ultimately replaced by a more simplified rating format. We at the City were about to take an environmental rating system to the Texas builders. Our experience with builders had been in the energy-efficiency realm, and in the mid-eighties, this was still a hard sell. To introduce the next layer of building considerations in the form of environmental consequences of building, we felt that an incremental approach would be needed to get us in the door. Even so, as I look back at that first rating system, the list was certainly pushing the envelope.

The Austin Green Builder Program emerged (the name was later revised to the Austin Green Building Program). To our knowledge, it was the first green building program in the world. The world, it seems in retrospect, was ready for this more systems-based, albeit simplified, market-ready approach than was initially conceived. At the 1992 U.N. Earth Summit in Rio de Janeiro, the City of Austin's Green Building Program was recognized as one of twelve exemplary local environmental initiatives—and the only recipient from the United States. The following year, David Gottfried, Rick Fedrizzi, and Mike Italiano founded the U.S. Green Building Council, acknowledging Austin's Green Building Program as one of the inspirations to establish a nationally based organization to advance green building. In just a few short years, the term green building had entered the public lexicon. USGBC's work on LEED began in 1995, further building off of the inspired conceptual framework that sparked Austin's ground-breaking initiative. And, as they say, the rest is history.

SOLUTIONS, NOT PROTESTS

The success of green building appears to be outpacing many other environmental movements. Renowned geneticist David Suzuki, named one of the 2007 "Heroes of the Environment" by *Time* magazine along with Al Gore, Robert Redford, and Wangari Maathai, expresses amazement at the adoption and progress of the sustainable building movement's transformation of the marketplace, compared to many other environmental movements. Suzuki is also impressed with the size and participation level of the community pushing the movement forward.[4] This success may be partly because green building differs from reactive movements oriented solely around protest. It provides a proactive solution to a complex web of problems, long-term profitability, and a positive approach people can get behind. Green building creates visible symbols and visceral experiences for how a sustainable world might look and feel, further feeding inspiration in the movement and an increase in supporters.

Leaders in the field have found ways to leverage their agenda within the building industry because of the tremendous resources already invested in design and construction activities. Most of the building projects that end up becoming green are development that is slated to happen anyway. With the appropriate vision, tools, and leadership, these resources can be shifted toward green rather than conventional building. Capital dollars and design team creativity can be captured to create increased levels of ecological integrity in the built environment. Green buildings can become generators, rather than consumers, of power and other resources. This turns the traditional paradigm for grid-dependent and minimum code-compliance building on its head.

SUSTAINABILITY GOES CORPORATE

Hand in hand with the maturation of the green building movement, sustainable business practices are becoming a key corporate value. Many Fortune 500 companies are now also rated on their corporate reputation for sustainability, including social factors, community and environmental responsibility, innovation, and quality of goods or services. Research is beginning to show that high marks related to sustainability issues can be directly correlated with corporate profitability. Never before has the understanding been clearer that our ecological prosperity is linked to our economic prosperity.

Green facility development, ownership, and tenancy are now understood as a key aspect of smart business practice. Consider the many examples. Toyota Motor Corporation not only markets hybrid automobiles such as the Prius but is also building green buildings to house its own employees. Toyota Motor Sales division's campus headquarters building in Torrence, California, uses a combination of strategies, including solar power, recycled water use, and high-efficiency equipment. The building outperforms Toyota's required 10 percent return on investment, reduces potable water use by 60 percent, and reduces energy use by 60 percent over code.[5] That all adds up to significant operational savings and an award-winning building that has received excellent media coverage, the latter of which also generates corporate value.

Yoshi Ishizaka, senior managing director of Toyota, seems to understand how all this not only protects the company's bottom line but also embodies a new business ethic. According to Ishizaka: "It is our actions today that determine the world of tomorrow. The results of those actions will directly affect the world that our children inherit."[6] Toyota is emblematic of a growing number of corporations that have enthusiastically embraced the green building concept as central to their good business practices. Governments, too, share many characteristics with corporate organizations. They develop, own, and manage facilities. They seek to protect the value of their assets and are concerned with risk management. They employ large numbers of people and share corporate concerns about employee performance, retention, and overhead.

WHY CITY GOVERNMENT?

Few entities hold more power to transform the face of urban environments than do city governments. These municipal jurisdictions define the boundaries of urban environs; permit building projects; provide critical safety, environmental, and social services; and are often the single largest owners of urban space, including public lands and rights-of-way. In addition, cities can often be large users of private architectural design and construction services. As major public developers and landholders, cities such as Seattle are significant players in the real estate marketplace. They can serve as clients for a huge number of design, construction, and development service contracts, with large market value. Not only is this impact seen in the architectural services arena, but the public works that result have a huge impact on the enduring fabric of the city. Green government facilities send a message to the public, who help to fund, and eventually visit, these places.

The City of Seattle, for example, owns over one thousand buildings, totaling nearly 7 million square feet. The operational impacts of maintaining these buildings are huge. In addition, it owns and manages 2.5 million square feet of parking and yard space, and nearly 215 million square feet of green and open space.[7] The City also owns the electric, water, and solid waste utilities that set utility rates and provide conservation incentives. The City permits land and building development within the city limits. As the keeper of the keys for building codes and most utility services, the City wields tremendous power over the building sector and the built environment.

As the first entity to formally adopt LEED™ (Leadership in Energy and Environmental Design) standards, the passage of Seattle's sustainable building policy in February 2000 sent ripples through the public and private sectors. The announcement of the policy was met with a flurry of press and public recognition. If Seattle had the courage to do this, who would step up next? Many other municipalities and jurisdictions followed suit by formally adopting LEED as Seattle did. Those using LEED now include the states of California, Maryland, and Washington, and the cities of Portland, Los Angeles, Pittsburgh, Dallas, and Boston, to name just a few. The Seattle policy has been replicated by many, and Seattle's Green Building Program hosts fact-finding missions from far-flung locales, including New Zealand and China, and from cities closer to home, including Vancouver and Boston. It appears that the courage and leadership demonstrated by Seattle paved the way for the widespread adoption of what has now become the premier green building rating system in the nation.

The link between public leadership and market transformation holds fertile ground for innovation and evolutionary change. The widespread adoption of green building by the public sector can easily create the tipping point toward sustainable cities. Government can lead the way, taking the initial risks and not only exploring how green building can financially benefit building owners but also demonstrating how it can provide environmental and community stewardship benefits. According to the U.S. Green Building Council (USGBC), as of December 2008: "Government owned or occupied LEED buildings make up 26% of all LEED projects. There are 1,151 LEED projects registered to the federal government, 1,516 registered to state governments, and 2,319 registered to local governments."[8] The government sector has a clear mission as steward of the communal good and public trustee of sensitive ecological systems, energy and water resources, public health, and high-quality, thriving urban and neighborhood environments. Not only does the public expect government to protect their health, welfare, and safety, but— as they become savvy regarding the urgency of a sustainable future— they also expect government to lead the way.

Trail blazing can be wearisome work. Those who follow the first pioneers can hope to find their path easier. Those who came first can provide a road map to help others find their destination more easily. I hope to spare other pioneers from having to entirely "reinvent the wheel" in creating green building programs. Armed with the tools this book provides, may your efforts go further, faster, and with fewer bumps. There is no singular pathway to success, and all I can do is share my own unique perspective. The endgame, if we are successful, is that the creative genius of others can build on what has already been done in order to raise the bar. Together, we hold the potential to collectively catapult us toward the future we envision.

This book begins by discussing how to build support for your program by gaining leadership endorsement through such techniques as establishing how green building can help to solve many urban and global sustainability challenges. Because creating green building policies and programs is a process of transformational change and innovation adoption, next there is a chapter on how to leverage and manage the change process in the green building industry and within your own organization. The following chapters provide examples and guidance on policy development, providing green building services (such as educational programs and technical assistance), and creating green codes and incentive programs. The book concludes with guidance on how to measure the impacts of green building programs to determine progress and justify your program. It takes a look ahead at opportunities on the horizon for green building programs. At the end of each chapter, I summarize takeaway lessons and tips that you can refer back to as you undertake policy and program development.

CHAPTER 2

Building Support for Green Building Initiatives

When faced with the task of developing a green building program, you may feel daunted. But take hope: green building is a concept that in many ways is easy to get others to rally around. It can foster a positive, visionary approach to environmental and social stewardship, reinforcing activities that take us in the direction we want to go, versus trying to stop people from doing undesirable activities. It can capture multiple benefits and attract a broad range of partners. Whatever your situation, whether or not you already have elected officials and managers that see green building in their city's future, there is no time like the present to get started. One parable about time goes like this: In an ancient land, an emissary at court presented the king with the gift of a fruit tree. When the emissary had left, the king called his royal gardener. When the gardener saw the tree, he said, "Your majesty, I must tell you that this tree will take many, many years to bear fruit." The king's response: "Then I command you to plant it right NOW!" The time to act is now, so let's get started.

This section of the book provides strategic guidance on gaining initial support and ongoing funding of a green building program. This includes identifying political and stakeholder advocates, justifying the need for a program, and locating the program within an organizational structure. This guidance can be used for programs that focus on internal policies for building projects as well as for programs focused outside the organization (the private sector in the case of government programs).

SUSTAINABILITY COMPETITIVENESS

Most cities are hungry for information about their vitality and competitiveness. One of the simpler indexes for green building is how many LEED projects there are in your city or region. The USGBC maintains a database of LEED projects that can easily be searched by state or city. Most mayors of cities that want to distinguish themselves will be very interested in how their cities compare to others in terms of number of green buildings. Both Certified LEED (completed) buildings and Registered (planned) project numbers should be examined. (Keep in mind that planned projects may never be com-

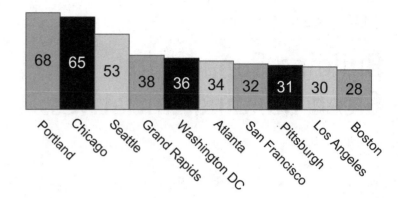

FIGURE 2.1 Top Ten Cities by Number of LEED-certified Projects (as of May 2009)
Many cities are competitive regarding the number of green buildings they can claim.
Data Source: USGBC

pleted.) These numbers can be reflected in relationship to total number of projects by certification level or total number of square feet, or viewed within the context of relative city size or population. (The USGBC regularly runs reports for the top fifty cities for Certified and Registered projects, as well as square foot data.) For smaller cities engaging in green building, different ways of viewing the data can be useful. For example, as shown in figure 2.1, Chicago, a city of roughly 2.8 million, was the number one city for number of LEED-certified projects as of May 2009. However, if you look at the same data including the top fifty cities, Burlington, Vermont, comes in at number thirty-five with ten LEED-certified projects. However, Burlington's population is a mere thirty-eight thousand. Per capita, Burlington is doing very well. Many smaller cities show up on the listing of the top fifty cities for LEED-certified square footage. Towns of fewer than ten thousand people that made the list include Sturtevant, Wisconsin; Morrison, Illinois; Pennington, New Jersey; and Bee Cave, Texas. Clearly, communities both large and small are investing in LEED.

Some cities are ranked according to broad measures of sustainability performance. A peer-reviewed study done annually by the organization SustainLane ranks the fifty largest U.S. cities according to benchmarks in sixteen areas.[1] These areas include air and water quality, waste management, water supply, housing affordability, and natural disaster risk. The SustainLane rankings also include how many LEED-certified projects exist within the city. Table 2.1 shows the 2008 rankings.

Such ranking programs can help identify areas where a city is doing well or needs improvement, and they may be viewed as drivers for green building initiatives. They can also be useful as a learning and motivational tool. If elected officials are not aware of such rankings, educate them with briefings or policy papers. The rankings can result in bragging rights and may help leverage political support.

Many of the indicator items are interrelated. With regards to such areas as energy or water performance, green building can build capacity, reduce demand, or increase resiliency.

TABLE 2.1. 2008 SUSTAINLANE U.S. CITY SUSTAINABILITY RANKINGS

Cities are listed by their 2008 rankings order. Numbers in parentheses denote 2006 rankings. This program ranks cities annually for sustainability performance and can be used to educate elected officials about how a city is doing.

1. Portland, OR (1)	14. Sacramento, CA (13)	27. New Orleans, LA (32)	40. Nashville, TN (42)
2. San Francisco, CA (2)	15. Washington, DC (12)	28. Los Angeles, CA (25)	41. Arlington, TX (41)
3. Seattle, WA (3)	16. Cleveland, OH (28)	29. Louisville, KY (35)	42. Long Beach, CA (30)
4. Chicago, IL (4)	17. Honolulu, HI (15)	30. Columbus, OH (50)	43. Colorado Springs, CO (26)
5. New York, NY (6)	18. Albuquerque, NM (19)	31. Detroit, MI (43)	44. Indianapolis, IN (45)
6. Boston, MA (7)	19. Atlanta, GA (38)	32. Phoenix, AZ (22)	45. Virginia Beach, VA (48)
7. Minneapolis, MN (10)	20. Kansas City, MO (18)	33. San Antonio, TX (21)	46. Memphis, TN (43)
8. Philadelphia, PA (8)	21. San Jose, CA (23)	34. Miami, FL (29)	47. Las Vegas, NV (27)
9. Oakland, CA (5)	22. Tucson, AZ (20)	35. Charlotte, NC (34)	48. Tulsa, OK (40)
10. Baltimore, MD (11)	23. Jacksonville, FL (36)	36. Houston, TX (39)	49. Oklahoma City, OK (49)
11. Denver, CO (9)	24. Dallas, TX (24)	37. Fresno, CA (33)	50. Mesa, AZ (47)
12. Milwaukee, WI (16)	25. Omaha, NE (37)	38. El Paso, TX (31)	
13. Austin, TX (14)	26. San Diego, CA (17)	39. Fort Worth, TX (46)	

LOCAL POLICIES

Many sustainability issues are geographically, bioregionally, or politically specific. Your region may be struggling with particular institutional, economic, social, or environmental issues that will have a high priority for elected officials. The significant 2009 update to LEED acknowledges regionalism by allowing for special additional credits by region, related to regional environmental priorities. For example, the desert Southwest region of the United States is facing pressing water issues. This may justify and inform special LEED credits and a green building program that emphasizes water conservation. These can build a support base for green building. If you don't know what issues are pressing in your vicinity, conduct research with elected officials, department heads, utility officials, environmental nongovernmental organizations', business leaders, or neighborhood groups. State and federal data may also be helpful, as well as resources within nearby colleges and universities.

Look for existing initiatives and policies that a green building program can use as a docking station or platform. Many public entities are likely to have comprehensive plans, policy goals, or environmental programs that can be linked to a green building program. Related policy precedents can help to grease the wheels toward green building adoption.

Seattle's mayor develops an annual Environmental Action Agenda (shown in table 2.2) that dovetails nicely with green building. A quick-reference, short menu of environmental goals creates shorthand for political priorities. This is extremely useful for communications with internal stakeholders who may resist change. When adversaries hear that the mayor or city manager has endorsed green building via the Action Agenda, it often quells opposition.

Many cities and large organizations have detailed sustainability directives related to all aspects of their operations within a comprehensive framework. These policies are sometimes organized into an Environmental Management Program (EMP). The EMP is a policy, management, and benchmarking tool. Seattle's Environmental Management Program manual states: "Environmental management is a dynamic process, based on a model of continual improvement."[2] As a starting point, the Seattle EMP used the ISO 14001 system, developed by the International Organization for Standardization and adopted by the American National Standards Institute, as its standard specification. The stated purpose of the EMP is to:

- ensure that the City of Seattle, as a corporate entity, incorporates a high level of environmental stewardship into its daily activities and complies with regulations

TABLE 2.2 MAYOR NICKELS'S SEATTLE ENVIRONMENTAL ACTION AGENDA

Green building is a key element of this political agenda and is useful for communications purposes.

	Lean, Green City Government	Healthy Urban Environments	Sustainable Community Practices	Smart Mobility
Agenda stated goal	Reduce human and environmental risks—and lower operating costs—of city government through resource efficiency, waste reduction, and pollution prevention.	Protect and restore ecological function, public health, and neighborhood livability through more sustainable approaches to managing both the natural and built environments.	Leverage city programs and services to catalyze and accelerate adoption of healthy, resource-efficient, environmentally responsible practices by households, businesses, and other institutions.	Improve mobility, environmental quality, and social equity through smart transportation services and solutions.
Green building link	Green building policy for city-owned green buildings can deliver reduced energy and water demands and utility costs for government.	Green building policy for private development can increase urban forest and habitat areas and restore watershed health through good construction practices, stormwater management, and good site design.	Educate home owners to buy green homes and remodel green. Provide assistance for businesses to invest in high-efficiency lighting and office equipment.	Reward infill development and discourage sprawl. Encourage bicycle and pedestrian activity through building amenities and site/road design.

- establish citywide environmental goals and policies and provide a framework for improved management and accountability
- develop and implement a municipal conservation program to make more efficient use of energy and water in City facilities
- establish a process for measuring and reporting annually on environmental performance.[3]

The process of creating the EMP included a review of City activities, products, and services that might have environmental impact, including release of pollutants to air, land, or water; production of solid or hazardous waste; contamination of land; adverse impacts to habitat, wildlife, human health, or quality of life; and depletion of natural resources. The Seattle EMP was initially approved by the city council in 1999 and includes policies and environmental performance indicators for fleet management, environmentally responsible purchasing, waste reduction and recycling, grounds management, chemical use, and green building. Many cities with progressive environmental programs or a central sustainability office will have EMPs, whereas others may not.

One reason Seattle's green building policy was adopted so quickly was the preexisting politically adopted framework within which the policy fit: the EMP. Elected officials will have their own perspective on environmental and sustainability issues. As election cycles may bring new players into the field, each can customize his or her agenda or priorities in green. Ensuring consistency across election cycles can be challenging. If you have done your homework in regards to building outside stakeholder support, this will aid ongoing support regardless of who is in office. In addition, make sure that departments or other organizations "own" the green building program. Consistent reporting on benefits of the program (discussed in chapter 7) also helps to ensure support that transcends the purely political.

ESTABLISHING A PROGRAM CONTEXT

While green building is a great idea, it must be justified based on what benefits it can deliver. Green building is a means to an end, rather than a goal without relation to other desired achievements. Before creating a structure or plan for a program, identify goals and issues, particularly those critical locally, which give the program a reason for existing. What is the program's raison d'être? It is important to ask the following questions (and to educate others about them): What can building green achieve? What benefits does green building deliver? These answers are multifaceted, but some will resonate more for your local context. It might also help to identify what larger, national and global issues reverberate for local stakeholders or elected officials.[4] Green building benefits can be mapped to local priority issues or problems. A politically or geographically specific context can give a program additional relevancy. Here are some examples of issues that may help to justify the need for a green building program:

- Minimizing impact on climate change (buildings in the United States account for 38 percent of total carbon dioxide emissions)[5]
- Growth management/smart growth (green building can help to reduce sprawl, protect valuable farmland, and create new development with a lower impact)
- Conserving energy and water (green building can reduce development-related operational demands for energy and water)
- Aging infrastructure or infrastructure capacity issues (green building can reduce demand on overloaded stormwater, water, or energy infrastructure as well as create new off-grid infrastructure capacity with on-site renewables, rainwater collection, or stormwater infiltration)
- Flooding and combined sewer overflows (CSOs) caused by combined storm and wastewater sewer challenges (low-impact development strategies can lower stormwater runoff and reduce peak flows that cause CSOs)
- Transportation planning, transit-oriented development, and commute trip reduction (site selection for green building development as well as the inclusion of commuter amenities can help to reduce single-occupancy vehicle trips)
- Public health and food security (green building can reduce dependence on coal-fired power plants, which pollute the air; protect indoor air quality with healthy materials; and encourage urban agriculture, improving the quality and security of local food supplies)
- Long-term fiscal responsibility (for public or private entities concerned with making sound financial investments with reasonable return on investment and protecting the value of building assets)
- Ecological health (green building can help to protect valuable habitat, protect air and water quality, and reduce the demand on limited environmental resources)
- Support for the local economy and job creation (green building can help to support local businesses and jobs by buying locally manufactured products and developing local green-collar job expertise in such areas as building energy management and retrofits)

Benefits of green building are shown in table 2.3 relative to the triple bottom line, and benefits at the various scales of utilities, ratepayers and building owners, or society in a broader sense. Many cities own their own utilities or at the very least have a vested interest in the utility capacity of their jurisdictions. Although the list here is extensive, it can be shortened to select those connections that will resonate most for local stakeholders, both public and private.

TABLE 2.3 GREEN BUILDING BENEFITS

	To Utilities	To Ratepayers and Building Owners	To Society
Energy Conservation	• Reduce peak loads and over-all demand for service • Reduce need to purchase power on the market during peaks	• Reduce utility bill and operating costs • Keep rates reasonable and predictable	• Extend nonrenewable energy resources • Reduce hydropower impacts to habitat • Protect air quality
Climate Change	• Reduce regulatory impacts of greenhouse gas mitigation • Protect against impacts of climate change, such as snowpack losses that affect water and hydropower supply	• Reduce possibility of in-creased flooding, sea-level rises, and unpredictable weather patterns • Prevent increased air conditioning	• Lower risk of sea-level rises • Lower intensity of flooding and hurricanes • Protect air quality • Reduce transportation impact
Waste Reduction and Recycling	• Reduce collection, transport, and disposal demand • Increase recycling of problem wastes • Extend service life of goods	• Reduce garbage and recycling disposal costs • Reduce construction costs • Reduce exposure to toxins	• Reduce pollution and carbon load from raw material extraction
Water Conservation	• Reduce overall demand for potable water and peak demand • Increase water reuse	• Reduce building operating costs • Reduce water and waste-water bills	• Maintain potable water supply • Reduce energy and pollution associated with treatment and transmission
Water Quality and Drainage	• Reduce demand and cost of wastewater treatment and transmission • Reduce combined sewer overflows	• Reduce on-site flooding • Improve site aesthetics and usable space	• Maintain ecological and habitat health • Protect endangered aquatic species
Regulatory Positioning	• Anticipate regulatory demand • Avoid noncompliance	• Anticipate cost of long-term regulatory demands with proactive approach	• Decrease economic impact adaptation to changing reg-ulatory requirements
Human Health and Safety	• Decrease work absenteeism related to building conditions	• Reduce staff–related overhead costs	• Improve health of society related to air, land, water quality, and toxic releases

BUILDING LEADERSHIP SUPPORT

For significant organizational change to occur, top-level decision makers must be engaged. Having elected official support is an important key to the initial success and continued vitality of green building and other change initiatives. While staff backing is also critical, change will happen much more quickly with official support than if from the grassroots only. Without endorsement from the top ranks, change initiatives ultimately flounder when they reach political or institutional barriers that can be removed only with executive-level support. Of course, mayoral direction will have important ripple effects down through the ranks of government.

Good leaders are able to present a compelling, inspiring vision of where they want to take things. Putting the situation within a greater context adds meaning and value. Two examples of top sustainability leaders whose vision has mobilized the masses are Ray Anderson, founder and chairman of Interface Carpet Inc., who turned his company into a global leader in innovation in recycling, closed-loop manufacturing, waste elimination, and product reengineering, and Jaime Lerner, Curitiba's former mayor, who is largely credited with turning the Brazilian city into a global example of pedestrian, bike, and transit access. Ray Anderson says:

> We look forward to the day when our factories have no smokestacks and no effluents. If we're successful, we'll spend the rest of our days harvesting yester-year's carpets and other petrochemically derived products, and recycling them into new materials; and converting sunlight into energy; with zero scrap going to the landfill and zero emissions into the ecosystem. And we'll be doing well . . . very well . . . by doing good. That's the vision.[6]

Most people and organizations tend to think about a future vision in terms of objectives or goals. Vision statements can create a common language that may serve as a rallying point for others; as such, they need to be stated in positive terms. For example, the vision statement "Create a sustainable energy future" resonates a compelling future vision, in contrast to the negative statement "Reduce dependence on fossil fuels." The positive statement is motivated by a desired positive future as opposed to envisioning stopping a currently undesirable one. Vision statements also tend to be more effective if a sense of ownership is created by including in the visioning process those who will be responsible for implementation.

If your elected officials and top managers are hesitant regarding sustainability initiatives, or if they wonder whether such change is even possible, one strategy is to show them real-world examples. For example, the Seattle-based organization International Sustainable Solutions hosts sustainability study tours that help public and private opinion leaders and decision makers gain inspiration by meeting with government officials in Europe, Central America, and Australia to visit model sustainability projects (see figure 2.2). They focus on city sustainability examples that can be replicated or adapted. The ability to see best practices that actually work is often just what the skeptic needs to become a sustainability champion in their own community. Consider sending your local mayor, council member,

FIGURE 2.2 European Sustainability Study Tour Group
Sending elected officials on tours to see green building in action can help gain their support.
Credit: Courtesy of International Sustainable Solutions

or city manager on one of these trips, or organize tours for them to see project examples that are closer to home. Look for examples through USGBC Web site listings of LEED projects or the Department of Energy High Performance Buildings database. Include city department heads and local building industry representatives, if possible. If tours either locally or abroad are not feasible, hold presentations and briefings about green building. Show how market transformation is occurring across the country. The USGBC Web site has some good, basic slide presentations that can be downloaded at no charge.[7]

It is also possible to invite representatives from other public sector programs, or green building experts, to speak to your elected officials. One strategy is to hold a public lecture, followed by a closed working session with a smaller group of staff or elected officials. Hearing firsthand how others are implementing green building projects and programs can be very useful in allaying fears. It is also important to make sure that honest discussion occurs regarding the challenges of implementation. This helps to build credibility and confidence.

Policy makers and elected officials can be educated regarding green building. Alternatively, professionals with expertise in green building can run for office. Design professionals do not traditionally consider a career in politics, but they should. Elected officials are in a key position to influence the urban environment as well as many public and private building projects (see box 2.1). A background in architecture, urban planning, landscape architecture, or an allied field can help elected officials make informed decisions in the right direction.

Dan Burgoyne, *Sustainability Manager, Department of General Services, State of California*

California has long been a leader in energy efficiency, green technologies, air emission standards, and other environmental areas. Its state government and many of its populated cities have stepped forward with bold initiatives for green building and for protecting the environment, human health, and natural resources.

In 1978, California established its Energy Efficient Standards for Residential and Non-residential Buildings (Title 24, Part 6, of the California Code of Regulations) in response to a legislative mandate to reduce California's energy consumption. These standards have been updated periodically since and continue to lead the nation in energy efficiency. Green building initiatives did not receive as high of a priority in the two administrations that followed until the turn of the twenty-first century.

In 2000 and 2001, then governor Gray Davis (1999–2003) issued two executive orders (California Executive Orders D-16-00 and D-46-01) that increased efforts to encourage that State buildings are designed, constructed, and maintained in a "sustainable" manner and to locate state buildings in existing urban areas when possible, revitalizing urban centers and using existing infrastructures. Resulting efforts led by California's State and Consumer Services Agency resulted in the development of the California Sustainable Building Task Force (SBTF).The SBTF brought together representatives from over forty state agencies and organized such efforts as establishing goals and initiating several landmark leadership green building projects, including

California's first state-owned LEED–Certified building, the Department of Education (part of the Capitol Area's East End Complex), which was awarded LEED-NC Gold in 2003. They also prepared a plan and report known as Blueprint 2001 (*Building Better Buildings: A Blueprint for Sustainable State Facilities*) and Blueprint 2003, which contained recommendations, action plans, and accomplishments improving State green building, and which led to development of a study and 2003 report entitled *The Costs and Financial Benefits of Green Buildings*.[1] This groundbreaking study determined that an average 2 percent incremental investment to green thirty-three buildings results in a 20 percent return on investment.

During the Gray Davis administration, much progress was made by the State in evaluating the benefits of green buildings, and the State got its feet wet with its first six LEED-certified buildings. Green building was encouraged, but not mandated, and a strong level of executive sponsorship was provided by Arnold Sowell, undersecretary of the State and Consumer Services Agency. Still, the statutes lacked specific mandates and measurable targets needed to institute green building statewide.

In 2003, Governor Arnold Schwarzenegger took office and immediately exhibited strong, active executive sponsorship of green building and other environmental initiatives. In December 2004, Governor Schwarzenegger issued Executive Order S-20-04, which established mandates to reduce energy pur-

Paul Schell was mayor of Seattle from 1998 to 2001. He was a former developer and dean of the College of Architecture at the University of Washington. His initial support for green building was instrumental. In the early days of LEED, he said:

> The actions we take reverberate. How we build our buildings, how they fit into the community, the resources they use, are scrutinized and sometimes celebrated, but almost never do they go unnoticed. Our goal is that city facilities will become models of sustainable environmental stewardship and healthy worker environments, and we think the LEED rating system provides the best standard for defining what constitutes a green building.[8]

Since 2002, Seattle's mayor Greg Nickels has continued unwavering support for both green building and climate protection. In 2008, he issued a mandate to "make Seattle the number one green building city in the nation." Such broad pronouncements help to develop an overarching mission and vision for a program. Encourage your elected officials to speak out about the opportunity that green building holds. Organize press conferences, and draft press releases for them. Offer to ghostwrite speeches and articles, and be sure to relate green building to the local situation. If nervousness exists over full-blown support

BOX 2.1 (CONTINUED)

chases from the grid by 20 percent by 2015, and for the first time mandated LEED-Silver certification for both new and existing state buildings. This also established a very high level Green Action Team to oversee progress on the governor's green initiatives. This Green Action Team consists of agency secretaries from five key state agencies and meets regularly to review progress. Throughout Governor Schwarzenegger's administration, he has appointed key leaders throughout state government who have supported his green building initiatives. Because this leadership and these expectations are enforced from the top, results have been dramatic and green building is becoming integrated throughout state government. Virtually all new construction and major renovations of state buildings larger than ten thousand square feet are now pursuing LEED-NC certification (currently 222 buildings in design or construction), already 60 existing buildings larger than fifty thousand square feet are pursuing LEED-EB certification, and more will follow. A total of more than 19 million square feet of state facilities is pursuing LEED certification as of the start of 2009, to eventually join over 5 million square feet of state buildings already LEED certified.

In 2006, Governor Schwarzenegger signed into effect the nation's first greenhouse gas reduction law, the Global Warming Solutions Act of 2006 (AB 32), which requires that the state's greenhouse gas emissions be reduced to 1990 levels by 2020.

In 2008, the California Air Resources Board approved a Climate Change Scoping Plan that identifies strategies for greening new and existing California buildings. These strategies included goals to build all new residential construction as zero net energy buildings by 2020 and all commercial buildings by 2030. Additional measures will address existing buildings. The governor also signed other legislation (SB 375–Regional Greenhouse Gas Emission Reduction Targets) into effect that will require future urban development to align with transportation infrastructures to further reduce greenhouse gas emissions. In 2007, California issued the California Green Building Standards Code (2007 California Code of Regulations, Title 24, Part 11), the first such code in the nation.

The effect of Governor Schwarzenegger's strong executive sponsorship, as well as the leadership of several legislators, has affected California green building much like a tsunami, spreading a wave of green building initiatives across the state at a depth never before experienced. This will likely have a long-lasting impact on California's building landscape. During this same time period, numerous local government jurisdictions have also exhibited leadership through the development and approval of green building initiatives, including public- and private-sector green building mandates.

1. Greg Kats, *The Costs and Financial Benefits of Green Buildings: A Report to Californias's Sustainable Building Task Force* (October 2003).

for green building, one approach is to implement a program as a "pilot." Pilot programs minimize risk for elected officials, implying that the initiative is only a test case. No long-term commitment is needed until the ideas have been validated.

BUILDING STAKEHOLDER SUPPORT

Many high-level officials will be reluctant to support green building initiatives if they are not sure of constituent support. Political endorsement from stakeholders is crucial in the process of creating and implementing green building programs and for securing high-level political validation. This can help address political or institutional resistance as well as increase the comfort level of elected officials in advocating for green building. Stakeholders can also provide key input into barriers and opportunities within the local marketplace. Insight into their "hot button" issues as well as their needs and desires can help avoid pitfalls; with such knowledge, details of policies or programs can be crafted to ensure their success.

Focus groups can also help bring together stakeholders for onetime sessions that provide key input or answers to specific questions. However, establishing good, ongoing relationships with standing stakeholder groups is well advised whether your current situation requires intensive advocacy or not. Even if the local political climate currently supports green building, the resistance that can be encountered as the program progresses and specific issues or budget challenges evolve can be offset by vetting ideas with trusted advisory groups.

Consider forming green building advisory or task force groups. These can be public or internal groups, they may be called "Green Ribbon" task forces, and in some cases they can take the form of formal commissions. Pennsylvania's governor, Tom Ridge, established a Green Government Council in 1998, whose task is integrating sustainability into the State's operations, including green building. Mayor Thomas Merino of Boston formed a Mayor's Task Force on green building in 2003, calling it "a group of public and private partners that will help us navigate the waters of environmental/high performance building in Boston, laying the groundwork for policy initiatives that will help us build a better Boston."[9] The group has gone on to develop recommendations and a report that provided guidance to the City of Boston on strategic green building actions. Seattle formed a mayor-appointed Green Building Task Force in late 2008 charged with preparing recommendations on how to increase the energy efficiency of new buildings by 20 percent. This fifty-member group was split into two subgroups, one to deal with existing buildings, and the other to deal with new construction. Be sure your stakeholder groups are a reasonable size to ensure effective group interaction.

Strong stakeholder groups can serve several key functions, including the following:

- Ensure that stakeholders feel their opinions are important and have been considered
- Build a group of industry allies and advocates of green building
- Assess needs and barriers within the industry in order to ensure program success
- Provide a sounding board for new ideas
- Gauge and build political support for green building
- Leverage resources and expand the resource base for green building program development
- Provide key recommendations to staff and elected officials

When forming stakeholder groups, consider including a wide variety of individuals that will be able to represent many viewpoints. Create representation from multiple players in the building industry, including developers, design professionals, contractors, real estate agents, lenders, building operators and owners, and tenants. Make sure different building types get represented, including commercial, institutional, multifamily, and single family. Professionals related to the markets represented by the different building types will have different needs and concerns. Key organizational partners should also be represented when collecting stakeholder input, including public sector representatives such as code officials. Such partners may include other government entities, utilities, nonprofits, and professional or industry associations. A list of key partners that should be considered for inclusion follows.

Private Sector/Business

- Developers
- Contractors and builders
- Design firms (architecture, planning, engineering, landscape architecture, interior design, and so forth)
- Chambers of commerce
- Local newspaper and magazine publishers
- Public relations/marketing firms
- Financial institutions, including local banks and representatives of national institutions
- Real estate agents
- Green product and natural food retailers

Academic/Learning Institutions

- Local universities and colleges
- Community colleges
- K–12 schools
- Job skills training programs
- Continuing education organizations
- Agricultural or university extension programs
- Research institutions

Nonprofit Organizations

- Grassroots green building organizations (for example, the Northwest Ecobuilding Guild in the Pacific Northwest)
- Environmental organizations
- Public health organizations
- Race and social justice organizations
- Sustainable community organizations

Professional Organizations/Local Chapters

- American Institute of Architects (AIA) local Committee on the Environment (COTE)
- International Interior Design Association (IIDA)
- U.S. Green Building Council (USGBC)

- Urban Land Institute (ULI)
- American Planning Association (APA)
- Master Builders Associations
- American Society of Landscape Architects (ASLA)
- Association of General Contractors (AGC)
- Building Owners and Managers Association (BOMA)
- International Association of Facility Managers (IFMA)
- National Association of Industrial and Office Properties (NAIOP)
- Tenants unions
- Contractor trade unions
- Real estate organizations

Government and Utility
- Local and regional utilities
- Utility-based organizations, citizen's advisory groups, and conservation groups
- U.S. Department of Energy and U.S. Environmental Protection Agency regional offices
- State government organizations, such as the Department of Health

Partnerships have characterized virtually every green building program across the United States. The Alameda County green building program has partnered with small nonprofits, such as Bay Area Built It Green, the local chapter of the National Association of the Remodeling Industry, and the State of California on training, industry networking, and building standards.

It may be difficult to get stakeholder involvement from those who oppose green building, but both supporters and skeptics should be included. Some stakeholders will be fearful that green building will "put them out of business" or decrease their competitive edge. Be patient with these adversaries. Listen to their concerns. Spend time educating them about green building and businesses who have gained from its success. These could include building owners whose overhead costs have decreased, or design firms whose business has increased as a result of new expertise.

DEVELOPING INTERNAL CHAMPIONS

Without champions to lead and implement change where the rubber meets the road, it is likely that nothing new will happen. As Chrisna du Plessis, a sustainable development specialist with the South African government, learned from local case studies on sustainable development in Pretoria, "the success or failure of policy implementation relies heavily on the personal commitment of a few local authorities, officers and councilors and the level of skill and resources available to the local authorities."[10] In Seattle, one of the most important champions during the critical initial phase of policy implementation was city architect Tony Gale. He was a daily inspiration and tireless policy advocate within the department that held responsibility for the greatest number of capital projects. Without him, I believe we would have a great policy sitting on a shelf in Seattle but no green buildings to show for it today.

Champions are needed at both the upper and lower ranks of any organization. If support exists at both levels, change can be initiated or supported at either end of the scale. At critical junctures, support at the opposite end of the scale can help overcome roadblocks and provide for ongoing advocacy. Regular communication between the advocates at different levels is important. Face-to-face meetings and telephone calls are vastly superior to e-mail communications, which can be misinterpreted or constrained due to the written record and publicly accessible format. In addition, good team relationships and mutual support are rarely developed via e-mail. Face-to-face dialogue is critical, especially during the early development of teams or trust-based working relationships. E-mail and calls can provide support later in the process, but be wary of coming to rely on them exclusively. Advocacy relationships among teams and between high- and low-level champions must be tended carefully. Without regular contact, support and trust can erode over time. Don't assume that someone who was an ally twelve months ago will continue to be an ally today, unless close ties are maintained.

Forming a team of internal stakeholders and champions to oversee program and policy development is critical. These teams should represent a broad diversity of internal organizational stakeholders. At the City of Seattle, we developed an informal Green Building Team that provided broad oversight, representing the perspectives of finance, environment, new development, building codes, and other interests. Since no single department was in charge of new capital projects, the Seattle Green Building Team became a venue to identify and track the City's new building development from ten thousand feet. Select team members based on both organizational representation and technical expertise. It is advisable to map out the organizational and operational environment in which your program will operate in order to make sure you have all the bases covered.

One word of advice is to keep the relative size of such teams large enough to provide adequate departmental representation but compact enough to function effectively. I find groups of larger than eight people difficult to manage and cumbersome for effectively voicing opinions, reaching consensus, and group learning. Manage departmental representation and communications flow through a single representative. This can eliminate duplications and can lower the communications burden for others. It can prevent green building project managers and their consulting teams from being inundated with information requests, which may exasperate them even if they support green building. Without this clearly designated chain of communication, interactions can easily become inefficient.

ORGANIZATIONAL POSITIONING

City government officials or managers may be faced with the challenge of program start-up. Staff champions for green building may also be tasked with preparing recommendations to managers or elected officials regarding program initiation. If you are starting a green building program from scratch, you may be faced with choices on where to locate the program within a public organizational structure, or a corporate structure. You may need to provide options on program placement to elected officials or executives, with pros and cons associated with each. If you are advocating for the program to reside within your own department, or that your position be relocated in conjunction with the program, it is advisable to bring in advocacy support that represents a third-party perspective.

The single most important issue in organizational placement of a green building program, especially at its start, is being within a group or department that has management-level support, preferably at the top. If, for example, the executive wants to locate green building in a department where the department head is not an advocate, there will be additional challenges. In addition, a robust program will be difficult to build if there is no staff-level support. Ideally, there must be at least one champion at both the management and the staff level. There will be fits and starts along the way, as there will inevitably be push back from some sectors either inside or outside of government. Resistance and concern may occur for a variety of reasons, including the following:

- Fears of increased government regulation or mandatory requirements
- Misperceptions that green building will increase costs and reduce competitiveness
- Competition for scarce budget or staffing resources, or attention to competing issues
- Anxiety about loss of constituent (voter) or citizen political support

It is important to ensure there is internal support for the program when things are going smoothly as well as when they are not.

Program positioning is likely to be entirely opportunity driven, in the same way that some green building projects are. If a good opportunity presents itself to create a program, based on management support, funding availability, or perceived need, don't spend too much time analyzing if this is the right fit. Competing issues and budget needs can cause such opportunities to evaporate if not tapped quickly.

Some opportunities regarding organizational positioning may be related to the nexus between program benefits and organizational priorities, as discussed earlier in this chapter. For example, a city-owned electric utility that has made commitments regarding climate protection or energy efficiency may suggest that the program be housed with them. It's important to remember that green building has multipronged benefits and that the relative priority of discrete sustainability issues may be affected for organizational positioning or the funding source. Think about positioning the program at a location that affords maximum connectivity to a broad range of green building benefits. If possible, avoid putting the program within a department with a narrow mission, such as a single utility, which may result in the program becoming pigeonholed. This might be achieved with placement in departments that comprise broad missions, such as those with functions of sustainability, comprehensive planning, neighborhood development, or building construction permitting. Broad support can also be ensured by building advocacy and funding support across multiple departments, regardless of where the program is physically located. Organizations that house some of the leading green building programs in the United States are shown in table 2.4.

Location within a Utility Department

Many green building programs, including Seattle's and Austin's programs, grew directly out of city-owned utilities. Publicly owned utilities, such as those providing electric or water services, are often good locations for green building programs. The Austin Green Building Program is located directly within the City's electric utility, and its performance is based on energy savings delivered by green buildings. Forward-thinking utilities, such

TABLE 2.4 ORGANIZATIONAL LOCATION OF GREEN BUILDING ———————
PROGRAMS IN THE UNITED STATES

Green Building Program	Location
City of Austin	City Electric Utility, Austin Energy
City of Chicago	Decentralized program spread across City Capital Projects, Building Permitting Office, Center for Green Technology
City of Portland	Portland Bureau of Planning and Sustainability
City of Seattle	Department of Planning and Development (originally decentralized and located within two City-owned utilities)/Building Permitting and Comprehensive Plan Office
City of San Francisco	Department of Environment

as Austin Energy and Seattle City Light, have been in the conservation business for years, offering conservation incentive programs, demand-side management, education, and outreach. One drawback is that alignment with individual conservation issues, such as energy efficiency, can make it more challenging to give additional priority to other green building issues, such as transportation or health.

Locating green building programs within utilities, especially those with existing conservation programs, can leverage resources available for green building projects in the form of financial incentives. It also provides a strong rationale for program funding and benefits. Even if the green building program is not housed directly within a utility, strong partnerships with utilities will be important. Utility conservation goals dovetail well with green building programs, which can reinforce management support and continuing financial investments in the program. Benefits of green building to utilities are multifold (as shown in table 2.3).

Location within an Environment/Sustainability Department

Some cities have centralized environmental departments or programs that cover a broad range of sustainability-related issues. One example is Portland's Bureau of Planning and Sustainability, which merged its previous Office of Sustainable Development with the city planning agency. The sustainable development functions are funded from multiple sources, including utility revenues, providing for a staff of forty. Areas of concern represent multiple aspects of sustainability, including global warming, energy efficiency, renewable resources, waste reduction and recycling, sustainable food systems, and green building. Seattle's green building program is also co-located with the city's planning functions, which can capture opportunities to integrate green building into zoning codes and planning for large public projects such as transit.

The broad umbrella approach has considerable advantages because it makes it easier to address the multiple issues of green building from an integrated perspective, recognizing and valuing synergies among different areas. Examples of specific strategies where this is true include green roofs benefiting stormwater flows and building energy efficiency, or on-demand water heating benefiting both water efficiency and energy efficiency.

Location within a Construction Permitting Department

There is probably no more powerful position for a market transformation of the building industry than within a construction permitting agency. This location allows direct access to building permit applicants, developers, contractors, and code officials. The Seattle program was initiated within the City-owned utilities but transitioned after five years to a consolidated program housed within the City's building permitting office. The City of Chicago integrates many of its functions within its Department of Construction and Permits and has created green building incentives as a part of the permitting process (see chapter 6). Access to and relationships with code officials who may be unfamiliar with green building practices that do not meet current code requirements can be critical. It allows the opportunity to provide advocacy to green building project teams or to prevent major permit process slowdowns that create disincentives for innovation. Over time, it can also help to eliminate code barriers. Working directly with permit applicants also gives staff insight into what it takes to accomplish green building within a particular regulatory framework and serves to illuminate where the code barriers lie.

Location within Capital Projects Offices

Programs that include an external focus on private development will not normally be located within departments focused on public construction projects. However, it is vital that some aspect of green building programming or staffing resides within such organizations if capital construction is expected to be green. Internal advocates will be key to understanding the organizational, political, and budgetary issues being faced. Some cities have a single department that deals with capital construction, making it relatively simple to create a staff point person and a focus on green. In Seattle, six separate departments manage their own new construction, renovation, and building operations. It is more challenging to influence so many departments. If each department is made accountable to deliver on green building policy goals or initiatives, this increases accountability and program success.

CROSS-ORGANIZATIONAL ISSUES

No matter where the green building program is physically located, it should work toward building advocates across a broad range of departments. If all green building functions are centralized, it may keep other departments from "buying in" and from building the advocacy and organizational change needed within their own organization. It is always important for green building programs to partner and collaborate across departmental organizational boundaries. Combined funding and staffing strategies are possible regardless of organizational location. The City of Seattle program receives programmatic and staffing funds from multiple sources, including electric, water, drainage, and solid waste utility revenues; the general fund; and building permit revenues. While there may be a downside, including having to meet multiple goals and report to a larger management group, the upside includes increased stakeholder engagement and access to broader political and funding support. Look for models and lessons learned from other initiatives in your organization that have been successful.

A governance and communications structure for a green building program should be established at the time the program is organized. Each city or organization will have a structure that is appropriate to its situation. Given the multiple funding sources for the Seattle program, a Green Building Steering Committee meets quarterly to oversee the development and implementation of the program's work program and associated budget. The committee includes representation from all the funding partners and from the City's Office of Sustainability, which provides a good line of communications with the Mayor's Office. The program structure was approved by the city council via a Memorandum of Agreement among the Steering Committee departments. The program reports not only to the Steering Committee but also to the city council annually.

Many cities, including Seattle, will have other programs and initiatives that preexist the green building program but are integrally connected. These will most often include energy and water conservation programs. It is helpful to reinforce and manage the links to other City initiatives since they are critical partners for funding, technical assistance, incentives, and cross-marketing. There are challenges associated with the cross-departmental relationships, however. These include sensitivity around identity and control of different programs, what programs receive priority funding, and jealousy of who is getting the most attention and accolades.

These issues can all be resolved, but it is good to be aware of them and sensitive to how they can create a minefield if not tended carefully. Previously, some partners at Seattle's electric utility felt uncomfortable with the green building program's role as a new-found star. They felt that they had been around for years doing conservation work in the trenches and that green building was a new kid on the block. They were nervous about losing funding to the new initiative, and about losing control of their own energy-efficiency programs that play an integral part in green building. It takes time to build trust and allies in the face of these issues. Patience is important, as is acknowledging the concerns of others. In addition, be sure to give lots of verbal and written acknowledgment and credit to partners. This includes both internal briefing materials and materials released publicly.

Good working relationships with a broad range of staff and a working knowledge of organizational goals that might not be solidified into policy can be quite useful. These may occur across a broad spectrum of departments, including utilities, human resources, facility management, and community service agencies. Seattle's Personnel Department became an important partner for the Green Building Program during the process of conducting post-occupancy evaluation of city-owned green buildings. Information was shared regarding the relationship between building occupant complaints, poor indoor air quality, and sick leave, which could be reduced by building better, green buildings. Once the department understood the relationship, they became additional advocates for building green.

PROGRAM FINANCING STRATEGIES

Two basic areas of funding are needed for green building programs: program service costs and costs for an organization's construction projects. (The latter topic is discussed in chapter 4.)

Green building services need budget allocations to support three key areas: staffing, program funds, and incentives. The staffing and program budget needs vary depending on the level of intensity of the program being delivered.

Your program and associated budget can be grown over time; everything doesn't have to happen at once. If there is a desire to focus on green building but also lack of focus or analysis on where to start, consider funding a part-time staff person first, who can then develop a proposal for a program and the funding needed for it. If securing initial staffing dollars is a challenge, alternatives exist, including securing a loaned staff person for a limited period. Some large organizations also have "executive loan" programs in which they loan out staff for specific projects. Another funding approach is to ask for "seed" funding for staffing from several organizations for a limited period. Grants are also a possibility to provide for staffing needs. While grants and seed funds can be very useful in the very early stages, it is critical to eventually secure permanent staffing.

Many green building programs start out with one staff person and then increase staffing levels over time to build a larger team. Smaller cities or programs may start out with part-time staffing and grow to a full-time staff or additional staff resources based on partnerships with outside organizations. Once the program is in place and the value is ob-

TABLE 2.5 GREEN BUILDING PROGRAM FUNDING SOURCES ────────────

Green Building Program	Funding Source
City of Austin	Electric utility revenues
City of Chicago	Electric utility multimillion-dollar settlement (based on poor past performance)
City of Portland	Solid waste and recycling commercial tonnage fees and franchise fees (In June 2000, the residential franchise fee was increased by 1.55 percent to offset a portion of the costs.)
City of Seattle	Combined funding from electric, solid waste, water and drainage utilities, permit revenue fees, and general fund
City of San Francisco	Garbage service revenues and fees via San Francisco Public Utilities Commission

vious, it will be easier to secure ongoing funding. Seattle's program grew over an eight-year period from part-time staffing and minimal program budget to a staff of six with a budget of almost $2 million. Less intensive programs might start out with few staff and a program focused on Web-based information and marketing programs without staff-intensive technical assistance. Over time, a more intensive program can include financial incentives and technical assistance services (see chapters 5 and 6). This discussion covers budget planning in only a very broad sense. Funding to back a green building program can come from several sources, including the following:

- General funds
- Utility revenues/conservation funds
- Public benefit charges
- Construction permit fees
- Special penalties or taxes

To demonstrate the range of funding strategies, funding sources for the programs described earlier are shown in table 2.5.

General Funds

If you have successfully garnered the support of elected officials, I suggest that you ask directly for dedicated general funds to support the program. General fund budget allocations will help to secure a long-term funding base and keep the program from constantly needing to justify its existence based on cost benefit. General funds are commonly one of the principal governmental or municipal funding sources that are the least restrictive in terms of covenants regarding their use. General funds are typically from such sources as sales tax revenues, building and occupational tax revenues, and court and parking fines. They tend to come from many different sources that funnel into one "big bucket" of general funds, with maximum flexibility in terms of freedom from obligation. One thing to keep in mind, however, is that in an economic downturn, budget from general fund sources will be scarce and more likely to be subjected to budget cuts.

Utility Conservation Funds

Many programs, including those in Seattle, Austin, Portland, and San Francisco, receive utility funding. Green building programs can be thought of as part of demand-side management. Conservation-related dollars are usually the source, financed from ratepayer revenue. In most cases, this occurs as a percentage of utility revenues set aside for conservation programs. One challenge of such funding sources is the ability to measure the value of the program to ratepayers and to ensure a funding nexus. For example, how much energy is saved by green building, resulting in an offset in the cost of capacity expansion to customers? Various utility types can provide funding, including electric, natural gas, water, drainage, and solid waste. San Francisco's Green Building Program, located in the Department of Environment, finances its programs from garbage rates and fees levied by the San Francisco Public Utilities Commission.

Public Benefits Charge

Another utility-based strategy is known as a public benefits charge. This may also be called a system benefit charge. This entails the levy of a special charge to ratepayers for a specific purpose that has public benefit. Typically, it is charged to all utility customers based on consumption. It can be levied and disbursed at the state or local level. Such programs provide continuing support for special programs, such as renewable energy investments, rebates, energy-efficiency programs, low-income support initiatives, and education programs.[11] Examples include Santa Clara's public benefits charge, which is used to finance energy-efficiency programs and purchases of renewable electricity. The City of Portland's green building program is partially financed from a solid waste and recycling commercial tonnage charge allocated to residential garbage customers.

Construction Permit Fees

A portion of green building program costs can be funded through building permitting offices and the revenues generated from construction permit fees. Be aware that these funding sources are also likely to fluctuate dependent on the real estate economy. As in the case of utility funding, a funding nexus between the funding source and the associated benefit to building permit applicants must be demonstrated. The City of Seattle's program uses construction permit fees to fund the portion of the program that provides green building technical assistance to permit applicants. Some jurisdictions are adjusting development fees to reflect the associated impact on infrastructure. Examples include Du-Page County, Illinois, whose development fees reflect a project's transportation impact, and Lancaster, California, which uses the site's distance from the city center to calculate fees.[12] Building permit fee waivers represent a permit-process incentive (see chapter 6).

Special Penalties or Taxes

In some cases, special taxes or penalties can be used to fund green building programs. Much of the City of Chicago's green building program is funded via a multimillion-dollar legal settlement that was made with their electric utility (based on poor past performance). Such opportunities may be rare, but be on the lookout for them. Another type of penalty can come in the form of a tax. For example, the City of Boulder, Colorado, has created a tax on energy usage that will be used to finance their climate protection efforts. The tax generates approximately $1.33 per household.[13] The City of Seattle's downtown density bonus program (see chapter 6) requires achieving LEED Silver certification. If the project fails to achieve the requirement, financial penalties are allocated, which will be used to fund green building grants or additional program services.

Partner Funding

Seattle's program often leverages resources by providing seed or partial funding for initiatives and then seeking partner funding. In addition, some programs that were initiated by City Green Building eventually transition to be led by other organizations. In this way, the ripple effects created by a public sector program are expanded throughout the marketplace. Partnership funding might include conferences and lecture programs, trade education, design competitions, tours, media, advertising, and demonstration projects. Partnerships can also represent in-kind resources. For example, in 2007, Thor Peterson, Seattle's residential green building staff member, partnered with Whole Foods on the Living Green educational series. Thor gave a series of Green Remodel lectures, while Whole Foods handled all the logistics, marketing, and hosting of the program. Thor also partnered with a local newspaper to provide weekly green building tips, published in their home section. Identify your strategic partner organizations and work with them on cosponsoring and cofunding programs in your shared priority areas. Such partnerships can also be with other municipal departments with complementary missions, such as departments of neighborhoods, parks, or libraries.

Combined Funding Packages

The above financing sources can be used in isolation or, in some of the more robust programs, combined to create a total funding package. An appropriate funding mix can build resiliency into a financial package, just as diversified investments are part of a robust financial portfolio. Thought of in this way, if one budget area is challenged, other sources may be able to pick up the slack. The City of Seattle Green Building Program receives budget from multiple funding sources. An example of their program budget breakdown is shown in figure 2.3.

While it may increase the administrative burden associated with budget management, funding the program from multiple sources offers an additional opportunity to broaden internal buy-in and support. For example, if the funding comes from different departmental budgets, each department has a vested interest in the success of the program and will stay engaged. The challenge for this funding model also lies in the need to please multiple funders, meet their needs, measure benefits to them, and provide reporting to more than one entity. Varying levels of detail are needed in providing evidence of the funding nexus.

The preferred method for receiving combined funding is to have the funds transferred annually or quarterly from the funding department to the receiving department.

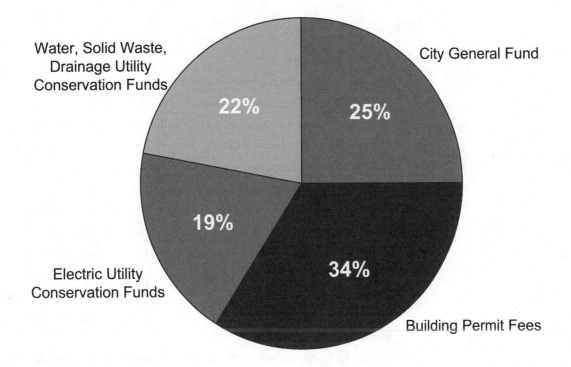

Water, Solid Waste, Drainage Utility Conservation Funds 22%

City General Fund 25%

Electric Utility Conservation Funds 19%

Building Permit Fees 34%

This may require the provision of additional "budget authority" for the receiving department. This budget authority authorizes them to actually spend the funds they are receiving. The first few years that the Seattle program used combined funding, each funder wanted detailed information about exactly where its funds were going, copies of invoices, and so forth. This was extremely cumbersome. Eventually, the finance department authorized what it referred to as the "budget allocation" method of accounting. This meant that there was funding and accountability at a very high level for an annual program of work, and funds were not parsed out individually to specific projects. This method provided general oversight but not micromanagement of the budgeting and program implementation process.

Following is a summary of key points and lessons from this chapter.

FIGURE 2.3 Sample City of Seattle Green Building Budget Allocation Consider multiple funding sources to broaden support and build budget resiliency.

Challenges to Building Support

- Lack of leadership at a high level (the primary challenge for creating a green building program)
- Resistance from inside government due to scarce resources or competing issues
- Citizen and industry push back regarding fear of increased regulations or loss of control
- Misperceptions regarding costs and benefits of green building
- Coordination challenges across departmental or organizational boundaries

TIPS

Tips on Building Support

- Become familiar with your local geographic, ecological, and political sustainability challenges and priorities.
- Demonstrate how green building can help to drive positive change for your community's sustainability challenges.
- Do research to determine how many green building projects, such as LEED, there are within your city and how this compares to other places.
- Utilize sustainable city rankings or other indicators of success to educate public officials about how your city is doing. Use these indicators as motivators.
- Find existing utility conservation programs, policies, or political documents (such as comprehensive plans) that can be linked to green building. Build a case for why they are connected.
- Garner support from top-level leaders, such as elected officials and department heads.
- Arrange for elected officials and opinion leaders to attend green building tours, or conduct green building briefings.
- Secure stakeholder support from a broad range of both internal and external building industry representation to provide political support and guidance.
- Be sure to include both supporters and skeptics of green building in stakeholder groups.

Tips on Developing Internal Champions

- Develop advocates at both the upper and lower ranks of management and staff.
- Maintain good ongoing communication between the upper- and lower-rank advocates.
- Rely on face-to-face dialogue rather than e-mail whenever possible.
- Ensure a wide range of champions across all stakeholder suborganizations or departments.
- Develop a team structure with broad stakeholder representation but consisting of no more than eight or so core members.
- Think of teams as brain trusts and repositories of institutional memory.
- Designate clear lines of communication to eliminate duplication and confusion.
- Foster an atmosphere of openness, trust, and frankness, coupled with confidentiality.

Tips on Organizational Positioning and Funding

- Locate green building programs within departments or organizations that have high-level management support as well as staff-level advocates.
- Consider locating programs within utilities, environmental departments, or building construction permitting agencies.
- Utilize grant or seed funding to launch programs if other resources are not available.
- Build a long-term funding base from multiple sources, including conservation funds, public benefits charges, construction permit fees, special taxes, and revolving funds.
- Seek partners to cofund programs and leverage resources.
- If multiple funding sources are utilized, secure budget authority to transfer and spend funds directly. Use a cost allocation method of budget management that minimizes administrative overhead.

CHAPTER 3

Change and Innovation in Markets and Organizations

G etting the lay of the land within your local green building marketplace will help you to target and customize your programs and policies. This chapter addresses how to target and manage green building changes both in your organization and within the broader context of the building industry marketplace. It also discusses some broad principles that influence both areas.

Understanding the dynamics of market behavior as the building industry moves through the process of adopting green building innovations can provide additional insight into the continuum of change and your place within it. Adopting innovations requires organizations within the marketplace to change. An appreciation of the unique dynamics of organizational behavior can help green building leaders navigate the change process within the institutions they inhabit, whether they are governmental or corporate organizations. Finally, handling communications within your organization, as well as within the building industry marketplace, requires attention. Managing relationships and awareness of green building within peer, building operator, and building occupant groups is critical. In addition, being prepared to deal with press and media inquiries is an important part of a good marketing strategy (and is discussed briefly at the end of this chapter).

MARKET POSITIONING

When beginning the strategic planning process for program services, there are many things to consider. Chances are that the initial phase of a green building program will not be able to cover every type of service or all customers. A variety of ways to target and prioritize services exists. One way to think about positioning programs within the design and construction industry is by the development or project type, which may also be referred to as a market sector. Market sectors include commercial, residential single family and multifamily, and institutional. Each of these market sectors has its own characteristics, service providers, and challenges. In some cases, the project delivery methods vary as well. Some sectors may have their own building codes and industry organizations.

It is important to understand the market dynamics of each sector, determining who the key decision makers are and where they get their information. In addition, we must assess the barriers and opportunities associated with each sector, which can become leverage points. An example of this is in the multifamily market sector—in particular, condominiums. The market in Seattle is somewhat overbuilt for condos, and the real estate market in general has slowed considerably. In addition, condominium buyers are well educated and likely to be aware of health and environmental conditions. A leverage point in this market might be helping the condo developer understand that building a green condo will represent a competitive advantage in a saturated market, a distinguishing feature for the developer's products. Green features related to health and a lower carbon footprint, in addition to healthy lifestyles related to neighborhood location, could attract buyers if marketed correctly. Another example is in the medical and laboratory sector. Energy costs for such facilities are huge. Targeting education or incentive programs for this sector can use energy conservation as the leverage point, or "hook."

Table 3.1 shows a summary of how various construction market sectors can be characterized and how decision makers impact these, using Seattle as an example. The focus for this table is new construction activity. Seattle is entirely built out, so there is very little new single-family construction. A significant amount of single-family construction activity still occurs as renovations of existing homes. With a desire to provide some type of educational service to home owners, Seattle's Green Home Remodel program was created. Thor Peterson authored a highly successful series of brochures, which have been replicated by many jurisdictions, including the City of Chicago.[1]

Another important program planning step is gaining insight into the local real estate market conditions. Do some research to determine market activity over the past five to ten years and, if possible, the projected development for the next ten years. This type of information is often available from chambers of commerce, business and real estate associations or publications, and market analysis consultants. Look for help from city staff involved in economic development, city or utility planning, or demography. Figure 3.1 shows building square footage projections for the City of Portland through the year 2050, which they used in planning and targeting their green building initiatives. Such data can help determine where the current and projected impacts occur, by building type. While the new square footages of commercial and residential building are fairly equal for 2020, by 2050 new commercial development in Portland is estimated to far outstrip residential development.

Historic building permit data can also be useful. Contact your local building permitting agency to pull this data and compile it into reports. Analyzing construction activity using permit data has several dimensions. Be sure to pull data on the number of permits issued by type, as well as by the construction value or square footage estimates. Different ways of viewing the data can be revealing. The number of permits alone can be deceiving. A single permit is not an indicator of the size or impact of a project. A single commercial per-

TABLE 3.1 DECISION MAKERS BY MARKET SECTOR————————————————————————

Understanding who the key decision makers are, and the conditions of the related real estate market, can help to pinpoint or target green building programs and messages.

Market Sector	Key Decision Makers	Local Real Estate Market Conditions for Seattle
Single Family Detached	Home owner (Market research shows women make most home purchasing decisions.)	Seattle built out; little new single-family construction Infill projects and remodels only Criticisms regarding large homes out of scale with neighborhood
Townhome	Home owner Developer	Significant portion of current construction market in neighborhoods Criticism regarding bland style, poor aesthetic
Multifamily Attached Apartment/ Condo	Developer	Significant number of new mid- and high-rise condos in central business district Mixed use with ground-floor retail
Commercial/ Office Retail, Speculative	Developer	Large number of high-rise construction projects in central business district Office, retail
Commercial/ Office, Owner or Tenant Driven	Owner, Tenant	Hotels Large corporate tenants (e.g., Amazon, Starbucks)
Institutional, Government	Owner, Officials for public funding approval process	Large number of government projects High activity in hospitals, medical facilities, universities, local schools Large corporate campuses Affordable housing
Planned Community	Developer, officials for public funding or entitlement approval process	Transit-oriented development Large-scale infill, such as public housing Greenfield development outside Seattle

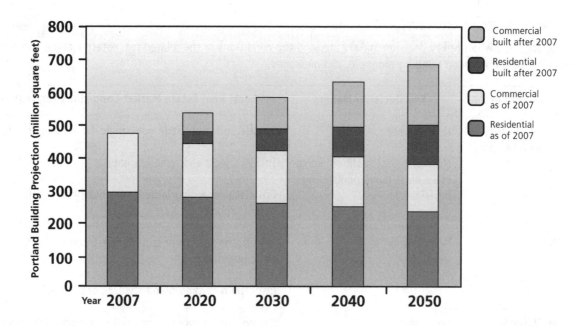

FIGURE 3.1 Portland Commercial and Residential Building Square Footage Projections through 2050(based on average growth rate projections from 2000 to 2006) Projected construction activity can be used to target green building programs for the most impact.
Source: City of Portland High Performance Green Building Policy Report, December 4, 2008
Credit: Image courtesy of City of Portland Bureau of Planning and Sustainability

mit for a high-rise project obviously represents a huge square footage compared to a single commercial permit for a strip center or a single-family residential building. The square footage represented by a project will drive the associated resource use impact, in both construction and operations impacts (for example, the amount of materials and construction recycling activity as well as the energy or water use and transportation impacts).

In Seattle, new downtown commercial construction was targeted with one-on-one technical assistance services, because of the small number of projects that could be served for the returned impact. Similar services targeted at a large number of smaller projects would naturally require higher levels of staffing and program resources, because of the larger volume of projects that would require personal assistance.

In times of economic prosperity, there will be more market activity related to new construction, as well as larger projects being permitted and built. During economic downturns, construction projects tend to be smaller and more focused on existing building renovations than on new construction. In slower real estate development years, services can focus on existing buildings and tenant improvements.

With the recent downturn in the real estate market, it will be more difficult to project real estate activity in the future. However, it's fairly safe to say that large, new construction projects will be limited because of scarce funding sources. Look for exceptions to this in the form of large institutional or nonprofit investments that may represent significant opportunities to integrate green building, such as the planned four-block project Jack's Urban Meeting Place, in Boise, Idaho, funded by the Simplot Family Foundation. Some sectors, such as health care and assisted living, will not be as severely affected by the economy. Renovation and remodeling projects, as well as tenant improvements, can also be expected to stay fairly strong. Families will tend to improve or renovate their homes to meet their needs, rather than buy new ones or sell the ones they have. In the office market, tenant improvements are likely to stay robust as tenants shop for less expensive office space in an increasingly competitive marketplace with high vacancy rates. Finally, improvements associated with energy efficiency are likely to be very well funded as a result of recent increases in federal incentives (see chapter 8) and the new administration's focus on climate disruption and green-collar, energy-related jobs. Upgrading existing buildings to decrease energy use is a market activity that is likely to grow, given its potential to reduce operating costs for businesses looking to trim their bottom line.

Often, opportunity lies in building on existing conservation programs or goals, which can bring added partners into the picture and leverage additional resources. Conservation plans from local utilities sometimes show where the most potential for conservation lies. Not all utilities have conservation plans, but the more progressive or larger ones will. If the electric utility sees huge conservation potential in a certain sector, this might suggest a key partnership. Other opportunity-driven actions may involve piggybacking on a large redevelopment project with high visibility and major impact. In Seattle, the High Point Community Redevelopment Project provided significant opportunities due to the huge scale of the project (over eight hundred new housing units), with an emphasis on affordable housing, and all by working with a single partner, the Seattle Housing Authority. Seattle Public Utilities— Seattle's drainage, solid waste, and wastewater utility—focused a significant green building effort on this project, providing several million dollars to implement and demonstrate low-impact development techniques, including natural drainage and porous pavement.

It is likely that most green building program services will address a variety of market sectors, not just one. Take the market sector analysis and other key factors into account when determining how much of your program resources (both budget and staffing) to allocate to each sector. This strategy was used to allocate Seattle's green building program resources (see figure 3.2 for an example).

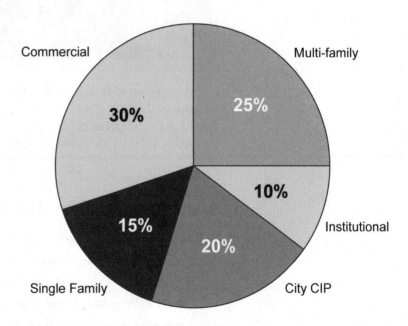

FIGURE 3.2 Sample City of Seattle Program Sector Resource Allocation Green building programs can address a variety of market sectors with varying emphasis. (CIP stands for capital improvement projects; see chapter 4.)

BOX 3.1 MARKET TRANSFORMATION THEORY ——————————————————

Green building adoption can be thought of within the context of market transformation theory. This well-known theory was first presented by Everett M. Rogers in his seminal book *Diffusion of Innovations*. In its application here, green building is the innovation, or new practice, that is being introduced into the marketplace, which may choose to accept or reject it. The innovation adoption process can be broken down into phases, with each successive phase representing a broader audience adopting the innovation as the marketplace becomes transformed.

The classic bell-shaped adoption curve (see figure 3.3) divides the marketplace into five groups: innovators, early adopters, early majority, later majority, and laggards. Innovators, represented by a very small 2.5 percent of the overall marketplace, are the first to adopt green building. They are risk takers who are able to cope with uncertainty and are willing to accept an occasional setback. The next group, the early adopters, are opinion leaders who follow the innovators' precedent. These are later joined by the early majority, characterized as followers who make deliberate decisions; the late majority, who tend to be skeptical and cautious; and finally the laggards, who are the most traditional group and the slowest to change and adopt new ideas.[1]

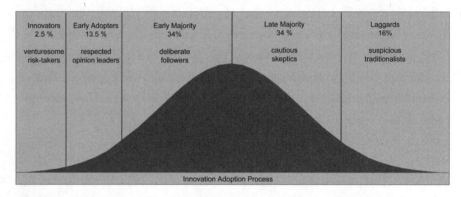

FIGURE 3.3 Innovation Adoption Process after Everett M. Rogers, Diffusion of Innovation, 2003
Green building adoption can be thought of within the context of the theory of innovation adoption and market transformation.

NAVIGATING CHANGE WITH EARLY ADOPTERS

This brief story provides some insight into how working with early adopters can foster acceptance of green building by others at a later time. Early in the implementation of the City of Seattle policy, there was a mix of optimists and skeptics. Some departments enthusiastically welcomed the change, while others initially seemed to view it as a nuisance. The departments that embraced the change had a can-do attitude. They immediately started holding strategy sessions with green building program staff, trained themselves about green building, and took steps to hire architects with green experience. Conversely, skeptics in other departments seemed to spend most of their energy contradicting the mandate and coming up with excuses for not going green. They seemed fearful of what might

Rogers defines diffusion as the communications process over time among members of a social system—in our case, members of the building industry.[2] The spread of the green building message throughout the marketplace represents industry members looking for ways to become comfortable with the degree of uncertainty and perceived risk that green building may represent for them. The impetus to undertake this change originates from the awareness that previous building practice fails to meet certain needs or solve certain problems. The innovation needs to be understood to represent a relative advantage in the marketplace, which could include increased economic profitability, sustainability, or social prestige.

Key to the adoption process is the ability to gain information through communication channels within the market system. Members of the building industry share information regarding the innovation. Attitudes toward the new idea must change in order for more people to adopt it into their practice. Rogers outlines five basic steps in the communications and decision process:

Knowledge → Persuasion → Decision → Implementation → Confirmation

This process is important for several reasons. First, it happens within the peer network of the building industry. Second, if the process is not successful, the innovation may be rejected in all or in part. People within the peer network of the building industry will look to others in the industry to assess their opinion of green building. Does it work? What are its relative advantages? As Rogers notes: "Mass media messages are too general to provide the specific kind of reinforcement that the individual needs to confirm his or her initial beliefs about the innovation."[3]

Advertising campaigns or other mass media strategies may help bring awareness of green building as a concept but will not lead to adoption of it. The latter must occur via the peer networks within the industry. Therefore, green building program staff should represent peers in the building industry and should seek to maximize opportunities for peer-to-peer exchange of information. The most well-known initiative that took this approach is the agricultural extension program created by the U.S. Department of Agriculture, which utilized a network of researchers connected to county extension agents. The extension agents brought the most recent scientific innovations to people in the field, using peer-to-peer, face-to-face communication and persuasion.

1. Everett M. Rogers, *Diffusion of Innovations*, 5th ed. (New York: Free Press, 2003), 284, 285.
2. Rogers, *Diffusion of Innovations*, 3.
3. Rogers, *Diffusion of Innovations*, 175.

happen if they failed or made a mistake. (For background on market transformation and early adopters, see box 3.1.)

While our instincts may tell us that we need to work harder to convert the skeptic group, this may prove unwise. Skeptics who are forced to adopt a change before they are ready will likely do everything they can to sabotage the effort. If people are determined to fail, it is unlikely that even the most well-intentioned assistance will meet with success. If the early attempts fail and word of this spreads, it can have a very negative effect on the initiative as a whole.

In those early days of the Seattle program, I was working harder and harder to push the skeptics to embrace a green building policy for which they were not psychologically ready. Memos and meetings became complicated maneuvering activities colored predominantly by jockeying for control and the upper hand. This became quite unpleasant and divisive, as the skeptics began to portray green building as too costly and competing with other, more important public mandates. As these problems intensified, I began to focus on them more and more. I was spending a lot of my time on the defensive, trying to defend green building and LEED, or being a watchdog toward those resisting the policy. I was becoming the "eco-police." Not only did I seem to be getting nowhere fast, but I was not having much fun. I was also spending less time with the pioneering teams who really wanted to do green building but who still needed help. I shifted my focus and started working more with early champion teams to turn in some very successful LEED projects.

If we look at social-based marketing strategy, working with early adopters is a necessary step to build successes and immediate wins. Skeptics need for others to take the initial risks before they feel they can follow. In addition, we should not ignore the early adopters, who are likely to need a concerted assistance effort in order to ensure their triumph. As the early adopter victories gain momentum and the word spreads, the skeptics will take note and will eventually follow.

As it turned out, the skeptics came along in the end. They just needed to embrace change at a different rate, and to watch as the early adopters took the initial risks. In one instance, one of the city's early LEED design teams was extremely resistant to adapting its designs to fit the policy criteria. Only a few years later, one of the architects was presenting at a conference and championing LEED as an excellent tool. This transformation happened within a relatively short amount of time. I was reminded to allow space for different individuals to change at their own rate. Some would change faster; others, slower. This does not mean the late adopters are "bad" people; they are just at a different place in the bell curve for innovation adoption.

PROGRAM PHASING

Understanding where your local marketplace is in terms of the innovation adoption curve is useful for targeting program efforts, phasing program development, and selecting communication tools. Assessing the market position within the adoption curve is a matter of judgment. If you determine that green building adoption is in its earliest stages, working to support the early innovators should be the priority. If the marketplace is further along, services for the early or late majority may be in order.

In the early stages of green building adoption, a few brave innovators will launch the first attempts. It is important that at least some of these attempts are perceived as successful. Case studies can be an effective tool for spreading the word about new green building strategies and successes. Of course, it is also important to be honest regarding failures, which will help to build credibility and ensure that continuous learning supports the ongoing evolution of successful green building strategies in your marketplace.

Green building program planning can respond and correlate to innovation adoption and to several basic strategies for reinforcing behavior change. Green building program activities can be planned in phased steps, starting with easy steps and progressing to more stringent actions over time, as market adoption unfolds. There are three basic phases for reinforcing market adoption and behavior change. First, remove barriers to eliminate excuses for not changing, and support the early innovators. Second, create incentives (voluntary adoption). Finally, create requirements (mandatory adoption). These topics will be discussed in more detail in later chapters.

These three distinct types of activities are most successful when done sequentially. In many cases, green building programs have started with voluntary measures in order to gently introduce green building concepts and create awareness. Next, incentives are provided to expand adoption and make green building more attractive to skeptics. The final phase of mandatory requirements may be implemented once the foundation of market adoption has been built and the industry has had a chance to become prepared by testing out green building during the voluntary stages. Over time, the process can begin again to address higher levels of green building achievement or to reflect advances in the field. The next phase includes mandatory requirements in order to capture the laggard group, who may not change as rapidly as is desired unless required to. Another way to approach this is to create code requirements that will provide a basic level of green building performance. Incentives can be created that add an additional tier over and above basic requirements to encourage deeper levels of green building. Several examples of goals related to the residential and commercial sectors, with phased action steps, are shown in table 3.2.

HOW ORGANIZATIONS CHANGE

As mentioned at the start of this chapter, managing change within the building industry and your own organization may benefit from some insight into how these respond to change. Changing the culture, values, or norms of any institution is a messy and often chaotic process. Any organization can be thought of as a system, with various pieces and parts that make up a larger whole. Many different components of the organization may function in a certain way only if other parts of the system play their role. In whole systems, performance depends on how all of the parts interact together. I have often found it helpful to work from a larger contextual understanding of whole systems theory to make sense of the organizational change process. My studies with Antioch University's Whole Systems Design Program have been highly valuable in the world of green building innovation adoption.

A system is a collection of parts that interact with one another to function as a whole. Each

TABLE 3.2 PHASED TACTICS FOR MARKET TRANSFORMATION

Consider how to sequentially remove barriers, provide incentives, and create requirements for each building sector you wish to target.

Market Sector/ Target Audience	Tactic or Strategy		
	Remove Barriers *(Lack of knowledge or regulatory barriers)*	**Provide Incentives** *(Cash, rebate, process, or disincentives)*	**Create Requirements** *(Regulatory and code)*
Residential Owner-Occupied Homes **Homebuyer, Purchaser of Condo or Townhome, Builders, Developers**	Real estate listings that include green home info Educational workshops and brochures on benefits Weekly newspaper tips Green building hotline Review plumbing, energy, stormwater codes for barriers Remove code barriers	Green product rebates Grants for green building certification Tax credits Accelerated permitting Fee waivers Impact fees	Integrate green building requirements into single- and multifamily building code Adopt Standard 189* Integrate greenhouse gas impacts into environmental review
Commercial Office and Mixed Use **Developer, Building Owner**	Case studies with cost benefit data Promote business case and marketing advantage Technical assistance Review plumbing, energy, stormwater, fire codes for barriers Remove code barriers	Incentive zoning with density bonus for green building Cash incentives for green certification programs Tax credits Packaged utility incentives Accelerated permitting Fee waivers Impact fees	Integrate green building requirements into land use and commercial building code Adopt Standard 189* Integrate greenhouse gas impacts into environmental review
Neighborhood and New Community Development **Developer**	Demonstration projects Green residential tours Review land use code for barriers Remove code barriers	Entitlement process Incentive zoning with density bonus for green building Cash incentives for green certification programs Tax credits Accelerated permitting	Integrate green building requirements into land use code Integrate greenhouse gas impacts into environmental review Create development covenants

*Standard 189 is a proposed code standard developed by ASHRAE in collaboration with the USGBC to create minimum code requirements for green building. It applies to all building types except low-rise residential.

individual element, as well as how it is arranged within the system, tends to be very important. Living things, mechanical devices, and even social organizations can be thought of as systems. Many systems depend on ongoing interactions and inputs from other parts of the system for the system to function as a whole. These interactive exchanges often occur as "feedback."

Feedback can be thought of as either positive, and therefore amplifying, or negative, and therefore dampening as a result. Examples of negative feedback loops include supply and demand in the real estate market, automobile cruise control, float valves, or population stress. Negative feedback works to cancel out changes, or negate them.

Positive feedback causes even more change to occur and amplifies the change. Common examples of positive feedback include interest earnings on investments, cell reproduction, or the accumulation of technological knowledge. Positive feedback is not always beneficial, as with the growth of cancer cells or algae blooms. What most positive feedback loops share is a rather explosive quality in that one initial modification can result in dramatic transformation. The terms *positive feedback* and *negative feedback* should not be confused with the terms positive or negative to denote having good or bad qualities.[2]

Systems theory tells us that, without chaos, little opportunity exists for change and innovation. Controlled, closed, and therefore stable systems are predictable but leave little room at the edges for experimentation, evolution, or adventure. With increased openness comes increased unpredictability, which may make people feel uncomfortable. Standard practices, institutional knowledge, and accepted norms keep us on familiar ground—we know how to think and what to do. Society and governance feel stable. These parameters are similar to negative feedback loops in closed systems: they give us guidance that tells us when to stop and how far to go, maintaining order. Negative feedback regulates, or damps, activity, keeping it within an accepted range. If we go outside the range, we are often not sure what will happen. However, it is at the intersections between what we already know and what we don't, that new thinking and innovation occur.

If a system begins to undergo a change process, the new modes of operating begin to bounce against the established system boundaries or rules. As this happens over time, the change process begins to swing more and more widely between the upper and lower limits, diverging wildly between stability and disorder. This pattern often feels increasingly chaotic.

When chaos begins to feel extreme to members of an organization, either fear or courage will prevail: fear of the threat of change and how it may affect those in the system, or courage to step into the unknown. Both directions can be thought of as adaptive processes, driven by different human emotions. In moments of such tension, I have found it immensely useful to remind myself, and others, about these basic laws of systems and the opportunity inherent in the chaos. People tend to relax after these conversations. I refer to it as "getting comfortable with chaos."

ORGANIZATIONAL CULTURE AND CHANGE

The natural rhythms, ebbs, and flows of the change process can be confusing, and people respond to change differently. In his excellent book *Leading Change toward*

Sustainability, Bob Doppelt notes that many people will respond with resistance because they fear a loss of authority, control, or prestige. They may also resist because they are completely stuck in a certain worldview or because the change is happening too fast for their ability to internalize it. Resistance can take many forms, including covert and clandestine or more overt and explicit. Covert resistance is particularly insidious and may take the form of people who are not just uncooperative but consciously attempting to undermine the change efforts. These hidden opponents may be extremely difficult to sniff out, whereas resistance that is out in the open is much easier to combat.[3]

Change may be much more difficult to navigate if you reside within an organization whose culture is extremely hierarchical or "command and control." Doppelt explains:

> Patriarchal organizations manage from the top down. Those at the top are the authorities. They are in charge of thinking and decision-making. Those at the bottom simply carry out the directives of the executives. Power is exercised through the use of hierarchical management and supervision. Because they view interactions from a purely vertical perspective, patriarchies see organizations as a collection of separate components, not as a whole system. Employees are seen as parts that can be exchanged for others, just as capital equipment may be upgraded, bought or sold. Stakeholders are viewed as thorns in the side, or more often than not, as major threats.[4]

With this hierarchical power system, fear of loss of control becomes endemic, passing its emotional energy down along the chain. In such rigid organizational systems, there is also little tolerance for mistakes. Mistakes are not viewed as learning opportunities and natural events for innovative organizations; they are viewed as embarrassments. Permission to make mistakes, which are inevitable, may help some of the more timid stakeholders to take risks. During the development of Seattle's sustainable infrastructure initiative under the leadership of landscape architect Steve Moddemeyer, the City's director of finance held a kick-off meeting with the core stakeholder team. He told them that the City was behind them 100 percent and that "It's okay if you fail." Explicit statements such as this can help staff who may be more concerned with accountability than innovation.

It is important to realize that with innovation adoption, everything won't always be perfect. There is the need for an ongoing feedback loop about what is working, what is not, and the ability to integrate this learning for continuous organizational improvement. Creating and fostering peer networks within your organization is a useful tool that can promote open internal communications and self-learning, as well as build the organizational community supporting green building. Working toward sustainability is a process, not an individual step, so plan to embrace the journey and your fellow travelers.

Another factor that may come into play with innovation change is the "rubber band effect," or what I call innovation backlash. The tension held by the rubber band lies between the desired vision and the current reality. As the organization is pulled further and further toward the vision, the need for the organization to change becomes intensified.

This creates a great deal of tension. Even if much progress has been made, the rubber band effect can sneak up to violently snap the organization back toward the status quo, as the previous rules attempt to dampen down the change. For those in the middle of the process, this can come as quite a shock. If you remember that the rubber band is able to stretch again, perhaps farther this time than the last, you can learn to be patient with some level of backlash and learn not to let it throw you completely off course. A long-term change process may contain a series of smaller or larger backlashes as the organization continues to move forward, perhaps two steps forward and one back at times. Perseverance will probably pay off in the end, so take heart and enjoy what you may learn along the way. Not all the lessons are technical ones; many are lessons about organizational development and the human condition.

MARKETING AND OUTREACH

Marketing, outreach, and other communications activities are techniques that can be applied to any aspect of your green building program or policy. Communications can be focused on a broad public audience, targeted specifically at market sectors or stakeholder groups, or focused internally within your organization. Outreach activities can help to support innovation adoption and both market and organizational change through fostering awareness, dialogue, and information-sharing networks.

Marketing and Branding

Marketing and advertising campaigns can be extremely useful for their ability to broadly distribute messages and increase awareness in the marketplace. In addition, a well-thought-out communications campaign can help overcome some of the primary barriers to green building adoption. McGraw-Hill Construction has conducted research on markets for green building that assessed some of the top obstacles, including lack of education, lack of awareness, lack of understanding of the benefits, disbelief of increased return on investment, greenwashing, and the perception that green building is too difficult.[5] Messaging programs can be developed that address these issues within various market sectors, such as commercial developers or home owners. Marketing can broadly promote the benefits of green building, or it can promote particular programs or tools.

When undertaking marketing, be sure to consider branding associated with your program as well as the language being used. To reduce confusion in the marketplace, it is wise to choose terms and use them consistently. For example, using both of the terms green building and sustainable building may create confusion. Choose one and stick with it. Green building is the most commonly used term, probably as a result of the huge growth of the U.S. Green Building Council.

Over time, Seattle's program was branded and named City Green Building. This name was used consistently with Web, print, and advertising materials. It is advisable to brand your program with a recognizable name, logo, and look and feel for published materials such as brochures and flyers. Make the name intuitive so that it will be obvious what the program is about, and try to avoid jargon and confusing language in all program materials. Use the look and feel consistently in the marketplace to build brand awareness and acceptance. While most programs will have few resources for traditional marketing and advertising, these dollars can be stretched by joining forces with partners with similar messaging goals. It helps to work with strategic partners so that the messages being delivered within a market are consistent, to avoid confusion. In the early days of Seattle's green building initiative, several key marketing partnerships were developed to provide broad, consistent messaging. Led by Lynne Barker, the City of Seattle, King County, and the nonprofit BetterBricks joined forces with the USGBC to create a powerful print marketing campaign to help brand green building and its value proposition. The resulting campaign, dubbed "Build Green, Everyone Profits," used corporate adoption of LEED as a method to build credibility in the marketplace.[6]

Peer Outreach

Developing peer networks within the green building industry or within your organization is a useful strategy for helping to foster the innovation adoption process. Connecting peers in the building industry can be accomplished via several outreach avenues. Organized events, such as lectures and public forums, can raise awareness regarding the work of the innovators in the building industry. Presentations to existing industry groups can also be very effective. The public sector can support such green building peer organizations as the local AIA Committee on the Environment (COTE) or local chapter of the USGBC, which tends to organize both educational and peer networking events.

Often, peers in the green building industry are pleasantly surprised when government or industry organizations lead the creation of peer networks, stakeholder groups, or other opportunities for people to meet one another and make connections. Social networking events may help bring together building industry opinion leaders and followers. Informal events can provide as much value as more formal ones. In the older generation of industry professionals, traditional avenues, such as formal invitations to public or private events, may be the most effective. Personal invitations that identify the individual by name can add gravitas to the situation, letting that person know he or she has been specifically selected for the value that his or her perspective and knowledge bring. For those who are from the newer generation or who have gravitated to recent social networking tools, other methods may be equally effective.

Internal Communications and Outreach

Attending to outreach and communications within your organization is an important step that may often go overlooked. Creating internal newsletters and organizing peer groups within your organization is a useful strategy for building staff support and knowledge networks. The successful adoption of Seattle's Green Building Program and policy within the internal workings of city government often relied on a fairly vast and dispersed series of relationships—knowing whom to call when and for what. Although such social networks take time to develop, they are important because they create a tribe of green building both within and outside the organization. The concept of community-based social marketing, developed by Doug McKenzie-Mohr, focuses on the fact that behavior change is most effective when it involves direct contact with other people at the community level.[7] In Seattle, we held monthly green building after-work visits to a favorite pub, where I saw amazing though seemingly random connections being made. I could not have planned for or organized such connections in advance.

More formal internal peer meetings were also important. These were often convened around particular topics or user groups, such as operations and maintenance issues, use of Forest Stewardship Council certified lumber, hiring green consultants, or green housekeeping. Sharing problems, solutions, and a broader perspective can help validate green building adoption. Each person needs to feel not only that he or she is part of the solution but also his or her connection to a larger whole, which adds meaning as well as an informal support group. Inclusivity can also help to prevent green building from seeming too much like a clique or an elite club that is difficult to join. Make sure a broad range of people feel included, whether they are policy analysts or building managers. Be sure to include those you consider to be adversaries or critics. They may be disarmed by your reaching out.

Outreach to both building managers and building tenants is an important part of a communications effort linked to new green buildings that your organization owns and operates. The need to educate also extends to building tenants within your organization. How much awareness do the new tenants have that they are occupying a green building? Do they know about the unique features of the building and the role they may play in helping to make sure these features function effectively? It's amazing how often this essential communication is overlooked. Building tenants may be more amenable to a broad range of functional issues if initial outreach has occurred that helps them to understand the building they occupy and encourages them to become a part of the solution. An initial welcome message in the form of a print or electronic newsletter, orienting tenants to the building and its green features, is highly recommended and can be part of a green building education program that can help to earn LEED credits. Periodic updates on green features may also be useful.

At Seattle City Hall, initially the toilets were flushed with potable tap water. Later, a rainwater cistern adjacent to the building was completed, and the system switched over to use the collected rainwater for flushing. This water was slightly discolored because some of the water overflowed from a green roof, causing tannins in the soil to leach into the water. Imagine the number of complaints received by tenants after this change occurred and no notification had been received. Simple signage in the restrooms explaining the water reuse system, why the water was discolored, and how much water is being saved can prevent this problem. One tenant education tool the City of Seattle has used is called the "Stall Times." It's a brief written update on building issues that is placed on the inside doors of toilet stalls. While this may sound like a rather odd communications tool, it is actually a simple way to communicate with all tenants. Building tenants are often the ambassadors to the building for visitors, so arm them with good information. Tenants who are privy to insights about operational issues may also be less likely to raise building-related complaints.

Press Preparedness

Be prepared for media attention, both negative and positive. Green building programs will inevitably attract attention, most of it good. Develop a media plan for each year with important milestones so you can proactively handle media attention and get it when you want it. Consider holding quarterly briefings with staff who handle public media inquiries. For organizations with a large number of green building capital projects, it is wise to prepare regular status reports as well as a template for press releases and project data sheets.

Public events, such as public press conferences, policy announcements, groundbreakings, or ribbon cuttings, will require you to be prepared for media attention. It is often difficult in the flurry of activity right before a public event to get the attention of elected officials, executives, and their media staff. Rather than handle this reactively, get prepared. Many competing messages often vie for attention. At times, the green building message can be lost among the many messages.

The best way to ensure that green building gets included as a key message is to provide public information officers with media-worthy facts well before they prepare their own press releases. This information should be kept short, digestible, and clear. Prepare short briefing materials and bulleted speaking points. Offer to hold one-on-one meetings with speakers and elected officials in advance of the press event to answer any questions they may have and to make sure they are comfortable with all of the speaking points. Here are some important facts to include: How will the project benefit the community? How will it benefit the taxpayers? How much energy, water, or other resources is the project expected to save? What are the most visible or fascinating green building features of the projects? This is the type of information that will be most likely to get featured. Does the project represent any "firsts"? How many other green building projects have already been built in the city? See chapter 7 for information on how to get data on the performance of green buildings that can be integrated into your press releases.

If you have the time, consider developing relationships with allies in the media, such as reporters who cover an environmental beat. These contacts can help to build positive press, to have articles written for which you can provide the content, and to dispel negative media. This is often called "earned media," and for good reason. It is dependent on spending the time necessary to cultivate and earn trust-based relationships with journalists.

Early in the growth of Seattle's LEED project portfolio, a negative story appeared in the local newspaper accusing our new LEED-Gold City Hall of being an "energy hog." While the basis of the story was unfounded, we did not have any data at the ready with which to refute the article. If negative media emerges and you are unable to respond quickly, this can be damaging to the reputation of the program and to green building in general. While you can't anticipate every inquiry, it is safe to assume that if you are out there making claims about how great green building is, there will be skeptics who will attempt to invalidate your message. While it is not necessary to respond to every complaint or negative comment, being armed with the facts will help you to handle the media on an ongoing basis.

Celebration and Ceremony

The process of market or organizational adoption of green building is not a sprint—it's a long-distance marathon. As such, take time to pause along the way, to mark accomplishments large and small, and to applaud your teammates and industry leaders. Paying attention to maintaining relationships takes more than simple communications; it requires respect as well as appreciation. Celebrating success is important to reinforce positive change along the long, and sometimes arduous, path to innovation adoption, and to build a strong and connected team of supporters who will play well together over time.

Celebration can be done in a formal way with public events, or with informal and private festivities. Over the years, our celebrations within Seattle's Green Building Program took many forms, including formal acknowledgment of the five-year birthday of our program, commemorative T-shirts and coffee cups, certificates of appreciation, awards programs, and letters of acknowledgment from the mayor. These are all useful tools to help supporters in the industry or within your organization feel appreciated. Such personal acknowledgments should not be underestimated, so take the extra time to make this happen. In addition, accolades may be even more important when things are not going so well, as opposed to times when they are. A discouraged or dispirited team may give up at a time when continuing to hold the vision is critical. In any case, try to make it fun. People who are genuinely enjoying the work they do, and one another's company, will have more capacity to maintain the enthusiasm that will be needed along the way.

TIPS

Tips on Managing Marketplace Change

- Take time to understand the state of your local green building marketplace.
- Identify decision makers and opinion leaders within your local building industry and what influences their decisions.
- Collect data on past, present, and future construction market activity. Target your efforts where the most impact will be made.
- Plan for activities that target a range of different construction sectors.

Tips on Managing Innovation Adoption

- Remember that different groups will adopt green building at different rates.
- Work with early adopters first, and make sure they succeed.
- Support the ability of decision makers to gain information through their peer network.
- Remember to incorporate the phases of innovation adoption into program phasing plans.
- Remove barriers first.
- Provide incentives second.
- Create requirements third.

Tips on Managing Change in Organizations

- Remember that organizations function as a complex system of interdependent parts.
- Try to get comfortable with the chaos of change. If the change process begins to feel chaotic, it helps to be reminded that this is where opportunity occurs.
- Be aware of the management culture of your organization (e.g., is it strongly top down?).
- Face resistance to change and fear of the unknown with patience.
- Remember to rely on your skills of courage, intuition, focus, and passion when navigating change.

Tips on Marketing and Outreach

- Create a clear and consistent brand and language for your program and its materials.
- Use marketing to address barriers, such as lack of awareness of green building benefits.
- Identify partners to coordinate branding and advertising programs.

- Provide outreach and support to green building operators and managers.
- Reach out to green building tenants with messages about green building benefits and features.
- Prepare a communications and press plan.
- Hold regular meetings with internal media liaisons.
- Prepare elected officials at public events with short, clear speaking points.
- Foster and develop relationships with the press.

Tips on Developing a Strong Green Building Community

- Help to foster peer networks through both formal and informal events.
- Manage internal communications to support an organizational network of green building supporters.
- Put effort into developing and maintaining personal relations with allies at all levels.
- Take time to recognize and celebrate victories and accomplishments.
- Create special meeting opportunities to communicate concerns and needs of adversaries.
- Provide social opportunities to build informal networks and ties.
- Build an inclusive community with open access and a limit on insider jargon.
- Keep everyone up-to-date with newsletters, informal information-sharing sessions, and training.
- Provide tenant education and building signage to help educate others.

CHAPTER 4

Developing and Implementing Policy for Publicly Funded Green Building

One of the most important tools for the green building change agent is policy development for green building. Green building policy can be adopted by public agencies or large corporate or institutional organizations to guide the development, renovation, and management of the buildings they own, operate, and lease. This shows that the organization is "walking the talk." While green building policy can be tied to various benchmark tools, most current policies are tied to the U.S. Green Building Council's tool called LEED.

According to the USGBC: "LEED initiatives including legislation, executive orders, resolutions, ordinances, policies, and initiatives are found in 44 states, including 193 localities (128 cities, 32 counties, and 33 towns), 31 state governments, 12 federal agencies or departments, 16 public school jurisdictions, and 39 institutions of higher education across the United States."[1] An excellent searchable database of LEED-based policies can be found at the government resources section of the USGBC Web site.[2] This chapter addresses policy that is designed primarily to affect publicly funded projects, including policy initiatives at the state and local levels. Similar approaches can be used across many different types of jurisdictions, depending on the legal mechanisms available.

Policy creation is more an art than a science. Many judgments will need to be made regarding the format, requirements, exact policy language, and adoption process. Policy variations will depend on the unique institutional, political, and economic realities surrounding the policy-making entity. Policy makers have multiple options for developing their own unique policy vehicle. The following section can be used as a guideline for some of the basic components that need to be considered.

One of the first steps in analyzing policy options is to determine what types of projects your organization undertakes, and how to turn these into green building opportunities using policy tools. Does your organization serve as a project developer and, if so, at what scale? Most public and some large corporate entities will undertake what is commonly referred to as capital improvement projects or a capital improvement program. The acronym CIP is often used for both terms. Such projects take capital dollars to make improvements to the built environment. (Capital purchases can also include equipment or other purchases that can be depreciated, but this type of activity is not covered in this book.) Capital improvements can include new buildings, upgrades to existing buildings, and infrastructure projects.

Scan the horizon of your organization. What development and tenancy decisions are in the immediate and long-term future? If large new construction projects are planned, then this should be your focus. In only smaller scale tenant improvements lie ahead, be sure your policy covers those types of projects. Most policies will guide some form of CIP activities. Entities that do not develop or own their own facilities can create policy for space that they lease from other building owners.

TYPES OF MANDATES

How can a planned CIP be leveraged toward green building? This represents an important policy question for the green building advocate or policy maker. Green building standards for publicly funded construction can take multiple forms, but they fall into two basic types: policy mandates and legal mandates. Policy mandates are clear executive directives but are not legally binding. Legal mandates are binding by law and require formal legislative action.

Policy mandates may be more nimble and can be adopted with a less cumbersome legal process. Policy mandates ultimately rely on political power and support for enforcement, and the repercussions for failure to comply are less clear. However, many jurisdictions are successfully implementing green building policy mandates. Legal mandates may seem onerous, which may make them more cumbersome to get adopted. The benefit is that they are enforceable by law and make the repercussions clear to those responsible.

Policy Mandates

Policy mandates often take the form of either an executive order or a resolution. In either case, they give direction from the highest executive within an organization, whether at the federal, state, municipal, or other top executive leadership level. Green building executive orders guiding public construction have been issued by many cities, including Albuquerque, Boston, Denver, Jacksonville, Salt Lake City, and Tampa; states, including Arizona, Colorado, Florida, Indiana, Maine, Massachusetts, Michigan, New Jersey, New Mexico, New York, and Rhode Island; and counties, including King County, Washington, and Monroe County, New York.[3]

Policy mandates may be issued by the executive or by other aspects of the governing body, such as city councils, commissioners, mayors, or city managers. Anaheim, Asheville, Athens, Austin, Berkeley, Seattle, Portland, and Sacramento have adopted green building policy via city council resolutions. Such actions are typically sponsored by a single city council member or commissioner.

In some cases, other public policy tools can be utilized as vehicles, such as in the case of the City of Rochester Hills, which integrated green building requirements into its Master Land Use Plan, or Seattle, which integrated its policy into the Environmental Management System for city operations. Policy can also be set by major public institutions, such as universities; quasi-public organizations, such as development authorities; and private entities, such as large corporate organizations or developers. Harvard University adopted Sustainability Principles and an implementation framework that addresses capital planning and construction as well as financial and budget planning.[4]

Legal Mandates

Legal mandates can take many forms that leverage the regulatory system to achieve green building goals, now and into the future. These forms can include ordinances, laws and by-laws, municipal codes, and state statutes. The governing assembly appropriate to the jurisdiction adopting the requirements must vote to approve the legal requirements. Often, the approving body is the city council, county government, or state legislature. These may include governing bodies at the federal, state, city, county, or town level, as appropriate.

TABLE 4.1 SELECTED GREEN BUILDING MANDATES COMPARISON

City Adoption and Date	Type of Mandate	Scope	Threshold	Referenced Standard
City of Austin 11/29/2007 (update to 2000)	Resolution	New construction, renovation, tenant improvements, additional guidance for small projects, existing buildings	New construction over $2 million, renovations over $300,000	LEED Silver with additional baseline standards
City of Chicago 6/2004	Policy	New construction and renovation	"Substantial" projects only	LEED Silver with Chicago Standard
City of Portland 4/27/2005 (update to 2001)	Resolution	New construction, tenant improvements, existing buildings	Receiving 10 percent or more City funding	LEED Gold new, LEED Silver existing buildings and tenant improvement
City of Seattle 2/14/2000	Resolution	New construction and renovation	Occupied buildings more than five thousand square feet	LEED Silver with additional baseline standards
City of San Francisco 5/18/2004	Ordinance, environmental code	All projects as of ninety days after adoption	Projects more than five thousand square feet	LEED Silver

Various approaches have been taken to developing green building law. Boston, Massachusetts, integrated its requirements for both public and private buildings into the local zoning code. The State of California created a Green Building Standards Code as a part of its state statutes, which affects all state buildings as well as state university buildings. Multiple states have adopted legislation mandating green building for public buildings, including Colorado, Connecticut, Florida, Hawaii, Indiana, Kentucky, Indiana, Maryland, Oklahoma, South Carolina, Washington, and Wisconsin. Many cities and counties have integrated green building laws for public construction into their municipal codes or bylaws via ordinance.[5]

Components of a Green Building Mandate

The following elements represent components of most green building mandates. Some elements are optional or represent variations on a theme. Customize your policy based on your organization's unique needs and opportunities. Table 4.1 compares different approaches for various cities.

Scope of Mandates

The first basic element of a green building mandate is the scope—that is, what type of projects will the mandate apply to? Critical scope areas that need to be covered should be established as a result of the project planning scan recommended earlier, to assess upcoming planned CIP activities.

Project Types

- *New construction.* Most mandates will apply to new construction projects that are owned by the policy maker. This can include brand-new construction as well as major renovations of buildings. Some projects may even include infrastructure. The City of Issaquah, Washington, has a policy that includes such infrastructure as pump stations, transmission facilities, and street improvements.
- *Existing facilities.* While many policies focus only on planned construction projects, many entities are focusing on the operational efficiency of their existing buildings. Even if these are not slated for major renovations other than normal maintenance upgrades, policy can be targeted at these projects. In addition, it is good to include existing buildings not only to capture these existing conservation opportunities but also to acknowledge that eventually any new facilities will need to be renovated.
- *Leased projects.* Some policies may apply to buildings that the organization does not actually own. This would comprise leased space in which tenants can set a policy standard both for the type of building they will lease a space in and the

tenant improvements they will be making. Typically, these policies will require LEED-certified buildings within which to rent space, and LEED Commercial Interiors standards for the tenant space. The U.S. Department of Energy states a preference for LEED Gold in the process of selecting leased office space.

- *Funded projects.* A policy may also apply to projects that receive public funding, such as schools, hospitals, or affordable housing. An example is the State of Colorado's Senate Bill 51, which includes within its scope any project funded with 25 percent or more state funds.

Project Threshold

A very important aspect of many mandates is the threshold that designates a measurable level or value above which the policy applies. This can be thought of as the policy trigger. Some policies do not address this issue and instead say "all" projects.

- *Project size.* The most common threshold used is project size, expressed as the number of square feet of the building. The most common threshold stated is five thousand square feet, but some thresholds are higher, such as New Jersey's, at fifteen thousand, and Boston's, at fifty thousand square feet. Consider the projects your entity tends to construct or manage, and set a threshold that will affect a reasonable percentage of these.

- *Cost.* Some mandates use project cost as the threshold. An example of this is New York City's Local Law 86, which sets a threshold of municipal projects costing more than $2 million. The threshold goes on to include city-funded projects of over 50 percent of the total cost, or at least $10 million. Alameda, California, uses a threshold of projects exceeding $3 million in construction cost. Miami–Dade County, Florida, requires LEED for renovation projects if the project costs more than 50 percent of the cost to replace the entire facility.

- *Energy demand.* While not a common threshold measure, building energy can be used. The State of New Mexico designates building energy use as one of its targets. Governor Richardson's Executive Order 2006-001 set a Silver LEED standard for all public projects over fifteen thousand square feet and/or that use over 50 kilowatts of electrical demand.[6]

- *Occupied projects.* Some policies may specify that they apply to occupied buildings, which would not include buildings such as warehouses. Occupancy can also be indicated by stating "conditioned space." This would preclude such facilities as non-air-conditioned or nonheated restrooms in parks. However, it is best not to refer specifically to air-conditioning because some occupied buildings may not have it, relying instead on natural ventilation.

- *Timing.* Some green building mandates will make a specific reference to their effective date, while most are effective from the date they are approved. Effective dates may be stated as a certain period of time after approval, such as ninety days, or the mandate may refer to all projects funded after a certain date. The latter will often relate to the timing of funding packages. In their green building ordinance, the City and County of San Francisco refer to all projects starting conceptual design after a certain date.

Referenced Standard

All green building mandates need to refer to a benchmark tool so performance can be measured.

- *Benchmark tool.* Most green building mandates reference LEED, but some also use Energy Star or Green Globes. The State of Maryland provides a choice between LEED and Green Globes. Green building standards custom fit to the jurisdiction may also be utilized, as in the case of the Chicago Standard for green building, and the Florida Green Building Coalition standards, which are referenced by the State of Florida.[7]
- *Subtools.* If different project types are referenced in the mandate, subtools within the chosen benchmark may also be referenced, such as LEED New Commercial for new construction, LEED Existing Buildings for existing buildings, or LEED Commercial Interiors for tenant improvement projects.
- *Performance level.* Once the green building benchmark tool has been selected, a minimum level of performance should be designated. This helps design teams know how far they need to go in order to meet the base requirements of the policy, even though they may well exceed it. The performance level is typically the LEED certification level or the number of Green Globes. Silver and Gold are the most commonly referenced LEED levels of achievement. The town of Greenburg, Kansas, has designated LEED Platinum as its performance level for all government-owned projects of over four thousand square feet.
- *Proof of performance.* Required proof of performance helps in ascertaining, or providing proof of, compliance with the policy standard. Some entities use an honor system and, if the mandate is a policy versus a legal requirement, do not require a formal certification process. Some mandate that projects be "designed to LEED standards." This is sometimes described with confusing jargon, such as saying the project is "certifiable." It is preferred to clearly require project certification, not only to take the burden of proof off the owner but also to aid in market transformation so that visible signals of industry adoption of green building will be seen. In addition, third-party verification can help to avoid any attempts at greenwashing.

Additional Requirements

In some cases, additional green building requirements may be called for, above and beyond the base requirement. Often, these entail making some of the normally optional benchmarking tool credits mandatory. Additional requirements are usually made in the areas of energy, water, or recycling efficiency. In addition to getting projects LEED certified, the State of Massachusetts requires "incorporating energy performance 20% better than the Massachusetts Energy Code and outdoor water reduction requirements verified by an independent 3rd party commissioning authority."[8] Harvard University sets additional LEED prerequisites and requires life cycle costing, energy modeling, and an integrated design approach.

Reporting

Some green building policy directives include reporting requirements, such as status reports on implementation success, green features, and cost benefits. Be clear regarding who should provide the reporting and when. Accountability for implementing the policy should also be outlined. (For more on reporting, see chapter 7.)

POLICY ADOPTION PROCESS

The policy adoption process will vary by jurisdiction and by the type of mandate. In general, policy mandates can be adopted more rapidly than legal mandates. In either case, building leadership and stakeholder support (as discussed in chapter 2) is critical. It is advisable to form an internal stakeholder group represented by people involved in budgeting and managing CIP projects. Ideally, they will have been included in drafting the policy, but if they were not, make sure to get their input before adoption occurs. An external stakeholder group can also be extremely helpful. Share examples of successful green building policies in other jurisdictions, especially those of a similar size and political makeup. Showing examples from the local area can also be extremely helpful. When the City of Portland passed its green building policy, staff invited several of us from Seattle to testify before the city commissioners regarding our own policy efforts. This proved an effective tactic for their successful adoption. Another strategy is to identify other policies and strategic goals that the policy helps to support.

If resistance is encountered when attempting to get a green building mandate approved, it may be necessary to negotiate the details of policy scope, level, and proof of performance. Is the threshold reasonable? Are the performance level and associated cost considered achievable by stakeholders? How does the proposed goal relate to what is happening in other jurisdictions? Some political leaders will be very competitive and want to exceed the standards set by others, while some will be satisfied with a level playing field.

Considerable time spent on process, including educating stakeholders, may be necessary. Plan to spend a lot of time giving briefings and public presentations. A fiscal analysis may be required, entailing an assessment of the upcoming capital projects that could be affected and the cost impact on these. In Asheville, North Carolina, the green building Resolution 07-91 qualifies its requirements by stating the need for a ten-year (or less) payback on energy savings related to incremental project costs.[9]

BUDGET IMPACTS OF MANDATES

While not all green building costs more, up-front costs are sometimes increased while financial benefits are seen in the long term. You will undoubtedly have to deal with the issue of the cost impacts of implementing green building mandates during the adoption process. As green building has taken hold in the marketplace, excellent data have become available. Several peer-reviewed, statistically significant studies provide a wealth of information on this topic.[10]

One study by Davis Langdon analyzed the costs of 221 buildings of a variety of specific types, including academic buildings, libraries, community centers, laboratories, and ambulatory care facilities. Both LEED and non-LEED buildings were analyzed. The study concluded that "there is no significant difference in average costs for green buildings as compared to non-green buildings."[11] Many variables influence costs for development, but green does not appear to consistently affect the cost any more than any other variable does. When describing cost impacts, one should never discuss first costs without including the long-term payback, or cost benefits, in the conversation. Another study commissioned by the CoStar Real Estate Information Group looked at data from 973 Energy Star buildings and 355 LEED buildings, totaling over 351 million square feet. They concluded, for example, that while LEED may cost 2 to 7 percent more, green buildings achieve higher rents and higher occupancy rates and are valued on the real estate market with a 10 percent higher sales price per square foot.[12]

Public entities, which do not sell or lease their buildings to others, may be more interested in long-term benefits for owner-occupied buildings. This includes decreased staff-related overhead costs in terms of reduced staff turnover and sick leave and increased worker productivity and satisfaction. Lower operating costs in the area of reduced utility bills are one of the most appealing and immediate benefits to owners of green buildings. The amount of time required to pay back initial investments for measures related to increased energy efficiency will be highly variable depending on local energy costs. Public building owners tend to hold ownership of their facilities in perpetuity, which allows them to consider longer payback periods than private developers, who may be looking for payback in between three and five years.

While cost benefit analysis is a useful tool for assessing the value of green building to the owner, caution should be used in relying too heavily on it, since it usually will not take into account benefits that may not be easy to assign cost. A variety of benefits may accrue to the owner or to larger society. Benefits to the owner might include better asset value preservation, positive public relations and increased sales, and reduced liability to lawsuits, such as from air quality health impacts to workers. Examples of benefits to society and the environment (also known as externalities) might include commute trip reduction, market demand for recycled content materials, water quality protection, and respiratory health benefits as a result of improved air quality. Many traditionally non-costed items have to do with quality of life or ecological impact.

Another area of benefit that is difficult to quantify is that of increased resiliency related to independence from the infrastructure grid, and disaster preparedness. One community that seems to fully grasp the deeper value of going green is Greensburg, Kansas (see box 4.1). After experiencing a disaster that virtually wiped out the city, they undertook a community planning process that resulted in adoption of a LEED Platinum mandate for all redevelopment, both CIP projects as well as private development. They have provided an inspiration and a model to others.[13]

FUNDING STRATEGIES FOR GREEN CAPITAL IMPROVEMENT PROJECTS

While budget strategies for funding green building programs, staff, and services were discussed in chapter 2, a separate funding issue comes into play for capital improvement projects. If there are increased costs for these projects, how will they be funded? Some believe that there should be no separate funding identified for green building and that the costs should be fully integrated into the construction budget. This approach recognizes that green building may not cost more and that, if green concepts are fully integrated into the building design, an additional line item in the budget holds little meaning. However, some may feel that additional budget tools are necessary or they will be faced with an unfunded mandate. Fees for green building certification programs are one of the cost increment areas that should be addressed. Here are a few possible approaches to funding green CIP projects.

- *Revolving funds.* Some governments may set up a permanent fund that is used as the source of low- or zero-interest loans. Public projects can access these funds for green building or energy and water efficiency implementation. The loans are paid back over time with the savings resulting from lower utility bills. The paybacks provide for a continuing reinvestment fund for green projects. This strat-

BOX 4.1 VISIONARY GREEN PLANNING IN GREENSBURG, KANSAS

Stephen Hardy, AICP, LEED AP, BNIM Architects Kansas City

On May 4, 2007, a two-mile-wide, EF-5 tornado hit Greensburg, a town of 1,389 in southwestern Kansas. The disaster leveled over 90 percent of the town's buildings, killed ten, and prompted the *New York Times* to claim that "nature had performed a coup de grace" on the Kansas town.

A second look reveals that this disaster was not the only threat to Greensburg's future. For decades, this rural Kansas town had struggled with an unstable economy. With few opportunities for the town's youth, Greensburg's population had declined. To many onlookers, Greensburg was known as a "dying town." Conventional wisdom held that the tornado had merely finished it off.

The citizens of Greensburg had a different idea.

Emerging from the rubble of their ruined town, they found that their buildings had been swept away but that the relationships that formed the bedrock of their community remained intact. Drawing strength from these relationships, the citizens of Greensburg decided to rebuild. The City of Greensburg created the Greensburg Sustainable Comprehensive Plan to face this challenge. The plan goes beyond disaster recovery and aims to overcome population decline and a struggling economy and create a framework for a socially vibrant, economically viable, and environmentally sustainable future.

The planning process began directly following disaster designation in May 2007 with a "Public Square" strategy to support long-term rebuilding and develop citizen leadership in Greensburg. The Public Square strategy created four sectors representing all aspects of the community: government, business, education, and health and human services. The planning team met regularly with the Recovery Action Team (a group of involved community leaders), the Kiowa County Business Redevelopment Group, City staff, Greensburg GreenTown (a nonprofit organization devoted to green development), the planning commission, and the city council to create recommendations based on the public square idea. In late December, a large community meeting of over three hundred people gathered input and vetted the recommendations of the plan.

The planning team learned a great deal about Greensburg from these meetings and discussions with community members. The community is proud of the rural quality of Greensburg, and they expect development projects to reflect the unassuming feel that they cherish. However, they understand that replicating exactly what they had before would be a step backward. Instead, the community sees the great opportunity presented by the disaster. They want to rebuild a progressive, inclusive town that provides jobs, education, and recreation to attract and retain a young generation of Greensburg residents.

Greensburg has made tremendous progress since the disaster (see figure 4.1). On December 17, 2007, the city council passed a resolution requiring all publicly funded buildings over four thousand square feet to be built to the U.S. Green Building Council's LEED Platinum certification level and to reduce energy consumption by 42 percent over standard buildings. As a result of this initiative, Greensburg is positioned to be home to the first six LEED Platinum buildings in the state of Kansas. The city has put in place economic development initiatives to attract green businesses to Greensburg. An innovative main street streetscape received full funding from the Department of Commerce, Economic Development Administration. This low-maintenance landscape uses innovative stormwater management strategies to irrigate native plants and filter runoff. The project is being studied as an alternative solution to stormwater infrastructure. It has been estimated that Greensburg's current energy-efficiency initiative could improve the overall energy efficiency by at least 30 percent. Greensburg is creating a plan whereby they get electricity from 100 percent renewable sources. This increases the percentage of renewable from 10 percent to 100 percent and eliminates carbon emissions from electric use fueled by coal power.

FIGURE 4.1 City of Greensburg, Kansas, Bird's-eye View of Rebuilt City
After being completely destroyed by a tornado, Greensburg, Kansas, envisions rebuilding itself to LEED Platinum standards.
Credit: Courtesy of BNIM Architects

Greensburg's commitment to sustainability has gained attention on the national stage. The Greensburg Sustainable Comprehensive Plan has won local, national, and international awards, including the 2008 ULI/*Financial Times* Sustainable Cities Award and the 2009 Daniel Burnham Award for a Comprehensive Plan.

egy can also help project managers avoid an arduous and competitive annual budget process to fund efficiency measures.

- *Conservation incentive packages.* Some states and many publicly owned utilities provide conservation incentives intended to reduce the initial costs of owner investment in water or energy savings. The incentive payments are seen as cost-effective purchases in conservation results that some utilities are required to meet. Even when a project is being developed by a city that also owns utilities that provide incentives, some projects may fail to take advantage of these resources.

- *Performance contracting.* This approach, which can be used for public or private retrofit projects, entails entering into an agreement with a private energy service company (often referred to as an ESCO). The ESCO analyzes and recommends efficiency upgrades that can be paid for through savings. The ESCO provides a guarantee that the efficiency strategies will meet or exceed the estimated savings. If the savings are not met, the ESCO pays the costs. The cities of Little Rock, Arkansas, and Redland, California, have utilized performance contracting for advanced energy systems and energy retrofits. Little Rock was able to save $320,000 a year with ESCO financing of a geothermal system and other energy retrofits. Redland retrofitted twelve buildings with an ESCO that guaranteed permanent annual savings of $450,000 paid back in seven years.[14]

- *Operations budget borrowing.* One challenge of publicly funded projects is the separation between construction and operations funding. Typically, the budgets for these are completely disconnected. In an ideal world, initial costs of efficiency measures could be funded from the operations budget, based on anticipated savings. This budget reallocation method is not easily accomplished, however, because of resistance by any budget manager to releasing funds to others. Ongoing funding for many public agencies and programs is dependent on the previous year's spending. If the program did not spend funds for its own programs in a given year, the funds may be reallocated in subsequent budget years. Some entities may be able to find a solution to this challenge.

IMPLEMENTING A GREEN BUILDING MANDATE

Once the goal of adopting a green building mandate has been met, the real work begins. Implementing a policy is not necessarily a clear-cut exercise, and there will be additional challenges along the way.

Seattle has been successful in achieving its green building policy in most cases. In the early days, there was often resistance from project managers or departments who were not enrolled in the idea of green building. I often received inquiries from staff asking what would happen if they did not achieve LEED Silver, especially considering this was a policy and not a legal mandate. My usual answer was that they would just have to explain to the mayor why they did not. This simple response was usually enough to provide some level of motivation. However, any inquiry regarding a new policy, even if it appears to be coming from a place of resistance, is an opportunity to create a new stakeholder relationship. Thank the inquirer for making contact, and offer to help procure training in green building. Hold a technical assistance session with the person's department or project team.

Some inquiries will regard projects that do not fall clearly within the scope of the policy. For Seattle, this occurred in the case of affordable housing projects receiving pass-through funding as well as in the case of small renovation projects. Neither of these was technically covered by the policy, but the inquiries provided an opportunity to encourage the spirit of the policy to be applied more broadly. Meeting only the credits that apply to the scope of smaller construction projects is one approach.

PLANNING AND MANAGING A LARGE CAPITAL PROJECTS PORTFOLIO

This section deals with organizations that develop, own, and manage a large number of buildings. Large CIPs allow for strategic planning of the organization's resources and needs and may also allow for debt stabilization and reduced borrowing costs. Packaging CIP projects into an overall program also allows for strategic communications and enhanced public relations. Major CIPs will require garnering public support and will often entail public hearings. Green building goals and requirements can help build public support. The benefits of adopting green building should be integrated into the communications plan.

For public entities with large capital assets, strategic planning for new investments must include an inventory of existing assets and the need for new assets. New projects must be recommended, justified, and evaluated. Projects are prioritized by comparing them with other proposals. Some public organizations have very sophisticated programs for planning CIPs. This often includes a value analysis, an analysis of the life cycle costs, return on investment, and other attributes of projects. The government of British Columbia utilizes an optional value analysis tool that defines value analysis as "an objective and systematic process for enabling the life-cycle costs (using the net present value of all costs, including initial capital plus operating, maintenance, demolition, renovation, and disposal costs)."[15] Their ministry of finance also provides a Green Buildings Checklist.[16]

Asset management is a comprehensive approach to projects that takes a life cycle perspective for making strategic decisions. It usually includes the funding, management, and performance assessment of each capital asset. Asset management has been applied to a variety of areas, including investing, information technology, public housing, and large infrastructure projects. Seattle Public Utilities has successfully used asset management in its capital project and major expenditure planning process. Each project must present its costs and benefits related to the triple bottom line of sustainability: social, environmental, and economic issues. Project funding is prioritized and approved according to these assessments. Projects with multiple sustainability benefits will rank higher. Following is a good example that reveals some of the benefits of an integrated approach.

Seattle Public Utilities undertook a reservoir capping program that was designed to protect water quality and drinking water safety. One of these projects was located in the Capitol Hill neighborhood of Seattle, an area where the Parks Department had coincidentally allocated resources to provide more park space. The opportunity to combine the two projects was attractive, leveraging funding and capturing multiple public benefits. The synergy between the projects became obvious: the reservoir capping provided environmental and safety benefits as well as provided a new source of land that could be used for additional public benefit. The project was ranked highly using the triple bottom line asset analysis for environmental, social, and economic benefit and had a high funding priority. The reservoir cap eventually became the site of the new Cal Anderson Park, a very popular and attractive park facility that helps to meet social and recreational needs of the neighborhood (see figure 4.2). In tough economic times, capital resources will be scarce, so demonstrating increased public benefit, leveraging of resources, and lowered operating costs via green building strategies will be a selling point.

For many large organizations, multiple facilities are needed to house the workforce or functions of a significant business or government operation. The types and sizes of the fa-

FIGURE 4.2 Cal Andersen Park, Seattle
This new urban infill park captured multiple environmental and social benefits by combining capital project budgets from two different departments.
Credit: Chloe Collyer

cilities owned may be quite diverse, as with city government, or they may be fairly consistent, as in the case of the retail sector. Regardless of the details differentiating the facility ownership, any large building owner needs to look on the portfolio of facilities as investments, as in more traditionally viewed real estate or investment portfolios. These portfolios benefit from a diverse investment strategy to minimize risk and from active management to monitor progress and needs for adjustment. Many building owners will recognize the capital investment represented by the buildings they own; fewer may see the connection between green building and the economic return of their long-range capital investments. Investors will have their own level of comfort with risks associated with investments. Most investors will tend to invest in a portion of assets that are at very low risk and another portion in assets that entail more risk.

For example, Seattle's green building investment represents a diverse portfolio of project types, sizes, functions, and green technology. Each asset varies slightly in its cost and its return on investment. With a diverse portfolio that is viewed as a group, versus a more narrow focus on only individual projects, diversity can strengthen the robustness of the entire building group from a cost and performance standpoint. One facility may cost more, on average to build to green standards, while others cost less. These fluctuations in cost will average out over time. In addition, some projects may perform at less cost than anticipated whereas others may entail higher than anticipated cost. The risk of individual variants is minimized through applying the risk to a broader group. This is a way of reducing at least some of the future risks to an owner. In addition, providing for more utility needs, such as water or energy on site, manages risks of rising utility costs over time or manages for unanticipated changes in the marketplace related to carbon, for example.

Successfully tracking the development of a green building portfolio is easier if you pay attention to the following key tips.

Create standardization for project registration. Create consistent language, or issue a naming protocol, when registering projects online with the LEED system or other systems. For a jurisdiction that may have many different subdepartments registering projects under their own names, this can save a lot of headaches later. If project naming is not done consistently, it will be difficult to search shared databases and get consistent information. For Seattle, the naming protocol that was eventually adopted started with "City of Seattle," followed by the department name.

Provide centralized project tracking. Create a spreadsheet or Web-based tracking tool for all green building projects your organization plans, builds, or completes. Keep all the critical project information handy, including LEED project number, date registered, name of the project administrator, name of your organization's project manager, and so forth. Eventually, you can record building completion dates, certification date, level of performance, and operational details. This tool is very useful for preparing reports.

Consider some of the online data management tools available for creating a centralized, accessible source of information for teams. SharePoint is an increasingly popular tool that an organization can host internally to provide a platform for document management, information storage and retrieval, shared workplans and activities, and more. For smaller organizations, consider utilizing Google Docs, which allows creation and management of online documents and for invited collaborators to view and have access to information. Other useful tools can be accessed with such products as Basecamp or Zoho.

Track important green features, lessons learned, and LEED credit documentation. You may want to keep a tally of what leading-edge green features each project has, such as green roofs, active solar systems, water reuse systems, and so forth. It can be useful to look up which projects have these features. Track important information regarding successes and failures. In addition, once documentation has been done and accepted for a particular LEED innovation credit, this can be referred back to as a resource for successive projects.

Create a single point of contact. Designate one person for tracking and reporting green building results. If a single person is in charge of this process, it will provide consistency in collecting and reporting data and can prevent redundancy. In addition, this person can work with the project team in sharing lessons learned from other projects in all aspects of project development. He or she can provide technical assistance and high-level review of LEED certification submittal packages in case experiences from previous projects will help smooth the process.

Some entities with large building portfolios track these results in relationship to their carbon output. Energy Star offers a Portfolio Manager that can track water and energy consumption of buildings across a large portfolio. The tracker tool can rate building energy performance as well as set investment priorities for building upgrades. It uses meter tracking to monitor costs, to benchmark performance, and to rate building efficiency. In addition, the tool can calculate a building's total greenhouse gas footprint as well as for a single owner's entire building portfolio.[17]

The USGBC provides a Portfolio Program for participants across market sectors, including government, financial institutions, corporations, institutional investors, retailers, higher education, and hoteliers. This special program for owners of large numbers of facilities is intended to provide recognition for organizations that have made a commitment to LEED and to, in return, provide them a high level of customer service. The Portfolio Program aims to streamline the LEED project documentation and certification process, creating an economy of scale for the owner. In particular, the program will help building owners with many similar facilities to create consistent green building standards for design, construction, and operations. A key feature of the program is the dashboard metrics tool for tracking aggregate environmental impacts linked to LEED online. Participants in the piloting of the program include the U.S. Army, the State of California, the University of California, Emory University, the City of San Jose, CB Richard Ellis, Kohl's, Starbucks, Best Buy, and USAA Real Estate.[18] (For more on measuring and evaluating the performance of green buildings, see chapter 7.)

TIPS

Tips on Policy Development

- Be sure you are "walking the talk" before you try to influence others.
- Assess the future construction trends for your organization. Inventory the near-term and long-term opportunities, and target your efforts accordingly.
- Determine the organizational, political, and economic realities. Select whether to implement a green building policy or a legal mandate.
- Select a clear policy goal regarding what projects will be affected and guided. Be specific as to project scope and threshold.
- Select a referenced standard and performance targets for the policy. Utilizing national standards, such as LEED, will add credibility.
- State who is responsible for fulfilling the policy, including reporting expectations.
- Look for other strategic plans, policies, and adopted priorities that relate to your efforts.

Tips on Policy Adoption

- Build support from top leadership in the organization.
- Identify a political champion for the policy adoption process.
- Involve stakeholders inside the organization with developing the policy and getting it adopted.
- Educate and organize community stakeholders who can help advocate for policy adoption, including government officials from other jurisdictions.
- Before the official adoption moment occurs, "take the temperature" of the situation. Is additional advocacy needed? Do you need to invite outside experts to testify?
- If cost impact analysis is required, be sure to include the long-term benefits as well as the initial costs.
- Consider alternative funding models, such as performance-based contracting, to help share the cost and risk of conservation investments.
- Encourage a commitment to regular performance reporting on the policy and its related impacts.

Tips on Policy Interpretation

- Expect inquiries regarding consequences of failing to meet the policy.
- Look on inquiries regarding how the policy applies to projects outside its scope as opportunities to further expand the program and stakeholder group.
- Encourage applying the intent of the policy to all types of construction activities.

Tips on Managing a Green Building Portfolio

- Consider using an asset management approach to planning and prioritizing your organization's CIPs. Include the social, environmental, and economic benefits.
- Review planned CIPs to determine the possibilities for combining projects or budgets or for leveraging benefits.
- Create standardized data and a project referencing system.
- Provide a centralized project tracking tool managed by a single person.
- Consider storing and managing documents at a centrally accessible online location.
- Track important green building features, project scorecards, and green documentation.
- Create a single point of contact for inquiries regarding the portfolio.
- Consider utilizing the USGBC's LEED Portfolio Program.

CHAPTER 5

Developing Green Building Program Services

This and the following chapter give guidance on how to develop a suite of program services and products, or a toolkit, to support market transformation of green building. These services and tools can be delivered by program staff, or consultants can be hired to provide them. No one model is best; however, it is advisable to have at least one staff person to oversee the program and provide leadership, coordination, and continuity. There are many excellent green building consultants who can assist with preparing educational materials, training, evaluating programs (discussed in chapter 7), or providing direct technical assistance. In order to determine when to hire a consultant versus delivering the service in-house, ask yourself whether staffing capacity or competency exist or whether outside expertise might provide increased value through added collaboration or third-party perspective, once you have determined what your needs are for your program. There are five basic types of tools within the program services toolkit, which can be thought of as a menu, with the ability to pick and choose for a customized program fit. The five types of tools include the following:

- Building design and certification tools
- Educational programming
- Technical assistance
- Incentives
- Building code requirements

This chapter deals with the first three types of tools within the service toolkit. These are the best place to start when developing a new program and can be thought of as your basic service platform. These approaches can help to reduce barriers to green building, such as lack of knowledge. Once these barriers have been removed with the help of the basic service platform, other types of tools can be built on the initial platform, creating a second tier (as illustrated in figure 5.1). This second tier includes incentives and green building codes, which are discussed in chapter 6. Building certification tools may also provide the basis for other parts of the toolkit, such as education or incentives.

An excellent compendium of program best practices can be found within the Green Playbook, created by Lynne Barker with a team of partners.[1]

FIGURE 5.1 Green Building Program Service Tiers Create an initial basic service platform with tools, education, and technical assistance. Then add incentives and code requirements as a second tier.

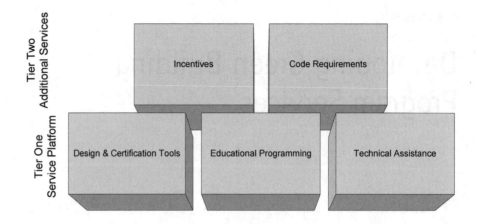

Who will be served by your green building programs and services? You can think of this group of people as your program customers or target audience. These customers can include people internal to your organization, such as capital projects staff or building managers, and those outside the organization, such as developers or architects working on private development projects. Program customers will typically be design and building industry professionals from a broad range of disciplines and may include a wide variety of projects. Developers, building operators, building owners, and allied professions of the building industry can also be included in the customer base or be specifically targeted depending on the goals of the program.

Each type of service and tool has its own characteristics, program delivery needs, and outcomes. Some will work better in particular market sectors than others. Each can be customized for the particular market sectors being targeted. Different service types will require varying levels of financial and staff resources as well as contact with customers. Some program services will necessitate spending one-on-one time with customers as opposed to providing services that do not require such customer "face time." For example, if executed correctly, a downloadable design tool can reach a large number of individuals without the need to sit down with each of them. Conversely, providing technical assistance is a very project-specific activity, requiring face time with individuals on the project team or the developer. The relative investment of time and resources needed to deliver a service can be thought of as the scalability of the service. You will need to consider the staff and program budget resources required for each piece of your toolkit, and the relative merits of each related to what you wish to accomplish.

Most programs will provide a mix of the different types of tools and services described here. Based on the program's context and goals, I recommend considering carefully how much of the program resources should be spent in each area. Seattle used a strategic planning process to determine how to allocate resources toward various program services, the results of which are shown in figure 5.2. This same type of analysis can be done for how resources are allocated by the market sector. In the example shown, only 15 percent of total program resources was allocated to education programs. In previous years, this was a much higher number because there were few other service providers in the Seattle market for green building education programs. Over time, many more education providers evolved, including the Cascadia Region Green Building Council and the local AIA Committee on the Environment. With other service providers in the marketplace, the program could focus less in this area. Conduct a market assessment to see what other service providers and partners exist in each of the service categories, to ensure that you are not duplicating what others offer. Such a survey can also reveal opportunities for strategic partnerships that can be used to leverage resources.

BUILDING DESIGN AND CERTIFICATION TOOLS

The most common green building tools in the marketplace are building certification programs. While some may argue that the purpose of these is not as a design tool but rather as a certification tool, they can be seen to fulfill both functions. If design professionals know the end target benchmark they must reach, it guides the design process. (See the last part of this chapter for more on the green building design process.)

Certification tools are important because they provide a "seal of approval" similar to organic food certification. The seal assures the buyer of certain standards and levels of

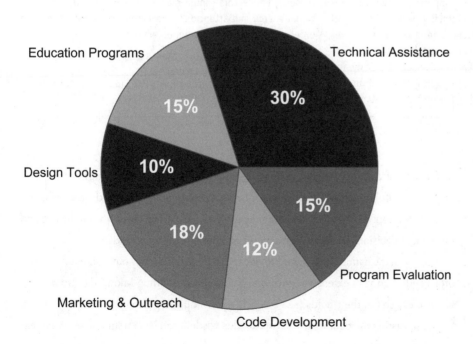

FIGURE 5.2 City of Seattle Green Building Program Service Resource Allocation Allocate resources for various program services relative to specific goals and the availability of other service providers in the marketplace.

Thor Peterson, LEED AP, MPA, Synthesis Consultants

Advancing green building, as with any effort at systemic change, is a complicated affair. It relies on various parties shifting behavior in concerted ways to result in a desired outcome. Simultaneously, it increases demand for green products and services and enhancement of the skill set, service, and product offerings of myriad players in the industry. Central to this transformation is linked knowledge: each person in the chain must be given convincing, quality, actionable information in order to result in behavior change.

Compounding this challenge, green building requires knowledge gleaned not only from architecture, engineering, and construction but also disciplines as varied as public health, toxicology, psychology, and botany. As the residential green building expert for the City of Seattle's Green Building Program, I was faced daily with the challenge of keeping up with a constantly evolving industry that was adding new discoveries to its toolbox of solutions. Green building's interdisciplinary nature also means that knowledge resides in a wide variety of locations, with no central repository. For the most part, the answers are out there; it just requires knowing where to find them.

Luckily, the green building community embraces a culture of information sharing and collaboration rather than proprietary and zero-sum competitive approaches. As a result, while the information may be atomized, it is accessible, and in fact, the custodians of that information are most often quite willing to share with others if the aim is enhancing the public good.

Illustrative of this was my participation in the development of the U.S. Green Building Council/American Society of Interior Designers REGREEN program. Intended to provide premium-quality information on green remodeling strategies for the average home owner, REGREEN was developed quickly and efficiently by assembling a group of topical experts from the private sector, nonprofit, and governmental realms. The process was facilitated by collocating the experts for multiple-day stints and facilitating rapid information assembly, compilation, and winnowing. The result was a quick distillation of the group's knowledge into information that served as the basis for the finished product. Using the USGBC's hallmark technical committee/public comment approach, the content was developed in a way that allowed for inclusiveness while retaining firm hold of technical expertise. The resulting guide serves as the basic text for a growing green remodeling resource, including Web seminars exploring specific remodeling approaches and scopes.[1]

Collective harnessing of intelligence, such as the process used to create REGREEN, is one valuable approach for transferring green building knowledge from its dispersed, atomized form into a synthesized whole. Also crucial is knowing where to find the knowledge sources. Key to success in my continuing role as a green building change agent is the ability to identify who to bring to the table. A common job responsibility among green building professionals is to be a "Connector," as Malcolm Gladwell described in his analysis of social epidemics, *The Tipping Point*.[2] Connectors, as the name implies, maintain a very large and diverse social network that allows them to bring together previously unlinked individuals. If our goal is true behavior change, we must strive for Connector status. Gladwell's framework describes a subset of individuals who naturally develop these large networks. Those of us who are not naturally disposed to being Connectors should realize that we must devote additional energy and attention to developing a robust network in order to advance our program objectives.

1. For more information on the REGREEN program, see http://www.regreenprogram.org/.
2. Malcolm Gladwell, *The Tipping Point: How Little Things Can Make a Big Difference* (Boston: Back Bay Paperbacks, 2002), 38.

quality and often provides impartial, third-party verification. Building certification programs are useful for large organizations or funders setting policy standards, real estate investors, developers, or buyers because they can provide a green index for purchasing and investment decisions, thereby increasing consumer or investor confidence.

Many of the national programs provide the advantage that they have undertaken a rigorous and often very extensive process to gather green building knowledge from a vast array of experts in their fields (see box 5.1). Green building expertise comprises many facets, so casting the net broadly to capture this wisdom can be extremely useful. For example, the REGREEN program, sponsored by the American Society of Interior Designers and the U.S. Green Building Council, convened a process to collect knowledge from a large group of topical experts in green home remodeling. Such breadth and depth of knowledge may not be available via a more limited pool of local expertise.

There are many different overlapping and sometimes competing green building certification programs and tools. Some of these tools are described briefly in table 5.1, which provides an overview of how different certification tools or programs apply to different project types. (A longer discussion of some of the different tools, with Web links to each, can be found in appendix B.) The field of green building certification is rapidly evolving, and by the time you read this book, the tool suite will no doubt have expanded. It is advisable for a green building program to assess the tools available for the target markets it wishes to influence and then make a deliberate choice in selecting tools that the program can link to. It helps to be clear about which tools are preferred by your program, in order to avoid confusion. This will be important later for program links to certification tools for other services and activities, such as education, incentives, technical assistance, and code requirements. Tools that are promoted voluntarily in the early program phase can become referenced standards later for mandatory requirements. Be prepared for subsequent phases that may include code requirements, even if the program is initially focused only on voluntary measures.

There are pros and cons to each of the design tools, and the process and cost to use them will vary. The tools also demonstrate a very wide range of green performance, highlighting the fact that green is a broad continuum from deeper to lighter shades. It is important to examine not only the overhead for using any tool but also the value being delivered and the accuracy of claims that use of the tool will result in a green building. While some consider the various tools to be competing and creating confusion in the marketplace, others consider them to serve unique niches.[2]

Other Design Tools

Many excellent tools have been created for a national and even international audience. Not all of the international green building certification programs that are emerging are discussed in this book, but I applaud our global green building partners. Local green building programs can link to nationally available tools or create their own design tools, which can be customized to local or regional conditions. An example of a nationally available tool is the REGREEN program, targeted at residential renovation programs, which was created by the American Society of Interior Designers and the USGBC. The tool provides guidelines and best practices, case studies, and a green product checklist.

Not all green standards or strategies will work everywhere. The skeptic may feel unas-

	Market Sector *(new construction unless otherwise noted)*	Tools
Residential	**Single Family Detached New Construction**	LEED for Homes NAHB Green Home Scoring Tool Local Homebuilder program (if available) Energy Star Homes Living Building Challenge
	Single Family Detached Remodel	REGREEN Local Homebuilder program (if available) Energy Star Homes
	Townhome	LEED for Homes Local Homebuilder program (if available) Living Building Challenge
	Multifamily (attached) Apartment/ Condominium	LEED for Homes (for Lowrise Buildings) LEED New Construction (for Highrise Buildings) Local Homebuilder program (if available) Green Globes Living Building Challenge
	Affordable Housing	Enterprise Foundation Green Communities
Commercial/ Office	**Commercial/Office Speculative**	LEED Core and Shell LEED Commercial Interiors Green Globes Energy Star Commercial
	Commercial/Office Owner or Tenant Driven	LEED New Construction + LEED Commercial Interiors Green Globes Energy Star Commercial Living Building Challenge
	Commercial/Office Remodel	LEED for Existing Buildings Energy Star Commercial Go Green Plus

sured by the attempt to apply a standard created without insight into local practicalities, perhaps wondering, "Sure, that works someplace else, but how can it work here where I live?"

Local green building programs can create their own design tools, which can be customized to local or regional conditions. Many local master builder or other associations have created their own residential green building programs and certification tools. Creating custom tools can also be useful for branding a program, providing consistent messaging, and assuring the local design community that green building will work for them. Tools

TABLE 5.1 (CONTINUED)

	Market Sector (new construction unless otherwise noted)	Tools
Institutional/ Specialized Sectors	Hospitals Medical Laboratory	LEED for Healthcare Green Guide for Healthcare Labs 21 for Lab Facilities Green Globes Healthcare Energy Star Healthcare
	Schools	LEED for Schools LEED Application Guide for Campuses Green Globes Schools Energy Star Higher Education and K–12
	Retail	LEED for Retail Green Globes Retail Energy Star Retail
	Government	LEED for New Construction LEED for Commercial Interiors LEED for Existing Buildings Energy Star Government
	Parks, Infrastructure	Sustainable Site Tool
Mixed Use	Planned Community Neighborhood	LEED for Neighborhood Development One Planet Living

can be provided in various formats, including fact sheets, detailed design guides, and case studies. Visuals in combination with text are most effective. Publication formats should include both online and print materials. Consider paper waste when printing large quantities; online publication may be preferable. Following are several rationales for developing tools that are specific to your program.

Regionally Appropriate Design

Regional appropriateness varies according to local conditions, including climate; sun, wind, and rainfall patterns; indigenous soils and plants; and local building techniques. The need to consider regional solutions that may not be one-size-fits-all is exemplified by the addition of new, regionally appropriate LEED Innovation Credits, contained in Version 3.0. Models for in-depth, practical regional tools include the Northwest Energy Efficiency Alliance's 56-page booklet entitled "Natural Ventilation in Northwest Buildings." This comprehensive primer provides climate-specific guidance for integrating natural ventilation in commercial buildings within northwestern climate conditions, with barriers, benefits, feasibility, and local examples.[3] Atlanta's Southface Institute publishes a 154-page manual called "A Builder's Guide to Energy Efficient Homes in Georgia," which is specific to the regional climate conditions.[4] Some examples of topics that might merit creating local design guidance focused on solutions suited to your region and climate include the following:

- Passive solar design for your latitude
- Natural ventilation strategies for your climate
- On-site stormwater management techniques suited to your soils and rainfall patterns
- Natural landscaping strategies for native soils, using plants well adapted to your climate

Local Building Codes

Some green building strategies may present challenges related to local code barriers. Even if there is only a perception that there are code barriers, rather than the existence of actual barriers, this still represents a hurdle that can be addressed. Predictability is an important expectation for building permit applicants. Assurance can be provided regarding what is permittable within local building codes with written publications or technical assistance.

There may be existing code publications that can have green building design guidance integrated into them. In Seattle, the Department of Planning and Development publishes a series of code guidance documents called Client Assistance Memos, or CAMs. The purpose of the CAM series is to provide user-friendly information on complex code issues. A special Green Building CAM series was created to highlight special topics. One of these publications was called "Rainwater Harvesting for Beneficial Reuse." This publication not only provides code guidance but also promotes the concept of rainwater collection by providing information on benefits, relationship to LEED credits, design considerations, system sizing, code issues, water rights issues, and a case study.[5]

Following are some examples of topics that might merit creating green building code guides:

- Building heights, solar access, and rooftop features, such as wind turbines or solar panels
- Green roof code guidance
- Advanced framing or other structural design issues
- Innovative energy solutions and local or state energy code
- Rainwater collection and reuse
- On-site wastewater treatment systems (gray and black water)

- LEED or other certification tool requirements in relationship to local code requirements

Financial Resources

Financial implications will affect the feasibility and cost-effectiveness of various design concepts. Since local costs may vary widely, home-grown tools may help encourage green building in your unique locale. Local and state incentives are important financial vehicles for decreasing the first cost of many green building strategies. However, awareness of such tools may be very low. Promoting financial incentives and alternative financing strategies may be very helpful to those entering the green building marketplace for the first time. A good place to start doing research on incentives for energy efficiency that may be available in your region is the Database of State Incentives for Renewables and Efficiency.[6] Examples of topics that might merit creating financial tools include the following:

- Local green building incentive programs, such as utility-based conservation incentives and LEED or other grants
- State and Federal tax incentive programs or state grants
- Local funders and lenders who specialize in green building
- Alternative financing models and local providers, such as performance-based contractors

Vendors and Consultants

Some tools may be created to make it easier for those in your green building market to find their way to materials or service providers that will help them achieve green building. Creating a network of businesses and services helps to build the local green community. You may consider publishing guides to help customers find local service providers. For example, the Northwest Ecobuilding Guild publishes an annual index of green building contractors and designers called the "Green Pages."[7] Another information gap that often exists is in the arena of where to procure green building materials, particularly those that meet the LEED requirements for products within a five-hundred-mile radius. The Northwest nonprofit Sustainable Connections publishes an online database called the Northwest Regional Green Building Products Matrix, organized around the CSI MasterFormat™.[8] The Santa Monica Office of Sustainability and the Environment publishes an index to local green building material suppliers.

Public entities need to be sure to include disclaimers while providing such information, to avoid the appearance that actual endorsements, recommendations, or guarantees are implied.

Examples of topics that might merit creating local resource guides include the following:

- Local and regional green building product manufacturers and suppliers
- Local and regional green design professionals and contractors
- Local and regional building materials recyclers

Case Studies

Case studies of local projects are an important tool to show your community that green building is feasible and can succeed. There may be particular project types, or projects that include certain strategies, that you are interested in promoting. Case studies can be fairly short, one to two pages, or more exhaustive profiles. They should include, at minimum, images, credits for the project team, details on green features, and LEED or other certification information. Also of interest would be data on project costs, cost/benefit information, design process, and information on how the building is operating and lessons learned, if available. It is recommended to use standard formats and data fields for case studies. Various case study formats already exist that help to create a larger body of knowledge within the industry. These include the following:

- High Performance Buildings case studies published by U.S. Department of Energy, Office of Energy Efficiency and Renewable Energy (see http://www1.eere.energy.gov/buildings/commercial_initiative)
- International Green Building Challenge, a research-oriented tool used for building evaluation, which uses a software program to account for local climatic conditions (see http://www.greenbuilding.ca/)
- Building Technologies Program's Zero Energy Buildings Database (see http://zeb.buildinggreen.com/)
- U.S. Green Building Council's LEED case studies (see http://www.usgbc.org/LEED/Project/CertifiedProjectList.aspx)
- Local USGBC chapter case studies (contact your local chapter)

EDUCATION PROGRAMS

Educational programs are a critical component of any market adoption strategy. The offerings in green building education have expanded significantly over time, so a good first step is to inventory what existing education programs exist in your area. Chapters of such professional organizations as the USGBC, the AIA, the Building Owners and Managers Association, and contractors and real estate professional associations may already have green building–related programming or an education series that a new green building program could be linked with. To reach home owners, try leveraging environmental education programs or green lifestyle programs connected with local natural foods stores or related businesses. Programs can be free or used as a fund-raising strategy to help support other programmatic efforts. Advanced registration and at least a nominal fee are advisable for education programs, because it increases the perception of value of the programs and gives more certainty to attendance numbers.

The purpose and range of topics that can be covered in green building education are broad. For example, the Cascadia Region Green Building Council offers a broad range of educational programming, including LEED Technical Review Workshops, "Green Skyline" tours, training on integrated design process, specialized training for commercial real estate brokers, and a "Transformational Lecture Series."[9]

Some training may be intended to inspire. Other sessions may be more technical and targeted at a particular outcome or audience. Programs can be geared toward the specific market sectors that have already been discussed, such as commercial or single-family residential audiences. The style of the presenters, the level of technical detail of the content, and the strategies for getting the word out about the event will vary for each market.

Presenters for professional audiences will need to have a good command of technical details and be prepared to answer fairly advanced questions. Conversely, presenters for a home owner audience should beware of using too much jargon. It is always a good idea to gauge the level of knowledge of any audience before getting into the details of a presentation. As the market has advanced in Seattle, home owners attending green building workshops have garnered a sophisticated level of green building knowledge. It may be necessary to create an introductory or "101" level of programming and a more advanced program as your market adoption unfolds.

Professional Education

Several pathways exist for professional-level programming. Programs can be customized to specific disciplines in the construction industry, such as architects, engineers, interior designers, landscape architects, contractors, or developers. This narrow approach allows for covering more depth of technical information pertinent to that audience. However, the value of bringing together an audience from a wide variety of disciplines should not be underestimated. Diverse disciplines must work together collaboratively in order for green building and an integrated design process to be successful. A rich dialogue can result from multidisciplinary programs and the ability to solve problems that transcend the boundaries of each profession. In a very successful workshop that the City of Seattle hosted in 2007, developers and their architects were required to attend training on mixed-use green building together. This not only allowed the opportunity for their alliance around green building to be strengthened but also increased the chances of success for their complex projects.

Educational content can be created to focus on many aspects of green building, including any of the building design and certification tools discussed earlier in this chapter. Project case studies make for particularly good training material, especially if lessons learned can be shared. Shining a light on lessons or barriers can be effectively linked with an interactive discussion following the session. Education sessions provide an opportunity to bring together the building community to share ideas and strengthen bonds. This needs to happen formally as well as less formally. Try holding a reception or networking event before or after any educational event. Providing food and drink is a subtle way of creating ties among people. Breaking bread with others in a setting without a formal agenda can help open people up, even if they come with a lot of pre-formed skepticism.

Accredited Programs

Programs that can lead to professional accreditation will appeal strongly to professionals in your marketplace. It is possible to bring national education programs to your local area, such as training programs offered by the national USGBC or AIA. You can often partner with these organizations, who will provide the content and trainers while you provide the venue, logistics, and marketing. Start with basic LEED or other green building training, and then add advanced training on other green building issues.

Programs can also be developed locally that contribute to gaining certified Continuing Education Units (CEUs) for a variety of organizations that have such requirements to maintain professional accreditation, including the Green Building Certification Institute (GBCI), AIA, the American Society of Landscape Architects, the American Institute of Certified Planners, real estate associations, and so forth. This broadens the attractiveness and appeal of the educational offering and will often ensure enrollment. The GBCI has become the credentialing body for continuing education providers that offer education that contributes to maintaining LEED professional credentials, and it is likely to serve a similar function for other allied green building programs in the future.[10] Partnering with providers of CEU educational programming can result in the creation of new, unique programs that support the goals of your green building initiative. For example, the Austin Green Builder program has offered referrals for builders based on participation in initial and ongoing training. Such referral programs are seen as extremely valuable in the marketplace. Public sector officials are barred from offering personal referrals, but participation in a training program can provide a credible basis for a referral.

Certification Programs

While not all certification programs require an examination, standards applied to the educational process can certify their value. The Sustainable Building Advisor program was developed in Seattle, originally as a partnership between Seattle City Light and Seattle Central Community College. Designed as a series of nine monthly sessions for professionals already employed in the building industry, the classes give a broad introduction to green building concepts and result in a practicum project. The program has been so successful that it has expanded to national licensing by local education providers. Programs have been offered on both the West and East Coasts as well as internationally.[11]

In 2008, the National Association of Homebuilders launched its Certified Green Professional designation, targeted at builders and remodelers. The program requires at least two years of experience and attendance at a two-day training course, management courses, and agreement to continuing education requirements.[12]

Vocational Training

Vocational training programs for green building have not received the same attention as professional education, but they are a critical link in achieving market transformation. For some, the green building movement appears elitist, available only to a wealthy and restricted set of home owners and architects. Van Jones, White House special adviser on green jobs, aims to change that while at the same time solving multiple economic, social justice, and energy crises. Writes Jones: "When many people hear the term 'green' today, they still automatically think the message is probably for a fancy, eco-elite set—and not for themselves. And as long as that remains true, the green movement will remain too anemic politically and too alien culturally to rescue the country."[13]

Without trained and knowledgeable people in the building trades, many green building strategies fail during construction implementation, even if designed properly. In Newark, New Jersey, a new green-collar, six-week construction skill training program was launched with a $85,000 grant from the U.S. Department of Health and Human Services. The sponsors of the program are the City of Newark, Laborer's International Union of North America, and the Garden State Alliance for a New Economy.[14]

Such partnerships among government, trade, and economic prosperity organizations hold great potential for an expanded focus on green construction skills training. Several progressive nonprofit organizations are leading the green-collar jobs charge, including the Apollo Alliance (http://apolloalliance.org/) and Green for All (http://www.greenforall.org/). Linking green building to job skills training also provides an important tie to economic recovery. A study commissioned by the Center for American Progress says that the United States can create over 2 million jobs within two years if investment occurs in a "rapid green economic recovery program." According to the study, a "$100 billion green-investment package would create four times more jobs than spending the same amount of money within the oil industry, and would reduce the unemployment rate to 4.4 percent over 2 years."[15]

Code Training

Developing green codes is discussed in chapter 6. However, it is important to note here that training should be offered to help building permit applicants understand code changes based on green building. People need to understand not only the specifics of the new requirements that will help them successfully gain a building permit but also the rationale for the changes. Providing such training can also help to build goodwill within the design community, who may often view building code officials as "the enemy" rather than a strategic partner.

Green code training can also help to provide a feedback loop to code officials, enabling them to understand challenges that may be faced by permit applicants. For example, in Seattle, Janet Stephenson designed a workshop series to help design professionals understand a new, more sustainable landscape code before its release. Each workshop in the series focused on a different technical topic related to the code change, presented by experts in their field. The series was very well attended and ended with a fun social event at a local pub, with a quiz on the knowledge gained during the series. Providing some hand-holding as a part of this code change process helped people to get more comfortable with the changes as they were occurring.

TECHNICAL ASSISTANCE AND COACHING

Competent green building technical assistance is one of the most important components of a successful program. It offers significant advantages to both service providers and service recipients. First, technical assistance services provides hand-holding for those new to green building, which is often critical in the early days of green building market adoption. Having a "go-to" source of personalized information can be invaluable. Developing a personal relationship with a green building expert can build confidence and trust. While labor intensive, the value of this service should not be underrated.

Second, technical assistance services provide a two-way street of communication that simple design tools or typical training programs cannot provide. The technical assistance service provider will learn from the real-world experience of implementing green building on an actual project. Theoretical exercises in green building, or case studies from different jurisdictions, are no substitute. Through an ongoing technical assistance experience with an individual project, the technical specialist will learn about the barriers to adopting specific green building practices, whether they are cost, code, or knowledge based. As the coach gains experience with more projects, his or her technical expertise is honed over time. Since green building is a rapidly evolving field, this ongoing learning and continual improvement is critical. Cross-fertilization can also result as lessons learned can be transferred to other aspects of the program, such as identification of code barriers and green code development.

Some additional benefits of technical assistance include the following:

- Reducing the perceived risks of green building and barriers, such as first cost
- Helping reduce code, permit, and institutional barriers to building green
- Building the field of knowledge and expertise regarding green building in order to support local jobs and businesses, export consulting services, and develop case studies and cost benefit information
- Increasing demand for sustainable products and services

Technical Skills

Technical assistance is one of the most resource- and time-intensive green building services. It requires extensive "face time" and a customized approach to individual needs. Limited technical assistance can be provided with a telephone or an electronic help line or quick information service that provides answers to individual green building questions. Such questions may relate to advice on product or technology selection, code questions, inquiries regarding where to see green building projects, or questions on where to get more help in the form of information on incentives. While the desire for such a service is usually validated by customer traffic, a more in-depth form of assistance will likely accrue greater value to the customer and to the program in the long run.

Thinking of green building technical assistance as coaching provides additional insight into the value it provides. A successful coaching experience also means that the coaches will be building their own skill set, with the ability to apply these skills to future projects. Coaching is likely to be an ongoing relationship, which may be developed over the life of a single project and, if successful, applied on a future trajectory to other projects.

Coaching as a form of technical assistance requires two distinct skill sets. First, technical knowledge of applied green building strategies and tools is critical. The second skill set relates to interpersonal relationships. Vast technical knowledge will be to no avail if the information cannot be shared effectively, with respect to the needs and values of the people and the project at hand. A good green building coach will need to have the following skills:

Technical Skills

- Green building technical knowledge, both universal and local
- Familiarity with rating systems and tools
- Knowledge of what is allowed by building code
- Knowledge of the financial resources available, such as incentives or tax breaks
- Ability to say "I don't know" when they don't, and to find information or answers they cannot provide

Coaching Skills

- Good collaborative, leadership, and negotiation abilities
- Good listening and communication skills
- Positive attitude, balanced with a realistic perspective on what is possible
- Ability to share complex information simply while avoiding jargon
- Skill in tailoring assistance to the needs of the customer
- Good follow-up and project tracking skills
- Persistence and flexibility

Seattle's green building program provides technical assistance and project coaching directly to construction permit applicants, developers, owners, and project teams. These services are extended to a wide range of project types, including commercial, institutional, multifamily, single-family, and city capital projects, with a more resource-intensive assistance level for the latter.

Service Levels

Establishing service levels for technical assistance helps in explaining what value the service provides and in measuring program performance. Seattle provides three general levels of service, which are described below, to seventy to one hundred projects per year.

Service Level 1

This is the most modest level of technical assistance and may entail one or a limited series of interactions with team members. Service includes the following:

- Education of the project team regarding service offerings, resources, and design tools, such as LEED or the local Masterbuilder Association residential green rating program
- Identification of core issues the project will need to address, including energy, water, stormwater, site planning, cost, design process, and so forth
- Referral to conservation incentive programs at local utilities
- Referrals to professional services and products via organizations or industry associations

Service Level 2

This is an intermediate level of technical assistance and may entail participation in design team meetings and workshops and developing customized assistance teams tailored to the project's needs. Service includes the following:

- Resolving code issues and detailed inquiries regarding green building features and strategies

- Creating and facilitating collaborative teams composed of representatives from multiple city departments, other service providers, and the project team.
- Attending design charrettes/workshops
- Developing relationships with design professionals, developers, contractors, tenants, and owners
- Coaching project teams in order to increase confidence levels to overcome barriers and risks
- Providing in-depth information on particular strategies and case studies or cost benefit information
- Working with construction permit staff in order to resolve permit challenges and enhance the skill set of permit staff

Service Level 3

This is the most far-reaching level of service offered and often involves participation in project development starting at the master planning or project planning phase. It includes extensive and ongoing project coaching and assistance through the entire permitting process and sometimes extends into the operations phase. Service includes the following:

- Facilitating and educating project teams and city staff in decision process improvement (early involvement with teams increases options and lowers cost)
- Facilitating permit review with project teams and permit staff (may involve working with a project through the entire design and review process, from early Master Use Permit submittals through Certificate of Occupancy)
- For city capital projects, may include hosting eco-charrettes, developing technical briefs for project teams, or providing customized education programs for specific projects
- May include tracking project results, such as energy or water use, compiling LEED score card data, or other postoccupancy information

DYNAMICS OF THE DESIGN AND CONSTRUCTION PROCESS

When providing technical assistance to green building customers, creating incentive programs, or implementing green building mandates, it helps to understand how the development process may vary. The design and construction process, as well as the design product, may differ somewhat from what we have traditionally come to expect in industry standard practice. Green design thinking should be integrated into each design phase, rather than being viewed as a separate design service or add-on. How do green principles affect each phase of the project development process?

Predesign and Master Planning

The impact of guiding principles established during the project planning phase is vast. Be sure to articulate sustainability as a key goal for any project as well as specific LEED or other benchmark goals. Master plan goals or project guiding principles can serve as a touchstone that design teams can return to again and again, and they can provide a course correction if design variations are proposed that move away from sustainability. Changing or violating a goal set forth in the project-planning phase is usually taken quite seriously.

The master planning process is also an excellent time to assess project elements that may affect LEED credits. This includes site selection options as well as plans to renovate or demolish existing buildings on the site. These must be determined at a very early phase, as some options will vanish further along in the design process.

Predesign also includes the development of a project scope and program. Consider the impact LEED or various design options will have on the scope and program. Does the program allow for adequate density on the site? Does it create opportunities to harvest site resources or capture alternate strategies, such as renewable on-site energy?

Consultant Hiring Process

As anyone who has ever commissioned a building architect or worked with a design team knows, selecting an architect or other design professional is perhaps the central determining factor for the end product. Hiring or assembling a design team for green projects is not that much different from any other architectural hiring process, except that another set of skills is added to those already needed. Many teams end up being chosen based on the architect alone. However, the other team members must be carefully considered for their experience and ability in delivering green solutions. Particular areas to pay attention to are landscape architects, commissioning agents, contractors, interior architects, lighting designers, and civil, mechanical, and structural engineers.

From the client perspective, for more predictable results and costs, select architectural teams with proven experience in green design and LEED. In order to determine level of experience, several options are available. First, look for other projects in the firm's portfolio. If there are built works that embody some of the sustainable design principles that are central to your project, consider actually visiting the projects, if possible. Set up an appointment with the owner representative or building manager. How well is the building actually working? How did client input get integrated into the product? Allow room for error with experimental buildings, but it is also a good sign if there has been some follow-up by the design team in the postconstruction phase. With new technology and practice, firms must self-critique their work to continue learning and improving their expertise and knowledge.

An important tool for consultant contracting is the project language used by the owner. Clear communication with bidders and consultants through specific language is critical in the development of a successful LEED project. This includes green building language in the Request for Proposal (RFP) and Request for Qualifications (RFQ) language, bidding qualifications, and consultant selection interview questions. Generally, be sure to ask for teams with LEED-accredited professionals, experience in delivering green projects, green design workshops, and design optimization to satisfy both cost and benefit requirements.

For design consultants, proposals should include your approach to achieving green design goals, life cycle costing, and specific conservation goals. Highlight green features of projects you have previously participated in. Don't assume you know what the client needs. Ask probing questions regarding what would define a successful green project for them. Identify priority issues for the client, such as health care clients who are concerned about patient and staff satisfaction, civic clients who are concerned about public perception, or a company who has experienced health-related air quality issues in the past and does not want to repeat them.

Look to work with other consultants who share your values and bring expertise to the table. For building projects where energy efficiency will be a focus, selecting a mechanical engineer to collaborate with will strongly affect the ability to integrate innovative concepts. While working with other consultants or contractors you are comfortable with due to a long working relationship, you may also need to consider trying different partners out in order to bring new problem-solving approaches to the drawing board or experience you may not have to the team. Being too comfortable with your tried-and-true subconsultants or design process may not help get to thinking "outside the box."

Finally, once a consultant team is in place, it is critical for the client and their team to include clearly articulated contract language that identifies what is expected by each consultant regarding sustainable design process and product. Services to be contracted may include green design charrettes, predesign analysis of factors affecting LEED credits, early cost estimating that includes LEED impact, LEED point achievement analysis, and certification package preparation and submittal. Contracts should clearly indicate the level of green building performance that has been set by the organization's policy or the project owner.

Contracting Models

The use of different contracting models may affect the success of delivering a successful, cost-effective green building. Requirements for public agencies to use a low-bid process for consultant selection is the least desirable option, as it may result in inexperienced contractors with no desire to achieve green buildings. Two of the less common models, which are most applicable to large projects, are discussed here.

General Contractor/Construction Manager. Application of a General Contractor/Construction Manager (GCCM) model means that the contractor is brought on at the beginning of the design process and helps to manage the construction aspects of the project from the outset. This gives the opportunity for much greater collaboration with the contractor and greater control related to green features, costs, construction sequencing, and a host of other aspects. Having the contractor at the table makes it more likely to successfully deliver such features as use of sustainably certified lumber, which may require long lead times in order to contain costs.

The projects that the City of Seattle has undertaken with the GCCM model have had a higher level of success in achieving LEED overall. This is probably due in part to the fact that the contractor was more involved but also partly to the fact that these tend to be larger budget projects with fees dedicated for energy modeling and additional commissioning. In addition, large contracting firms tend to engage in GCCM contracts and may have additional expertise or resources devoted to sustainability.

Design/Build/Operate. In this variation on the more familiar design/build model, some public entities are using a method that also includes operating the building as part of the contracted services. With a much larger package than construction alone, this creates greater competition among potential contractors. One distinct advantage of this approach is that the contractor has a vested interest in designing and building a facility with the lowest possible operating costs, which means the contractor is also sharing a portion of the risk with the client. The contractor will be responsible over the useful life of the facility, or a designated period, for commissioning, warranty repair, and operating/maintenance. Two examples of publicly funded green buildings that have used this option are the Seattle Public Utilities Cedar Water Treatment Facility, designed by CH2MHill, and the University of Washington's Benjamin Hall, designed by CollinsWoerman.

Early Design Process

The early design process usually includes the predesign, schematic design, and design development phases. Some green projects with high goals for innovation may require additional time during the predesign phase to do additional research. Three key elements will help to ensure a successful green design process: a green design champion, a design charrette, and an integrated design process.

Every project needs a designated green design champion. This means not that others are not expected to take responsibility for green thinking, but that there is one go-to person who will ride herd on all the green features, process, and design documentation. This person needs to have a take-charge attitude but also be a good cheerleader for the team.

The design charrette, or design workshop, is an early workshop that includes the entire design team, the client, and other stakeholders. The purpose is to set early goals and to explore initial design concepts while all options are available. As design progresses, doors begin to close on options that could have been considered earlier. Ideally, an early charrette should be held before schematic design begins, and then a series of shorter design charrettes can be held as the design develops. Include the management and report-

FIGURE 5.3 Design Charrette Led by the Architect
Provide technical assistance with design workshops for the entire team held early in the project development process.
Credit: Courtesy of CollinsWoerman Architecture and Planning, Seattle

ing of this workshop in the design team's scope of work. It is best to have the lead designer run the workshop or select the person who will (see figure 5.3).

Use the session to think big picture. Avoid going to the LEED score card right away! The only thing that is useful from the score card at this point is the categories and perhaps the design intent statements. Skipping directly to the score card will likely cause the team to miss innovation opportunities and focus too soon on details. Participants should include tenant representatives and operations staff. It is important to run the workshop with the awareness that it may include people with a broad range of knowledge regarding architectural design or green building. They should not have to feel embarrassed for whatever their knowledge level might be. As many have observed: "There are no dumb questions, only dumb answers." In any event, try to avoid jargon during group process.

Having representation by future building occupants can be key to making successful decisions that will affect the quality and performance of the work environment. Issues such as lighting, privacy, ceiling height, amenities, and more can benefit from occupant input. In addition, if occupants feel they were represented during the design process, they are more likely to feel that their participation in the process legitimately influenced the final design result, and their sense of involvement may reduce tenant complaints as well as help smooth over future potential dissatisfaction with certain aspects of the building. These players should be considered distinct from high-level client groups, such as executives, even if these include future tenants. This representation needs to occur both at the high level and at the staff level, from within the lower ranks of the client organization.

Failure to include building operator input can spell disaster for the operational success of a project. Building managers have practical experience and technical knowledge that can greatly aid the design team. Their experience and professional knowledge should not be undervalued. For example, failure to consult management staff who would later be responsible for maintaining the green roof at Seattle City Hall resulted in their having no accommodation for tool storage, requiring them to haul them up through a roof hatch for every use. A simple detail could have made the roof maintenance more efficient and less cumbersome.

One key quality of design teams for green projects is the close interaction of a team from a wide range of disciplines. Often, the best design concepts come from integrated design solutions that work beyond traditional disciplinary boundaries. One key to high-quality design results is the breadth and depth of the cross-disciplinary team. All consultants should be willing, if not eager, to participate in an integrated design process. Integrated design is fairly complex. An excellent new book on the topic, *The Integrative Design Guide to Green Building*, has been written by 7group and Bill Reed.[16] This design approach addresses the ongoing collaborative process of the design team, which may entail expanded early exploration of design options, and the subsequent dialogue that deals with the synergy among different design options and concepts.

Once the project design begins to emerge from the schematic phase, there will be a group of LEED credits that are sure bets because they are not too costly and they fit the project well. There will be some credits that are definite "no's" and there will be a set of green building ideas in the "maybe" category. All of these will not be likely to make it into the final project due to budget limitations. Use a selection process based on rough cost projections and cost "bundling," or grouping design strategies with functional relationships. Compare various cost bundles from a first-cost and a long-term cost perspective. Some strategy bundles may even cost less. This process can be used to select a suite of green building options that make the most sense for the project.

There should be a green design check-in meeting with the entire team at the beginning and end of each design phase. If a green building certification program score card is being used, how is it going? What is going well and what needs additional attention and problem solving? The client should be present at these meetings. If certain green design goals are not being met along the way, it will be too late to make changes once the project has reached the next phase: preparation of construction documents.

Construction Documents

This later phase of the design process focuses on the development of construction documents and design specifications. Most decisions have been made, and now the technical documents necessary to execute the design must be developed. Once the project reaches the construction documents phase, the toughest work related to design is done. However, there are still some keys to writing specifications that are the most likely to get the results the client wants. It may be tempting to use contract language designating many of the green elements as "alternates" or "add-alternates." This is not advised. A better approach is to put the green elements in the base bid package and to allow materials or approaches that are not green, or that will fail to meet LEED credits, only as alternates. This better integrates green elements into the overall design from both a philosophical and budgetary standpoint. If green elements are singled out as alternates, they won't be considered essential to the project. In addition, bidders may take advantage of the opportunity to pad the bid price for such elements, either in the hopes that the client will not elect to use the alternates or from fear rather than actual knowledge of the cost of these items.

Other important contract language may pertain to the use of materials and products that will meet LEED requirements, such as low-VOC (volatile organic compound) or recycled content materials. In such situations, it is greatly preferable not to use such language as "or equivalent." While this may seem to cover the bases legally, it can result in products that are not at all equivalents being substituted. To an uninformed contractor, the high-VOC adhesive may seem equivalent to the low-VOC product. Even one such substitution on the job site can result in the loss of an entire LEED credit, even if the intent of the credit was substantially met. In such cases, the specification should read "alternate only as approved by architect."

Construction

The construction phase is where the rubber begins to meet the road. If the contractor has been on board during the design process, the transition to the construction phase is more likely to begin smoothly and with a high priority on green construction practices. Regardless of the level of green expertise by the primary contractor, make sure that all participants in the construction process have attended a preconstruction meeting that explains the green building goals and their importance. Require all new subcontractors and any workers new to the job site to go through an educational briefing on green design goals before they begin work. If awareness and a common knowledge do not exist among everyone on the job, errors can occur that may jeopardize LEED credit attainment. Site substitutions can occur that do not meet the specifications. Vigilance is necessary to prevent this situation.

The construction phase is a good opportunity to promote green building to the public that will be passing by the site. Post signs explaining the green building goals and features and their benefit to the community.

Postconstruction

The postconstruction, or occupancy, phase of a new green building holds its own challenges. If building managers have been included in the building design process, this can avoid a lot of headaches later on. If there are unfamiliar building systems, do not hand the keys over to the building manager and walk off! Too often, the responsibility of managing the new buildings is turned over to these professionals with no orientation or support. Training programs should be developed for each building operator, and additional support should be provided to operations staff during the initial occupancy and "shakedown" period, when kinks in the system are being worked out. If possible, commission the project and give operations staff a chance to experiment with building systems before tenants move in. Training sessions on building systems can be provided by contractors, project engineers, or equipment suppliers. In addition, it is important to provide tenant education, as mentioned in chapter 3.

TIPS

Tips for Developing Green Building Program Services

- Create the first tier of services in the form of design tools, educational programming, and technical assistance. The second tier of incentives and code requirements can be added later.
- Conduct a market assessment to determine who else is providing green building services or programs. Consider partnering with these organizations.
- Assess which services to provide and the relative funding and staffing needs of each. How does this create an overall service package and funding breakdown?
- Become familiar with the green building rating certification tools in your market.
- Select the tools that best fit your needs, and connect your program to them.
- Consider developing custom design tools suited to regional climate conditions, local building codes and incentives, and local project case studies.
- Consider creating education programs to help overcome barriers, such as lack of awareness of green building strategies for success.
- Provide educational programming that is customized to different target markets or building industry disciplines.
- Review training opportunities your program can connect to, such as USGBC LEED training modules, professional accreditation or certification programs, and vocational training for green construction skills.
- If special green code requirements exist, create training to support their successful implementation.
- Provide technical assistance via a hotline or more staff-intensive services with individualized one-on-one support.
- Ensure that technical assistance staff have both robust technical knowledge and good coaching and people skills.
- With a full technical assistance program, considering establishing various service levels.

Tips for Green Building Clients

- Establish green building goals as part of the predesign or master plan process.
- Integrate green building language into RFPs and RFQs.
- Hire consultants with green design expertise and passion.
- Consider alternative contracting models, such as GCCM or design/build/operate.
- Hold an early design workshop focused on the "big picture."
- Allow design teams to choose their own sustainable design subconsultant or design charrette facilitator.
- Get design input from future tenants and building managers.
- Do not accept sweeping claims regarding the huge cost impacts that green building or LEED may have. Ask to have any claims backed up with facts, including long-term operational impacts.
- Post educational signage during construction and after the project is complete.
- Create both a building operator and tenant education program.

Tips for Green Building Designers

- Make sure there is a designated green champion on the team.
- Establish cross-disciplinary teams and an integrated design process.
- Make sure green design goals, such as LEED level of performance, are clearly established and agreed on by the client and design team.
- Don't focus on LEED goals too early. Remember that many excellent sustainable design strategies will not get points in LEED.
- Utilize early "cost bundling" to compare alternatives and select the best design options.
- Make sure the LEED credits being pursued make sense for the project and the site or region.
- Do not use "alternates" or "add-alternates" in green construction document language.
- Make sure that all contractors and subcontractors are educated at the construction site.

CHAPTER 6

Green Building Incentives and Codes

I n the 2007 Green Building Survey commissioned by the National Real Estate Investor organization, 75 percent of corporate users of real estate services and 80 percent of real estate developers said that government incentives for green building influence their decisions.[1] This chapter addresses how to create voluntary incentives and mandatory requirements for green building, primarily in the private sector. Over 70 percent of the survey respondents have noticed an increase in green building initiatives, yet small numbers have actually taken advantage of these initiatives. This arena is fairly new and is rapidly evolving.

FINANCIAL INCENTIVES

Incentives are an excellent strategy for modifying behavior, making the types of activities we want to see more attractive. Incentives are sometimes a strategy that removes barriers, such as initial cost. First costs for green building have come down significantly and will probably continue to do so over time. However, the first costs tend to be higher in markets where green building has not been broadly accepted or adopted. Bringing monetary incentives to the table can help augment the budget for a development project. It can shorten the payback period for investing in green building, since some project features may have a longer payback period than is acceptable. Cash incentives can also provide a carrot to builders or developers, particularly if they are in the early majority group of innovation adopters. People in this category tend to be very deliberate about their decisions and may be carefully weighing whether to try out green building or not. Many factors may influence this decision, but if they feel they are receiving support such as incentives, it can tip the scale in the right direction.

A wide variety of incentives exist that can help to increase the level of investment in green building. Financial incentives involve a monetary reward, such as cash or rebates, in exchange for a particular outcome or course of action. Other incentives may provide a financial value but are not directly awarded to the beneficiary as cash.

One important service a green building program can provide is an index or listing of all available incentives for projects within their jurisdiction, with a description of the details and eligibility requirements. This should include local, state, and federal level programs. These tend to change frequently, so be sure to schedule regular updates of the information. Incentives can be compiled into a searchable tool. An excellent index of incentives related to energy is the Database of State Incentives for Renewables and Energy Efficiency.[2] It may not include everything, but it is a good starting point and can be linked to from local program Web pages. In addition, the USGBC posts a useful listing of government-based LEED incentives.[3] Much of the information in this chapter uses this document as the source. Check in with all local, regional, and state-level governmental or utility-based organizations to compile information on all the pertinent incentive programs or tax rebates your customers might be eligible for. Get to know the regional nonprofit funders in your area to see if they support green building through grant programs.

Grants

A variety of local and national programs provide grant-based incentives for green building innovation. For example, the City of Portland operates a Green Investment Fund, which accepts proposals annually for projects that push the limits for water conservation, stormwater, waste minimization, energy efficiency, and toxics reduction. More than $2.5 million has been awarded over a seven-year period. The total annual awards average around $425,000, and the funding given to individual projects is flexible. Eligible projects include public or private endeavors. Proposals for projects in the conceptual or schematic project phase are encouraged. The innovations for recipient projects have ranged from a community center constructed with salvaged shipping containers, a zero-energy floating home with an innovative micro-hydro system capturing energy from the flows of the Columbia River, and a project with a "living wall" system that processes stormwater.

The program is supported by the City of Portland and the Energy Trust of Oregon and was first championed by Portland commissioner Dan Saltzman, who comments: "Supporting new green building products, technologies and practices is core to the city's comprehensive economic development strategy to grow and develop sustainable industry in the region. The Green Investment Fund is a prime example of what we can actively do to promote innovation in the field."[4] National organizations that provide green building grants include the Home Depot Foundation and the Kresge Foundation. Home Depot Foundation is investing in grants totaling $400 million over the next ten years to projects focused on green affordable housing and community trees/urban forests. Kresge Foundation provides grants to nonprofits for green renovations, historic preservation, and leading-edge new construction projects focused on LEED Platinum, the Living Building Challenge, or zero energy.[5]

Local incentive programs can be developed that specifically relate to national or local building certification tools. The cities of Portland and Seattle offered LEED incentives during the early days of LEED adoption in their area. The incentive provided $15,000 to $20,000 to projects achieving minimum LEED performance levels. The programs were very useful in helping early adopters overcome the initial hurdles to achieving LEED. At the time, building professionals may have heard of LEED but had never actually used it. There was a considerable learning curve as well as anxiety about whether using the tool would be successful. The recipients of the incentive signed an agreement stating that they would pay the incentive back to the City if they did not achieve LEED certification. Portland's incentive was funded via solid waste and recycling funds; Seattle's, via energy and water utility conservation funds.

The Seattle incentive required the project to be in the early phases of design (no later than schematic phase) and also required a green design charrette. The ideas behind these requirements were twofold. First, projects that set green design goals early tend to be more successful and to incur a lower cost for achieving green building. Second, projects that engage in early goal-setting workshops and collaborative design tend to result in better project outcomes. Peter Dobrovolny, Seattle's commercial green building expert who created and led the City's LEED incentive program, is known for working tirelessly and patiently with design teams, playing the green building champion for project teams that have none. Regular check-ins and reminders are often needed to make sure projects are successful, and the public/private partnership process allowed Peter to do that more effectively because it changed the City's role from a passive to an active one. King County of Washington State has continued the LEED Incentive program, with the following funding levels (see table 6.1).[6]

Other cities with LEED grant programs include Santa Monica, California, and El Paso, Texas. The El Paso program provides grants to LEED projects at project completion, based on a minimum number of LEED credits. The grant level increases as the LEED score goes up. The grant is capped at the top end with a $400,000 grant for LEED

TABLE 6.1 KING COUNTY—— LEED INCENTIVE AWARD LEVEL

LEED™ Certification Level	Funding Level
Silver	$20,000
Gold	$25,000
Platinum	$30,000

TABLE 6.2 BUILT GREEN INCENTIVE AWARD LEVELS ——————————

Built Green is the local home builders program of the Masterbuilders Association of King and Snohomish Counties in the State of Washington.

King County and City of Seattle Built Green Incentive Award Levels

Built Green Certification Level	Single Family (one unit)	Multifamily Development (four or more units)	Community Development (ten or more units plus communities certification at the three-star level)
Four-star	$2,500	$5,000	$10,000
Five-star	$5,000	$10,000	$15,000

Platinum multistory buildings that have been 50 percent vacant for five years. This last criteria connects green building with economic development.[7]

Local green building certification programs, such as those offered by local home builder organizations, can also be aligned with incentives. The local Master Builder program for the Seattle area, Built Green, can qualify developers for cash incentives of up to $15,000. The incentive awards range from single-unit homes to up to four-unit multifamily projects. Projects must achieve the upper tier ratings within the program, which require third-party certification. (The lower levels do not.) The program is funded by the King County Department of Natural Resources and Parks (Water and Land Resource Division) and Seattle Public Utilities (see table 6.2).[8]

Energy, Water, and Other Incentives

Many incentives are available that focus on specific aspects of green building. These are most often related to energy and water efficiency but may also include drainage and solid waste issues. Most are offered at the local level, but some exist at the state and federal levels. Such incentives should be leveraged toward green building projects.

A referral program for such incentives is an important tool for green building programs. However, some of the existing programs may not dovetail well with green building tools such as LEED. I suggest working with local program officials for energy and water conservation incentives to modify their program requirements to map to tools such as LEED. For example, Seattle Public Utilities has a long-standing program of water conservation incentives aimed at building retrofits. Through a collaborative process with their program staff, they realized that the rapid adoption of green building in their marketplace could help them to capture additional water savings. They created a new water conservation incentive for new construction. Typically, their approach had been to fund a portion of the cost of individual plumbing fixtures, such as low-flow toilets or urinals. LEED uses a whole building performance approach, which calculates the total building savings. The new incentive included a performance-based incentive that could be linked directly to LEED documentation materials for water conservation; the incentive pays $10 per gallon per day saved. This makes it very easy for LEED projects to apply for the incentive without a lot of additional paperwork, which in itself can be an incentive.[9]

The unique utility-based incentive adopted by Pasadena, California's water and energy utility provides up to $100,000 in rebates for buildings or individual electric meter customers that invest in energy efficiency resulting in a minimum of 12 percent efficiency above energy code (Title 24). One month's electricity savings is rebated for each percentage above code that the building performs, using a whole building performance method.[10]

There may also be incentives related to site development, including installing efficient irrigation systems, using native plants, amending soil with compost, converting impervious surfaces to landscaping or porous paving, or controlling and treating stormwater flow. Portland's Clean River Rewards program provides a stormwater utility discount of up to 100 percent of the discharge fee for managing stormwater from roof and paved areas on site.[11]

Financing and Insurance Incentives

Other incentives linked to green building are beginning to appear in the marketplace. Fireman's Fund offers a special insurance package for both personal and commercial properties that meet certain green criteria.[12] ShoreBank Enterprise Cascadia is a nonprofit community development financial institution that serves the Oregon and Washington region. They are an affiliate of Chicago-based Shorebank Corporation. Among other things, they provide alternative green building commercial loans for rehabs, multifamily, mixed-use, and infill projects. Their program is designed to "offer a higher advance rate against appraisals."[13] New York State provides low-interest loans for LEED-qualified energy-efficiency measures and green building materials. These are offered at 4 percent below market rate.

One of the more creative programs is the City of Berkeley's FIRST initiative, which provides City-backed loans for green building improvements. Financing is made available for installing rooftop solar collectors, in partnership with a third-party administrator, Renewable Funding LLC. The program assists property owners to repay the cost of the improvements over twenty years, as part of a voluntary increment on their property tax bill. Much of this cost is covered by the energy savings, which home owners can preview through a calculator provided by the Renewable and Appropriate Energy Laboratory at the University of California, Berkeley. A fixed interest rate covers the entire twenty-year period, and if the property is sold, the repayment obligation is assumed by the new property owner.[14]

Tax Incentives

An excellent strategy for creating green building financial incentives is through the taxation system. Tax benefits that accrue over a multiyear period may get the attention of builders and developers better than one-time incentives. Tax credits may also be more valuable than equivalent tax deductions. Tax credits have a dollar-for-dollar value, whereas a tax deduction normally reduces only a percentage of the tax that is owed. Tax incentives may be administered at the federal, state, or local level. Thus far, they have included credits for property taxes, business taxes, and personal income taxes.

New York State broke new ground in 2001 with the creation of the green building tax credit, a business and personal tax credit for owners and tenants of green buildings. The program counts a percentage of the allowable costs for green building in hotels, office buildings, and multifamily buildings of more than twenty thousand square feet and can be applied to new construction, renovations, whole building, or tenant spaces. The tax credit has a special focus on energy efficiency, fuel cells, photovoltaics, and greener refrigerants.[15]

Maryland, New Mexico, and Oregon have also enacted tax incentives. The New Mexico program includes LEED for Homes. The Oregon program, provided by the Oregon Department of Energy, is quite comprehensive in regards to alternative energy systems, such as wind, solar, and ground-source heat pumps. It includes energy loans as well as residential and business energy tax credits.[16]

Multiple counties and cities have also enacted property tax incentives for LEED-certified buildings. These include Baltimore and Howard Counties, Maryland; Chatham County, Georgia; Cincinnati, Ohio; and Honolulu, Hawaii. Some of these programs are dependent on location in a designated priority reinvestment area or enterprise zone. The time periods offered range from one to ten years, and the value of the incentive ranges from the full tax amount to calculated percentages of the total tax or total cost of the building. In some cases, the incentive increases as the LEED certification level increases. In Chatham County, for example, the tax incentive is at the full level for the first five years and then tapers off by 20 percent per year until the tenth and final year.

At the federal level, the Energy Policy Act of 2005 (EPACT) provides energy tax credit programs for home energy-efficiency improvements, residential renewable energy systems, and hybrid vehicles. New commercial buildings or reconstructed buildings that achieve a 50 percent reduction in energy use qualify for a range of federal tax deductions up to $1.80 per square foot. Partial deductions are also available for lighting, HVAC, and building envelope improvements. The Emergency Economic Stabilization Act of 2008 (P.L. 110-343) extends and amends the 2005 legislation.[17] The energy tax credits now include renewable energy incentives for public utilities and energy production businesses or financial investors, tax credit bonds for state and local government greenhouse gas emissions reduction programs, credits for residential home builders to help finance energy-efficiency measures, and credits for real estate developer project bonds for green building and sustainable design.[18] In addition, a mortgage buy-down program that would reduce interest rates contingent on meeting specific energy reduction targets is the centerpiece of a proposal called 14X Stimulus, sponsored by the nonprofit Architecture 2030 and other partners. State and local governments would adopt the plan by using public funding to help lower mortgage payments, simultaneously providing for energy efficiency and green-collar jobs.[19]

GREEN BUILDING CODES

In their excellent paper entitled "Institutional Efforts for Green Building," Alex Wilson and Doug Webber provide a backdrop for the need to address green building code reform:

> Building codes and zoning laws are established to protect the public by ensuring that practitioners are adhering to rules of good building practice. As minimum legal requirements, both building codes and zoning regulations have tremendous impact on the sustainability of the built

environment. As codes were historically developed to protect people from the immediate life-safety hazards of the built environment, they often neglect the bigger picture impacts that the built environment can have on human health and the environment at large.[20]

There are several basic approaches to using building codes to create widespread adoption of green building. The three categories described here are (1) removing code barriers, (2) creating code incentives, and (3) enacting code requirements. These could be done sequentially or concurrently. Code officials are another form of stakeholder that must be included in the collaborative process of green building adoption.

Code Barrier Removal

The first and most important step is to conduct an assessment to determine what code barriers to green building currently exist in all building-related codes (land use, building, energy, stormwater, structural, plumbing, and so forth). Developers and design professionals may blame code barriers for their failure to adopt green building. The barriers may be real or perceived, but in either case they are still barriers. It helps to work with stakeholder groups to find out what barriers they are encountering. Gathering input from permit applicants can be extremely useful and may reveal some barriers that would not be immediately obvious otherwise. Some code barriers may not prevent a feature being approved, but instead represent process barriers, such as taking more time to get the permit approved. This represents both a time and cost impact to the developer.

A stakeholder workshop conducted by the City of Chicago generated a list of 175 barriers to green building.[21] In late 2008, the City of Bellingham, Washington, announced a government initiative to remove green building code barriers with four steps: (1) a city/industry collaboration to identify and rank code barriers, (2) development of a work plan to address the barriers and pilot incentives, (3) implementation of at least five early actions to repair code barriers within the first twelve months, and (4) coordination with the County to address barriers within codes that they administer.[22] The Cascadia Region Green Building Council conducted a code barrier study for two public entities in Washington State, using case studies of projects and analysis of obstacles in the land use, development, and building codes.[23]

Many of the most widespread and difficult code barriers for buildings appear in energy and plumbing codes. Many green building innovations related to building systems appear in these two arenas. Energy codes tend to be complex, and prescriptive energy codes may discourage innovations or the testing of new technologies. Energy codes that allow modeling may also present problems because new energy-efficient equipment may not have been tested enough to provide performance-standardized data that will be acceptable to the code requirements.

Plumbing code officials tend to be some of the most conservative. This is understandable since they are protecting public health and the safety of the municipal drinking water supply. Water reuse systems and on-site wastewater treatment may be very difficult, if not impossible, to get permitted in many jurisdictions. In Seattle, Lynne Barker and Al Dieteman worked tirelessly over a multiyear period to get the local public health officials to accept rainwater collection systems. Eventually, they were able to create a model rainwater harvesting code that was acceptable to the code officials and presented a pathway to success for permit applicants. Another challenge with some alternative systems, such as on-site wastewater treatment, is that the permitting agency may require detailed engineering models or designs to demonstrate that the systems will work. For smaller projects, the cost of the engineering services effectively becomes the barrier. Fully developed code language that tells permit applicants what they need to do to have their plans accepted is a key asset. The acceptability of innovative stormwater systems is subject to many of the same barrier issues as wastewater. If stormwater systems fail, public safety is at stake.

There are often code barriers within land use codes that relate more to site development techniques. Many land use codes require wider streets and larger parking areas than necessary. This effectively enforces much larger areas of impervious coverage than needed and emphasizes "car habitat" versus open space with human or environmental benefit. Some land use codes guiding subdivisions may require large lots that reinforce sprawl, or that result in excessively large houses as a result of the relationship between land costs and return on investment for the developer.

Keep track of all code barriers that you encounter. Many of these will surface if your program is providing technical assistance to green building projects. One benefit of this type of service is that it helps public representatives to see how things are working in the field, what works and what doesn't, and what code barriers need to be addressed. Some code changes may be minor and will be relatively easy to fix. Others may require complex, cumbersome code change processes. Prioritize the code barriers to be addressed, with those that are easy to fix or will provide the most benefit if removed rising to the top. While some code barriers to green building are entirely legitimate, beware permit applicants who try to get code variances for their project just because it is green when the code departure being requested is not really directly associated with green features. Some of the valid code barriers that may typically arise include the following:

- On-site wastewater system ability to meet plumbing code and public health standards
- Rainwater collection system ability to meet plumbing code and public health standards
- Allowable rooftop coverage for items such as rooftop solar collectors
- Building height limits for wind turbines or solar collectors
- Natural ventilation system ability to meet energy code

- Large internal atrium ability to meet fire code[24]
- Low-impact development ability to meet stormwater code
- Narrow roadway design ability to meet fire code
- Small parking lot ability to meet parking requirements

Several incremental strategies can be used to address transformation of the building codes. These may be best suited to very complex and challenging code barriers. Pilot projects and alternative code approval pathways are a good way to initiate the code transformation process. Assigning projects a "pilot" status can help to designate them as experimental and may remove some of the perceived risk associated with deviating from standard code compliance. The purpose of pilot projects in this case is to test the new design strategy in the field, learn lessons regarding its successful application, and then take these lessons learned into the code modification process.

It is challenging to get code officials to approve projects that are at variance with the legal codes they are tasked with enforcing. Their job responsibility and accountability are to enforce the codes as they are. They are often unwilling to take risks unless they are protected from repercussions for doing so. For this reason, it is helpful to develop special pilot status designation within the permitting agency. In addition, the fears and anxieties of code officials related to testing something unknown can be addressed with a special pilot project status. No obligation to accept similar projects is implied, nor is a precedent for future projects necessarily being set at that moment.

Special code compliance pathways to support pilots or innovative projects can also be created to augment this process. Such programs should have a clear purpose, parameters, and expectations for code compliance staff. The program should have a name that clearly sets it apart from standard process. With such special service categories, code officials have a clear directive from upper-level management to approve innovative projects. This can provide permission to modify existing standards, and it releases staff from the normal level of accountability involved with enforcing codes to the letter of the law. Of course, the public health, safety, and welfare should always be protected, and the standards should be modified only if the permitting agency sees some value or public benefit, such as increasing the adoption of green building in the marketplace. Such programs can be created for particular technologies or design goals that the jurisdiction may wish to encourage but that often encounter barriers. Performance standards that must be met can be established for new technologies, such as gray-water reuse systems. Special programs can also be created for zero-energy buildings or any of the barrier issues listed above.

In Seattle, the Street Edge Alternative project was implemented by Seattle Public Utilities to test new greener approaches to residential roadway design (see figure 6.1). The

BOX 6.1 AN ODYSSEY OF CODE BARRIER REMOVAL ———————————————————————————

Clark Brockman, *associate principal, director of sustainability resources, SERA Architects, Portland, and* Ben Gates, *Central City Concern*

Central City Concern, an affordable housing provider in Portland, Oregon, houses some of the lowest-income people in the city's metropolitan area. To improve the economic situation and living environment of its tenants, they decided to pursue the Living Building Challenge (see appendix B) for their newest multifamily project under development. The Living Building Challenge is an ambitious green building performance benchmark that has only sixteen requirements, such as mandating the achievement of net zero energy and water performance. Our team identified Net Zero Water as one of the most challenging requirements, due to the complex regulatory environment that surrounds public water use. Achieving the goal requires significant water reuse strategies, all of which are currently characterized by jurisdictional challenges or barriers.

With grant funding from the Bullitt Foundation, Enterprise Community Partners, the Cascadia Green Building Council, and others, our team set out to document the regulatory path required for a building to meet the Net Zero Water and Sustainable Water Discharge requirements of the Living Building Challenge. Our mission was to accurately "map" the regulatory landscape in Oregon surrounding water use and reuse. At this point, we perceived that actual policy change was out of reach of this project's scope. We had no idea of the odyssey we had undertaken.

We started the process by developing an initial "straw man" diagram of all of the regulatory hurdles and barriers known to exist by our team of sustainability focused professionals (SERA Architects, Interface Engineering, Gerding Edlen Development, and Central City Concern). We then started meeting with regulatory officials, one at a time, at both the city and state level, encouraging them to correct the diagram as they saw fit through the lens of their particular agency. We heard

enough differences and inconsistencies in our one-on-one meetings to compel us to bring everyone together into one room at the same time to review the diagram with us one last time.

This meeting proved to be the linchpin moment in the study. We came to find out that all of these regulatory officials had never convened all at once to discuss policy—ever. In so doing, our team had unwittingly created a vehicle for accelerated policy change far beyond our expectations. We heard officials saying things like: "I always thought you (your agency) would never allow that—if your team is ok with it, we could be fine with it as well." This happened again and again during the ninety-minute meeting, charting a dramatic course of statutory policy change that would be initiated by Oregon's Plumbing Board over the next six months—without any legislation. By the time we submitted our report, three of the required appeals regarding rainwater and gray water reuse had been eliminated. More changes are still in process as of this writing.

Our team's task was simply to map the challenges and barriers so that all design teams in the state would have good information about how to pursue a Net Zero Water building in Oregon. Not only did we accomplish this, but we succeeded in convening a constructive dialogue among code officials that effectively provided institutional block busting. We had acknowledged unnecessary code barriers to water reuse and started a process of removing them. An important lesson was learned in how bureaucratic silos and lack of communication are part of the barrier. The results have surprised everyone, and we now hope to apply this methodology to water policy change in a variety of states across the country.

Excerpted with permission from Central City Concern, *Achieving Water Independence in Buildings: Navigating the Challenges of Water Reuse in Oregon* (March 2009), http://ilbi.org/resources/research/water/oregon.

project consisted of a single residential block. It allowed a narrower street, traffic calming, and a different approach to on-street parking. Instead of traditional curbs and gutters, drainage was handled using intensely planted drainage swales to more closely mimic the way natural systems deal with rainfall. The resulting street had an 11 percent less impervious surface than the street traditionally required by code. Permit approval was aided by designating the project as a pilot or "alternative" approach. A measurement and evaluation program was implemented to test the project's success. After two years of monitoring, results showed that the total volume of stormwater leaving the street had been reduced by 99 percent. The approach is being implemented in other pilot areas, with plans to amend the code to allow widespread adoption of the strategies.[25]

FIGURE 6.1 Seattle Street Edge Alternatives Project (SeaStreets)
Seattle used a special pilot program to test innovative drainage and roadway design strategies. The successful performance monitoring results provide justification to modify development codes.
Credit: Courtesy of Seattle Public Utilities

Code Incentives

Building and zoning codes provide a useful framework for creating incentives to green building. While such incentives may hold financial value to the recipient, they do not require the same kind of funding and financial outlay required by many of the strategies discussed in the section on Financial Incentives. Code incentives can also be considered an incremental step towards code requirements for green building, helping to pave the way for widespread adoption.

Code-based incentives (or disincentives) can take on a variety of forms. I'll discuss two types here: those focused on particular development features, and those focused on the code approval process. Some code incentives focus on very specific design strategies that the public permit agency is striving to encourage. Others will provide incentives for green building as a holistic concept. In Seattle, examples of the specific strategy approach include the following:

- Green roofs allow for a reduction in sizing of stormwater detention tanks.
- Rooftop solar panels allow for a height increase over the normal building elevation limit.
- Landscape code, called the Seattle Green Factor, gives bonus points for green roofs and rainwater collection.

Many jurisdictions have adopted a density bonus program that allows for greater building sizes than those normally allowed by code in return for comprehensive green building performance. Most cities and counties tie this to LEED certification, including:

Acton, MA, Arlington County, VA, Bar Harbor, ME, Cranford, NJ, Nashville, TN, Pittsburgh, PA, Portsmouth, NH, Seattle, WA, and Sunnyvale, CA. The first entity to adopt a LEED-based density bonus was Arlington County, Virginia (see box 6.2). These programs are often tied to what is known in zoning parlance as the Floor Area Ratio (FAR). The FAR is the limit to the amount of construction allowed in a given area, represented by the total building floor area as a percentage of the size of the land parcel. FAR limits are often combined with height limits. The density bonus can allow increased height and FAR in return for public benefit.

A good rationale for programs such as the green density bonus is that increased building densities will increase the load on infrastructure systems including energy, water, drainage, and transportation that support the building, and building green will offset some of those loads. Programs may apply only to certain designated zones such as downtown areas or specific neighborhoods where increased density is sought.

Code Disincentives

A very few programs have created disincentives for not adopting green building. Arlington County, once again, created a green building fund that is utilized for education and outreach purposes. The program is funded by a surcharge applied to all development projects that do not receive LEED certification. There may be financial penalties for failing to meet the agreed upon requirements of code incentive programs such as the green density bonus, described in box 6.2. Seattle's LEED density bonus program levies stiff fines for nonperformance based on the number of points by which the project fails to achieve LEED Silver and the construction value of the project. The penalties are deposited in a green building fund.

Some disincentives are for development projects that contribute to sprawl, or have an undue impact on transportation infrastructure services. Sometimes called a "life-cycle infrastructure charge," or development impact fee, this approach can help to stem greenhouse gas emissions associated with transportation, and the cost to extend public transit further and further away from employment centers. Two entities that are taking this approach are Lancaster, California, and DuPage County, Illinois. In Lancaster, development fees are based in part upon the distance of the development from the city center (the further away from the center, the higher the fee). DuPage County bases development fees on transit infrastructure impact and traffic creation.[26]

Permit Process Incentives

A large part of the cost for development encompasses the expensive and often slow permit review process and associated development fees. Code barriers can slow down projects attempting to integrate innovative green features. Many jurisdictions have developed programs that reduce development fees or expedite the permitting process, in return for

Joan Becker Kelsch, LEED AP, environmental planner, Arlington County

In an attempt to reduce the environmental impacts of a large-scale new construction, Arlington County, Virginia, implemented a pilot green building density incentive program in April 2000. LEED was relatively new and untested in the region, but Arlington's commitment to smart growth, transit-oriented development, and general environmental awareness made the small urban county located next to Washington, D.C., a prime candidate to try something new. What started as a pilot program in 2000 has grown to a successful way to encourage environmentally responsible construction.

The original pilot program provided a bonus density incentive to new office buildings in exchange for a LEED Silver certification. Between 2000 and 2003, only one building chose to participate. To encourage broader participation, Arlington expanded the project in 2003 to include all types of large development (office, multifamily residential, and mixed-use projects) and allowed increasing density bonuses for increasing LEED levels.

Project development teams who wish to request bonus density in exchange for LEED certification must agree to a specific LEED certification level and must register the project with the USGBC. As an enforcement mechanism, the developer must post a bond. The bond is held until the project achieves its LEED certification, at which point it is released back to the developer. The bond is calculated based on the size of the bonus density awarded to the project. If the project does not satisfy the requirements of LEED and does not achieve USGBC certification, the bond is released to the County.

Throughout construction, County staff members review the LEED components to ensure appropriate progress. Building permits will not be issued unless the project shows adequate progress incorporating LEED components.

Between December 2003 and December 2008, twenty-four buildings were approved as part of the green building bonus density program, and many have started construction. Of these, two projects have been completed and have successfully achieved their LEED certification. The twenty-four buildings that were approved with the LEED bonus represent 64 percent of approved commercial office space and 24 percent of approved residential units. Eleven buildings were approved with bonus density for LEED Certified, nine with LEED Silver, one with LEED Gold, and one with LEED Platinum. The remaining two projects are affordable housing projects using the local green home rating system. (It is important to note that most of the buildings approved in this five-year period have not been constructed yet.)

Because the market is trending toward green and buildings are achieving LEED certification more frequently, we will be revising our policy again in spring 2009. We offer lower bonus density for LEED-Certified and Silver buildings and slightly higher bonus density for LEED Gold and Platinum projects. A small additional bonus is available for residential projects to encourage LEED certification for apartment and condominium buildings.

For more information, contact Joan Kelsch, environmental planner, Arlington County, Virginia (703-228-3599 or jkelsch@arlingtonva.us).

---

adoption of green building. Such programs exist in Chicago, Costa Mesa, Gainesville, Santa Cruz, San Diego, San Francisco, Santa Monica, Scottsdale, and the counties of Howard County, Maryland; Hillsborough County and Sarasota County in Florida; Marin County, California; and the State of Hawaii. In focus groups conducted by the City of Seattle, developers consistently asked for accelerated permits as a green building incentive. Sometimes called "green lights for green permits," or priority permitting, the requirements and benefits for these programs vary. Some require designated levels of LEED achievement, LEED Accredited Professionals on the design teams, or achievement of green features using other systems, such as Green Globes or custom checklists.

Fee waiver programs vary by jurisdiction and may occur as refunds after project certification occurs, cover the costs of LEED certification, or require initial payment into a green building fund that is later refunded if requirements are met. The value of some waivers increases according to the level of LEED achievement. Other participant

benefits in green permit programs may include marketing, such as signage for project sites, or other forms of publicity.

The City of Chicago's green permits program, one of the most comprehensive ones in existence, qualifies participants with a menu of green features organized into three benefit tiers. Achieving more features within each tier further shortens the review period and reduces development fees. Different project types—including residential, institutional, industrial, and commercial—have their own criteria. Key areas of focus include green roofs, renewable energy and cogeneration, natural ventilation, exceptional water management, extra affordability, accessibility, and transit-oriented development. With expedited permit review, the review period can be reduced from four months to as short as four to eight weeks. Projects are qualified by an initial green review with program staff.[27]

One major Chicago project that participated in the green permit program was the Hines 300 North LaSalle project in downtown Chicago (see figure 6.2). As reported by Architectural Record, the 1.3 million–square-foot project was permitted in just thirty days. Designed by architecture firm Pickard Chilton, the

FIGURE 6.2 300 North LaSalle
This 1.3 million-square-foot project took advantage of Chicago's green permit program and was permitted in just thirty days.
Credit: Image courtesy of Hines

project has such innovative features as the elimination of water towers with the use of condenser water supplied from the Chicago River, and a 50 percent green roof. The vice president of construction for Hines, Scott Timcoe, noted that they applied for the program because "there is a huge construction boom in Chicago—sometimes getting a permit can be really laborious."[28]

While the construction market is slowing down with the recent economic downturn, green permit programs can still deliver value to projects with more early review by city staff and the integration of cash-incentive packages at the early stages. In addition, Chicago and other programs include the assignment of designated review staff to projects throughout the entire permit review process. In many organizations, a different staff member is assigned at each stage, with no continuity from start to finish. Designated permit staff with knowledge of green strategies and the ability to champion the project throughout the process can shorten review times. Education programs can help to foster code review staff who are more familiar with green building strategies.

Code Requirements

A surprising number of entities have moved toward green building requirements via building codes. Such programs do not have to replace incentive programs. Rather, they can be used in concert. Basic levels of green building performance that are accessible to the marketplace can be required. Incentives can be layered on top of this to encourage green buildings that go further and deeper. Code requirements take on a variety of forms. Once again, some cities have chosen to create their own customized requirements, and others are docking to existing tools, such as LEED. Some cities are making their mandates specific to certain aspects of the LEED performance requirements.

For example, the City of Santa Cruz created a green checklist with a minimum point requirement. Permit applicants fill out the checklist, and if they do not meet the threshold, they do not receive a permit.[29] The City of Boulder created a rating system called Green Points that creates point requirements for residential projects and now requires all commercial buildings to demonstrate energy performance at 30 percent beyond the LEED-referenced standard.[30]

Cities that have adopted or are considering adopting mandatory LEED standards include San Francisco, Boston, Baltimore, Chicago, and Pasadena. Mandating LEED is in some ways a shortcut to reviewing code barriers and eliminating them and to creating specific code requirements. Over time, permitting agencies should be looking to a more robust and in-depth approach to the greening of building codes. For one thing, tools such as LEED are subject to change; as this happens, the mandate that has been issued will automatically evolve, perhaps in unintended ways. This must be carefully tracked. In addition, without the barrier removal process, it is possible that the permitting agency will end up with standards that are at odds with one another.

Some cities are looking at using a new green code tool called Standard 189 to address this problem. The Standard 189 tool is being created in a partnership between ASHRAE (American Society of Heating, Refrigeration, and Electrical Engineers), the USGBC, and IESNA (Illuminating Engineering Society). It is a model code that is intended to be applied to all buildings except low-rise residential. The purpose is to provide a basic level of green building code requirements with mandatory criteria in all of the LEED topic areas, simple compliance, and a complementary tool for other green building programs. It provides both prescriptive and performance-based options. Standard 189 can be integrated into existing local building codes in its entirety or selectively.[31]

Other interesting examples exist of code requirements that deal with specific areas of green building. Energy efficiency has a lot of activity in this arena. The City of Aspen levies a charge on excess energy use in residences and commercial buildings. The Renewable Energy Mitigation Program, administered by the Community Office for Resource Efficiency, sets strict energy "budgets." For example, homes with outdoor pools and spas or snowmelt systems must install a renewable energy system or pay a mitigation fee. The fees are used to fund renewable energy systems elsewhere.[32] To deal with the energy use of existing buildings, some cities—including Berkeley, San Francisco, and Sacramento—require the use of energy audits. Portland, Austin, Denver, and Seattle are considering similar measures. Some cities are considering sweeping changes to their energy codes in order to meet the 2030 Challenge (discussed in chapter 1). In May 2009, Washington State governor Christine Gregoire signed Senate Bill 5854, which requires that state energy codes be amended to meet the 2030 Challenge requirements.[33]

Requirements to increase the recycling of construction demolition waste are another key code development area. Orange County, California, and Portland, Oregon, have mandatory recycling. Portland found that simply requiring a construction recycling plan resulted in increased levels of recycling, even with no other requirements. Other jurisdictions, including Boulder, Oakland, Chicago, Glendale, and San Francisco, have incentives for construction demolition recycling via a deposit program in which refunds occur if desired levels of recycling occur. Chicago's requirements were phased in, with the minimums for construction waste recycling advancing from 25 percent to 50 percent.

Quite a few code changes have addressed cool roofs, or programs that require roofs that reflect the sun's heat without increasing solar gain into the building or increasing the urban heat island effect. This strategy can address climate change as well as energy efficiency. The Cool Roof Rating Council provides a useful index of codes supporting cool roof design strategies. It also references rebate programs for cool roofs, which are offered in California, the Carolinas, Florida, Idaho, and Texas.[34]

In Chicago, all planned developments must include a set percentage of green roof and advanced energy efficiency. A few exceptions occur to ensure that these projects are not being discouraged, including affordable housing projects and grocery stores in what is termed "food deserts." A tiered set of requirements is provided, with more advanced levels of green roof, energy, and building performance for projects that are publicly funded via empowerment and enterprise zones, bank participation loans, and other publicly negotiated projects.[35]

A fairly new approach to building codes, known as form-based codes, offers some potential for integrating green building requirements. Form-based codes focus more on building massing, detailing, and layout than on building uses. They attempt to provide an integrated land development regulation that folds zoning, public works standards, urban design, and architectural guidelines into one document. A free access tool known as SmartCode Central provides free downloadable code modules that can be adopted and modified by local jurisdictions. A sustainable urbanism module created by Doug Farr is also available, which includes food production, renewable energy integration, light pollution reduction, and more.[36] King County, Washington, is conducting a pilot project on form-based code that puts a high priority on green building and low-impact development requirements. This project attempts to integrate these into each code module rather than creating a separate part of the tool related to sustainability.[37]

Incentives and Codes for Greenhouse Gas Reduction

As climate disruption has been increasingly recognized as a planetary crisis, building permitting agencies are now examining the role they may play in regulating greenhouse gas emissions. Several leading examples for such approaches have emerged from the Pacific Northwest. King County became the first county, followed by Seattle, the first city, in the country to require disclosure of greenhouse gas emissions as part of their environmental review process. All major development projects that trigger environmental review under the Washington State Environmental Policy Act must fill out a worksheet that is a first U.S. attempt to estimate the carbon emissions impact from a regulatory standpoint. The worksheet attempts to calculate emissions that will result in three key areas: embodied energy impacts, transportation impacts, and building operational energy use impacts. At this point, the process is only one of disclosure, but the logical pathway would entail setting thresholds that would establish when the amount of impact is enough that it requires mitigation. With the explosion of attention to the regulation of carbon and the possibility of carbon trading, this area of green building regulation is one to watch.

The City of Portland has proposed a High Performance Green Building Policy that includes creation of a carbon feebate program for commercial and multifamily buildings.[38] The feebate combines financial penalties for conventional construction, waivers for moderate green strategies, and incentives for deeper green projects. This program uses LEED and the Living Building Challenge as benchmarks to be applied to multifamily buildings of greater than five thousand square feet and commercial buildings of greater than twenty thousand square feet. The tiers of performance and associated financial incentives are shown in table 6.3. Rewards are onetime payments, require verification of green building performance, and vary based on the level of green performance and building gross square footage. Fees are also onetime payments. LEED performance-level requirements include the overall rating as well as minimum requirements within energy and water credits.

The proposal also targets residential single-family construction with a performance goal of having all new construction meet green building standards and be certified under the local Earth Advantage program, or LEED for Homes. These performance goals apply to homes of over twelve hundred square feet and are phased as listed here. If the performance goals are not met, a green building feebate will go into effect.

Portland has proposed an innovative tiered "feebate" program that combines fees for conventional construction, waivers for moderate green building, and rewards for highly green projects.

Feebate Options	Green Building Standards	Minimum Requirements	Feebate
Reward	Living Building Challenge	Net zero energy and water documentation (one year)	$2.58–$5.15 per square foot
Reward	LEED New Construction 2.2 LEED Core and Shell 2.0 LEED Schools LEED Retail	Platinum certification, PLUS: EAc1 + Eac2: 10 points WEc1 + WEc3: 4 points	$1.03–$2.06 per square foot
Reward	LEED New Construction 2.2 LEED Core and Shell 2.0 LEED Schools LEED Retail	Gold certification, PLUS: EAc1 + Eac2: 8 points WEc1 + WEc3: 4 points	$0.51–$1.03 per square foot
Waiver	LEED New Construction 2.2 LEED Core and Shell 2.0 LEED Schools LEED Retail	Silver Certification, PLUS: EAc1 + Eac2: 5 points WEc1 + WEc3: 2 points	Not applicable
Fee	None		(–) $0.51–$1.03 per square foot

Source: City of Portland High Performance Green Building Policy Report, December 4, 2008

- In 2009, 20 percent of new homes certified
- In 2010, 30 percent of new homes certified
- In 2011, 40 percent of new homes certified[39]

In one of the most ambitious and targeted climate action plans in the United States, the City of Chicago has outlined twenty-six actions for mitigating greenhouse gas emissions, with specific carbon reduction goals for each, and nine actions for climate adaptation. The actions are organized into four broad themes, including energy-efficient buildings, clean and renewable energy sources, improved transportation options, and reduced waste and industrial pollution. The city brought together what they felt was the best collaboration possible, using researchers, scientists, and analysts to ensure that the program was based on robust analytics and measurable outcomes. Using advanced satellite imaging, urban heat island "hot spots" have been identified. These neighborhoods will be targeted with programs and grants for energy-efficiency retrofits, green roofs, and tree planting. A significant effort is being made in Chicago to increase the energy efficiency of existing buildings in the context of climate action. Seventy percent of the proposed greenhouse gas reductions are in the area of building and other energy use. A green office challenge has been launched that targets the fifty largest high-rise buildings to compete with one another to achieve energy-efficiency reductions.

Climate actions extend to stormwater and landscape infrastructure. A city watershed plan will pinpoint neighborhoods that have specific flooding problems, which are expected to increase with extreme weather events resulting from climate change. These areas will be targeted with grants for increased permeable surfaces and rainwater collection systems, and an expansion of the City's Green Alley Program using pervious paving and high albedo concrete. The City is also working with nurseries and landscape ordinance officials to integrate a new plant list that addresses the fact that the City's plant hardiness zone is changing as a result of increasing temperatures.[40]

Other Considerations

Models and recent initiatives in green building incentives and code development offer many lessons. I encourage you to consider carefully other dynamics of green building adoption that may be difficult to anticipate. On the one hand, we should take care in moving too quickly to mandate technically specific green building innovations, in that this approach assumes that technology will not change and is stagnant. Market transformation is dynamic and holds many shifting variables. In an interesting 2002 article from the California Energy Commission, the authors note that narrowly defining market transformation variables may limit our thinking: "Policy and program designs should do as little as possible to limit the breadth of innovation. It may be that there is one best technology to solve a problem right now, but to mandate its use is to kill the development of any other competing technologies."[41]

We must also take care that the regulations we enact do not create what Stephen J. Dubner and Steven D. Levitt, the authors of the book *Freakonomics*, call "unintended consequences." They describe unintended consequences as the sometimes contrary effects that are created from well-meaning legal reforms. They argue, for example, that the Endangered Species Act (ESA) of 1973 may be creating negative unintended consequences: "One notable wrinkle of the E.S.A. is that a species is often declared endangered months or even years before its 'critical habitats' are officially designated. This allows time for developers, environmentalists, and everyone in between to have their say at public hearings." Regarding protection of the endangered pygmy owl, for example, "landowners near Tucson rushed to clear their property for development rather than risk having it declared a safe haven for the owl." Some are beginning to see the possibility that more harm may be coming to species as the result of the act that was designed to protect them, sometimes as a result of people "gaming" the system.[42]

An example of a different type of unintended consequences in the green building arena was the advent of energy-efficiency requirements back in the 1970s that did not take into account the need for indoor air quality. The new standards advanced energy performance, but by ignoring the existence of toxins in building materials and the need for ventilation, a condition called "sick building syndrome" emerged as another problem, resulting from the more airtight buildings. This unintended consequence speaks to a need to understand the complex systems in which we are operating, and examine the links between different spheres of cause and effect. This is not to say that we should not mandate actions for the good of society but that we should also be aware of the complexities of the marketplace, innovations, and building systems. One need only look at the catastrophic collapse of the real estate mortgage system to see that some forms of regulatory intervention can fail in unintended ways.

On the flip side, the rate at which we are despoiling our precious resources and paving every acre of land in sight must be halted if we have any hope of our future quality of life. While this book suggests many strategies for approaching the adoption of market adoption of green building, can we afford to bide our time while we create incentives, hoping that they will tip the scale toward getting people to do the "right" thing? Perhaps it is too late to hope that any of that will make enough of a difference. Our regulatory requirements usually lag far behind scientific and technological advances, so we cannot afford to be too cautious. The Precautionary Principle tells us that if there is even the possibility of a threat to the environment or human health, we should take action, even if cause and effect have not been proven scientifically.[43] From this perspective, perhaps it is time to mandate green building aggressively and broadly. We must use the legal mechanisms we have available to shift our course, and we must do it rapidly.

TIPS

Financial Incentive Tips

- Create a tracking system to keep up with all code barriers you encounter.
- Create an index of all available incentives for your area.
- Develop grant sources for green building projects.
- Consider providing cash incentives to reward use of the green building tools you endorse.
- Look at the possibility of creating incentives tied to economic development, such as for vacant or previously foreclosed properties.
- Work with local utility incentive program representatives to match green building criteria requirements (such as those used in LEED) to their program documentation submittals.

- Partner with regional funding organizations to help them offer green building funding products.
- Consider providing tax credits or tax incentives tied to personal and business taxes, property taxes, or income taxes.

Code Barrier Removal Tips

- Discuss code barriers that exist with stakeholders and permit officials.
- Review energy, plumbing, stormwater, fire code, and parking code requirements in particular.
- Create special pilot project or innovative project status to help unique projects navigate the permit compliance pathway.
- Convene stakeholder groups and discussion sessions with code officials. Get them to compare notes to find out where the barriers lie.

Code Incentive Tips

- Provide additional code flexibility for features you want to encourage, such as rooftop solar collectors or wind turbines.
- Assess neighborhoods targeted for increased density. Offer a density bonus tied to green building requirements.
- Create incremental steps in the incentive requirements to encourage higher levels of performance.
- Implement penalties for failure to perform in incentive programs by falling short of requirements.

Code Penalty Tips

- Consider use of development impact fees to force new development to bear a proportional share of the costs of providing infrastructure or other services.

Code Incentives

- Consider giving permit fee waivers.
- Look at how permit review times can be shortened to provide a reward based on time.

Code Requirement Tips

- Look at the potential of tying code requirements to one of the existing green certification tools.
- Consider docking your existing commercial building codes to the Standard 189 tool.
- Do an assessment of your energy codes to see if they are up to date and how

close they come to helping meet important energy-efficiency goals, such as the 2030 Challenge.

- Explore the idea of mandating code requirements for specific areas of priority for your region, such as cool roofs to lower urban temperatures, or minimum construction demolition recycling to extend landfill life.
- Consider the next generation of green code requirements or incentives that may relate to greenhouse gas emissions impacts.
- In order to phase in requirements, place voluntary goals and if they are not met by a certain date, follow with mandatory provisions.
- Direct green building penalties into special funds to encourage green building.

CHAPTER 7

Measuring Program Impacts

Green building holds the promise of delivering many benefits, but how do we know if we are getting there? Measuring and evaluating the impacts of green building programs is an important activity that helps to justify the programs' existence as well as verify that they are having the intended effects. It is wise to establish some performance targets for a program during the initial planning stages, as well as set expectations regarding how often progress toward these targets will be reported. How will the program's success be measured? Performance measures must be established, with indicators that can be used to assess progress. The types of measures can vary widely, as well as the amount of effort required to gather the information. Measurement and evaluation is a well-discussed field. What I will present here is not intended to be an exhaustive resource for designing and implementing evaluation programs. Rather, it is an introduction to some of the basic approaches and is intended as a starting point.

When designing an evaluation program, review the initial program justification (discussed in chapter 2). What is the program's mission, and how will you know if the mission is being accomplished? What are the key results that are desired? If energy or water efficiency is pivotal to the program's success, then some attempt must be made to measure these.

There are two different approaches to evaluating green building programs. The first type of evaluation involves measuring actual program activities, such as educational workshops or technical assistance. The second type measures the impacts of green buildings themselves. Each can be used separately, with the results combined into an annual results report. Some programs may choose to use only one of the approaches. I will discuss each type individually.

Most of the evaluation discussed in this chapter relates to general and ongoing program evaluation needs, although the resulting data can also be used for periodic strategic planning. One exception might be the evaluation of building performance, which I'll discuss at the end of the chapter. Special evaluations may be done periodically for singular purposes. These may occur during times of major change when market conditions, priorities, or budgets are shifting. Significant changes in the economy, population, agency reorganizations, infrastructure crisis, losses in revenues, or changes in elected officials may trigger special evaluations that can be used for strategic planning purposes.[1]

TABLE 7.1 GREEN BUILDING PROGRAM PERFORMANCE METRICS BY CITY

Various cities will have varied approaches to measuring program performance.

Green Building Program	Performance Metrics
City of Austin	Number of projects assisted Number of square feet of program participation Number of people trained Number of information requests provided Energy savings, modeled for commercial buildings
City of Chicago	Number of industry professionals and residents trained Number of green permits issued Number of acres of green and solar roofs Number of acres of pervious and green space Number of hotline calls Number of visitors to green building center Number of City-owned LEED buildings Predicted energy and water savings/LEED scorecards Cost/performance of several City LEED projects
City of Portland	Number of industry professionals, residents, and staff trained Number of permitted projects receiving technical assistance Number of certified green buildings in Portland Number of City-owned LEED buildings Utility savings and waste reduction from City green building projects
City of Seattle	Number of projects assisted Number of LEED commercial and green residential projects (local MBA program) Number of green affordable housing units Utility savings, waste reduction, carbon dioxide reduction, and so forth from LEED projects Number of deconstruction projects and building relocations
City of San Francisco	Number of industry professionals and residents trained Number of professional firms being influenced Number of permitted projects receiving technical assistance Number of City-owned LEED buildings

DESIGNING THE EVALUATION PLAN

Designing and implementing a measurement and evaluation program can be complex, time consuming, and expensive. Although evaluation is important, its cost and level of effort must be viewed in balance with other program activities. With the Seattle program, there was much pressure to prove the value of the program, in order to justify the ongoing program budget. While this is perfectly normal and it is important to be able to respond to these demands, it is easy to lose sight of other key issues at hand when faced with political and budgetary pressures to perform.

Keep in mind the appropriate balance between doing an activity and measuring its impact. If 75 percent of your time goes toward measuring the impact of activities done in the other 25 percent of your time, things have gone out of whack. While this may sound obvious, the situation can easily move in this direction if you are not careful to manage expectations for evaluation. While different levels of effort are required for various types of evaluation (discussed below) overall I suggest that no more than 20 percent of the program (nonstaff) portion of the budget be spent on measurement and evaluation. Program staff are unlikely to have all the skills needed to conduct a full evaluation, so outside consultants can be hired to assist with this specialized expertise. In addition, using third parties to conduct program evaluation removes the bias that may occur if such activities are handled only internally.

Each green building program will have its own customized set of performance measures, which are selected from a broader menu of possibilities. For a flavor of the variety of performance metrics being used by different programs, see table 7.1. As you can see, most of the programs combine some evaluation measures related to program activities with measures related to green building performance.

One of the first things to consider when designing an evaluation program is the intended purpose. What is the goal, and who is the intended audience? There may be more than one purpose and audience, as shown in table 7.2. Different evaluation measures should be matched to the intended purpose and audience.

TABLE 7.2 INTENDED PURPOSES AND AUDIENCES FOR EVALUATION

Be sure to consider the audience, as well as the purpose, of your evaluation program.

Purpose	Audience
Sustainability performance • Prove that green building is having the intended impact • Determine positive or negative trending and in what areas	• Stakeholder groups • Building industry • Researchers
Political and managerial • Justify the existence of the program and its associated resource investment • Provide for accountability to upper-level management and funders	• Elected officials • Managers • Budget officials • Citizens
Planning and development • Gain insight for long-range strategic planning, including tracking historical performance and major shifts over time • Improve or fine-tune the program	• Managers • Program planning staff • Program delivery staff

What performance goals is your program attempting to achieve? Performance targets can represent a progression that can be phased over time. For example, you may set a goal of affecting 10 percent of all building permits this year, 15 percent next year, and so on. They may be based on historical data, surveys, or what is happening elsewhere. The performance targets should relate to the program goals and objectives. Objectives may relate to program inputs, which are the resources used to deliver a program, including dollars spent and staff time used. The targets often also include outputs and outcomes (discussed in the next section). At the end of the day, program evaluation measured against established targets will tell us how effective the program is, if the targets and indicators of performance have been well chosen and all the needed data are available. Effectiveness can be thought of as the extent to which the outcomes are achieved. Various types of data can be used to measure and evaluate performance, including surveys, independent observation, anecdotal data, ongoing program tracking data, and special reports or research.[2]

Great resources are available from the organization Sustainable Measures. They provide a database of sustainability indicators used by many different organizations, which can be searched by topic. When assembling your performance measures, it is wise to consider selection criteria. The criteria provided by Sustainable Measures are as follows:

- *Relevant*: show something you need to know about; they are relevant for policy makers, businesses, residents, and so forth
- *Understandable*: including by people who are not experts
- *Newsworthy*: attractive to the local media
- *Reliable*: statistically measurable, logical, and scientifically defensible
- *Timely*: based on accessible information while there is still time to act[3]

You must also determine how the data will be collected, used, and tracked. Who will be responsible for managing the data over time, and what administrative tools will be used? Databases that can be converted into reports are one of the most useful methods.

A new program—called the STAR Community Index—helps cities track the sustainability performance of their city as a whole (see box 7.1).

OUTPUTS AND OUTCOMES

Different activities in the program or building industry can be described as outputs. Outputs are usually very specific and measurable program activities, such as the number of education sessions delivered, the number of publications released, or the number of customers assisted. Outputs, if properly chosen, are generally a proxy for the larger benefits that justify a program's reason for existence. They cannot in and of themselves show what is being accomplished. For example, showing an output of how many brochures are

Lynne Barker, *LEED AP, STAR Community Index program director*

As the imperative to address the economic crisis and climate change becomes ever clearer, the STAR Community Index promises to chart a clear path toward meaningful action by local governments. Planned for release in 2010, STAR is a voluntary rating system modeled after the LEED green building program. STAR will use a consensus-based approach to develop options that cities and counties can choose to make their communities more sustainable and livable. STAR will also help communities shine when they achieve significant success. The partnership behind STAR includes ICLEI–Local Governments for Sustainability, an international association of governments committed to climate protection and sustainable development, the USBGC, and the Center for American Progress, a think tank based in Washington, DC.

Just as LEED transformed the building industry by getting a wide spectrum of interests to agree on specific improvements that define green buildings, STAR will rely on volunteer committees drawn from a broad variety of government and private organizations to identify effective actions on all three pillars of sustainability: environment, economy, and society. The committees will also determine scientifically valid, cost-effective ways of evaluating progress.

There will be a point system tied to various measures and an award system for cities and counties that achieve certain point thresholds. Like LEED, STAR is not a ranking system; there will not be a "first place" or a "last place." But the ratings will recognize local governments for their achievements and encourage them to make continual improvements. They will also be able to compare their progress with actions in other communities.

STAR's founding partners believe that adoption of this program will lead to more innovation and efficiency because it will encourage collaboration. With a common agenda developed through a broad-based consensus process, municipalities will be more likely to share best practices and lessons learned.

STAR aims to lower program development and administrative costs for local governments. Further savings are likely because communities won't have to develop their own strategies or sort through disparate programs in search of ones that can be adapted to local conditions. Instead, cities and counties can focus more of their scarce resources on implementing projects that make a real difference.

To encourage action in small municipalities with tight budgets, STAR's benchmarking system will be freely available over the Web. Performance standards will be tied to readily available data whenever possible. For more information, see http://www.star communityindex.org/.

distributed does not really show whether or not anything different happened as a result of this or whether anyone's behavior changed. However, outputs are very useful for indicating how program dollars and staff time are spent. Output numbers tend to be fairly straightforward and represent data that are gathered relatively easily.

Outcomes are the *impact* that results from outputs. They are often very difficult to measure. What happened as a result of the workshop or the green building assistance that was provided? Did the workshop attendees, or customers, exhibit a change in their behavior or practice? This same thinking can be extended to the performance of green buildings themselves. Building a certain number of LEED buildings or green roofs is an *output*.

TABLE 7.3 EXAMPLES OF OUTPUTS AND OUTCOMES————————————

Outputs are easier to measure and are usually a proxy for the larger intended benefits. Consider including a combination of both output and outcome measures in your program evaluation.

Output (Activity)		Outcome (Result)
Green Building Workshop	⟶	Attendee Behavior Change
LEED-certified Building	⟶	Building Performance Change

The resulting *outcome* of these activities is represented by the amount of water or energy saved by the building or feature, for example (see table 7.3).

Once again, it is extremely challenging to go beyond measuring outputs to measuring outcomes of green building programs. Often, correlation and causation can become confused. *Correlation* may show that two incidents have a relationship to one another, whereas *causation* means that one event sets off or triggers the other. Confusing correlation and causation can cause credit to be assigned to something in error or blame to be laid on something undeservedly. For example, green building program activities, such as incentives or technical assistance, may have contributed in some way to a LEED project certification, but in most cases many other factors beyond the program itself caused a LEED project.

It helps to have some performance measures in each of the areas of outputs and outcomes. Programs with very small budgets may be able to afford only measurement of market transformation and program outputs, however. It may be possible to assemble utility information and green building savings based on data that public utilities can provide at no cost. A simple, low-cost survey of customers who have received green building services or information may also be useful.

MEASURING MARKET ACTIVITY

Seattle's program mission is stated as follows: "Make building green standard practice in Seattle." Assessing the adoption of green building innovations in the marketplace by looking at overall market activity is one way to measure progress toward this goal. Green building market activity can be measured in various ways. How the market changes over time is the key, so this type of evaluation must occur over a multiyear period. Start with a baseline, and track changes over time. Any city or town can track how many certified green buildings there are within their local community. In this case, the term *green building* is used broadly and would imply a holistic approach to building practices represented by programs such as LEED. It would probably not include a building that is only energy efficient but would include one with multiple green attributes. In some cases, if a particular green building strategy is of importance to your organization, you may choose to measure this. For example, if your organization is interested in green roofs, you could measure the total number and square footage of these within your city.

Compiling data on how many buildings in your community are certified over time using any of the various green building programs is one way to measure market transformation. You can measure program participation as well as actual certification. LEED project data from the USGBC online database can be sorted geographically by state or city.[4]

But it may be useful to conduct your own local tracking to be sure you are getting the most accurate and up-to-date information. This can include the status of projects within your own capital project portfolio as well as all market activity. There are some anomalies in the USGBC data set to be mindful of. There may be some project information that is not available, in the case of building developers who are not willing to release their information publicly. The geographic specificity of data may also be misleading, as for Seattle, where several projects not actually within Seattle proper show up in a data search. (One of these is owned by the City but not located within the City limit; another is at the regional airport, which is also beyond the City limit.)

If you track registered as well as certified projects, it is important to be aware of how this may play out over time. Projects that register for LEED may never be completed or may fail to achieve certification. Data on actual project certifications are the most useful in determining success. However, project registration numbers will give you insight into the trending in your and other markets. Program participation, as well as project certification, can reveal adoption of green building practices.

Another indicator of market transformation related to LEED is the number of LEED Accredited Professionals within your region or within your specific organization. The number of design firms and developers in your region who are implementing green building may be a useful indicator of market transformation. How many firms include green building services in their marketing materials and on their Web sites? It may also be insightful to see how many members of industry organizations such as the USGBC exist, and track this over time.

Presenting information in different ways is useful for tailoring results for different audiences or in revealing trends that may be obscured by looking at the data in only one way. Including not only the total number of projects but also the number of square feet or number of dollars invested in green building is one example. If you have a good number for square feet, it is possible to apply industry standard information for average building cost per square foot to get a total dollar value of investments.

Building permit data may include the project construction value. If you have access to building permit data and can influence how it is tracked, create a mechanism to track the planned use of green building certification programs. With this information available, green building permits can be analyzed relative to the total number of permits. However, this will not take into account projects that are permitted but never completed, the impact related to project size, or the time lag between permitting and project completion. Once again, be sure the amount of effort you are spending on evaluation is in balance with other program activities. Do not become so stymied by the analysis process that you end up in "analysis paralysis."

A very important point to keep in mind regarding tracking market activity is that it cannot usually be *directly* correlated to a green building program's activities. If the program provides education, technical assistance, or incentives, it can be said with some level of certainty that there is some correlation. The program's activities are likely to be moving the market toward increased adoption of green building. However, without extremely exhaustive analysis, which is normally beyond the means of most programs, green building market activity cannot typically be said to be a direct accomplishment of the program. Rather, the program probably contributed to the market change. Other market factors will also be at play, including consumer demand, lower operations costs, and others. Green building programs can contribute by helping to increase consumer demand and by raising awareness regarding the opportunity to lower operational costs, for example.

MEASURING PROGRAM ACTIVITY

Green building program services (such as those described in chapter 5) should be tracked and measured. These activities—including education, technical assistance, publications, and incentives—can be measured as outputs that are useful for program reporting. With a well-developed work program, a certain number of activities will be planned for the year ahead. In the case of education programs, the number of events delivered, compared to what was planned, can be reflected. For educational events hosted by the program, the type and number of events and the number of attendees should be recorded. Exit surveys of attendees can provide additional insight into the outcomes being created by the session. In addition, educational events for which the program provided sponsorship or other support should also be represented.

The associated outcomes of educational programming are more difficult to assess. The purpose of some green building educational events is to raise general awareness or provide inspiration, thus creating behavior change toward increases in green building activity. Targeted and customized green building training for professionals can be thought of as a form of performance support. Helping to sustain performance excellence of professionals in the building industry should enable them to create green buildings more successfully, faster, and less expensively.

Any training program should be evaluated at least minimally. Four levels of evaluation, as established by Donald Kirkpatrick, start with simpler assessment methods. Each successive level builds on information that is gathered at the lower level.[5] The first level of evaluation simply assesses participant reactions to the experience, which can also be thought of as customer satisfaction. It includes such questions as whether the participants liked the program or thought it had relevance for them. A positive response does not guarantee learning, but it certainly increases the chances of it. Simple paper evaluation forms can be used at the end of the session. Alternatively, with the advent of such low-cost online survey tools as Survey Monkey, a follow-up survey can easily be sent after the fact with automatic results analysis.[6]

Levels three and four involve assessing whether learners have changed their behavior by applying their new learning, and if so, what the outcome of changing their behavior has been.[7] A positive outcome might include an improved design process, increased adoption of new technologies, reduced operational costs, and so forth. The fourth level of assessment attempts to determine what participants actually learned. Did the training change their attitudes or increase their skill set? Pre-tests and post-tests can be used at this level. The third and fourth levels are challenging and probably beyond the scope of most programs' evaluation activity. For one thing, the timing of doing this type of assessment is not clear because it is hard to say when someone will use new knowledge.

The same types of tracking and reporting can be done for technical assistance and incentives. For the outputs, how many projects, or clients, were assisted or received incentives? What are the participation rates? What types of projects were related to the assistance? Another way to measure this is by representing how many square feet of projects received assistance. Providing technical assistance to one high-rise building project will likely have a bigger impact from a conservation standpoint than a very small building. If possible, the technical assistance services or incentives can be assessed using the four levels of assessment described above.

MEASURING GREEN BUILDING IMPACTS

Measuring program activities and measuring market activity are important evaluation tools. What they will not be able to reveal is what the true impacts of green building are. Are the buildings that are being built "green" delivering different results from those that are not? Are they saving more energy and water? Are they producing less waste? Is their return on investment improved? Are the people who inhabit them more satisfied or productive? Proof of concept is a logical next step if green building is to continue to expand. We must begin to measure whether or not we are truly moving closer to sustainability via the green building movement, and we must use this information in a process based on feedback loops and continuous improvement. LEED offers a point for a measurement and verification program that analyzes actual building performance, but this credit has not experienced high uptake in the marketplace due to the level of effort required. LEED for Existing Buildings can be expected to get increased traction in this arena.

Measuring the impacts of green buildings can yield data that are useful in several ways. First, if your program includes a green building policy for capital improvement projects, you will want to conduct some kind of evaluation of those particular buildings. What is the policy delivering? For broader programs aimed at market transformation, if you are measuring the number of green buildings being built, this is a useful output number. But what is the outcome? It is useful to know the impact that is linked to the activity.

Building performance analysis is a science unto itself. This section of the book is not intended to be an exhaustive source of information on building evaluation. Rather it will provide a snapshot of two basic approaches, as well as several examples based on my experience with the City of Seattle. Measuring the performance of buildings can be done with two basic approaches: (1) measuring the anticipated performance based on the design or (2) measuring the actual performance based on operations data. The former is relatively easy compared to studying operations and can be done much more quickly. The outcomes regarding building performance are mostly realized long after a project is complete, requiring a long-term analysis period. However, actual performance data are highly preferable, partly because the models we use to predict performance are commonly flawed.

Evaluating Anticipated Building Performance

Design tools such as LEED are extremely helpful in estimating the future performance of buildings. The LEED scorecard represents a wealth of information regarding what performance standard the building was designed to meet. However, it is important to realize that such performance projections will have limited accuracy. Designs seldom perform exactly as intended. Many variables will come into play, including the accuracy of energy modeling, changes in the finished project that are not easily documented, building manager or occupant behavior, and so forth. All that being said, what is intended to occur by design can still be very revealing regarding changes in market behavior and design practice as well as trending related to anticipated building performance.

How does one collect design-based information for analysis? If green building projects in your jurisdiction have received utility incentives, some useful data should exist. Work with your local utility to gain access to their information. The utility will probably have done an analysis of the design to capture anticipated savings results, as the basis for providing the incentive. In other words, how much water or energy is the incentive expected to save? How many tons of waste will it divert from the landfill? Gathering this data can be very useful for compiling anticipated energy or water savings from green buildings. You may need to compare how green building projects performed in comparison to those that pursued energy or water conservation in isolation. For green building programs located within utility organizations, this is a basic starting point.

For more comprehensive design data, look to green building program certification materials. Seattle developed a reporting tool and methodology, in collaboration with Paladino and Company, that utilized completed LEED project scorecard data (the design case) to project conservation results. Completed LEED scorecards and selected credit documentation were collected from willing building owners. The study focused on selected LEED credits that were of the most interest to the funders. The goals of the Seattle study were as follows:

- Understand the LEED credit performance of Seattle buildings relative to the national average credit achievement
- Identify the most commonly implemented sustainable design strategies and project their future impact on City service infrastructure
- Identify sustainability opportunities that are not currently being addressed by Seattle buildings (this information may then be used to shape future City programs)[8]

The methodology used to project impacts will be very specific to your location, taking into account such details as local utility costs. After such a methodology has been completed, future LEED scorecard data can be uploaded and reported. Variations in credit achieve-

FIGURE 7.1 Water-efficiency Achievements of LEED-certified Buildings in Seattle
Research can help demonstrate and quantify the benefits of green building. Analyzing LEED project credits can reveal how different strategies are used and how much water savings can be expected from each.
Source: LEED Certified Buildings in Seattle: Analysis & Projections. 2006. City of Seattle and Paladino and Company
Credit: Image courtesy of Paladino and Company and City of Seattle

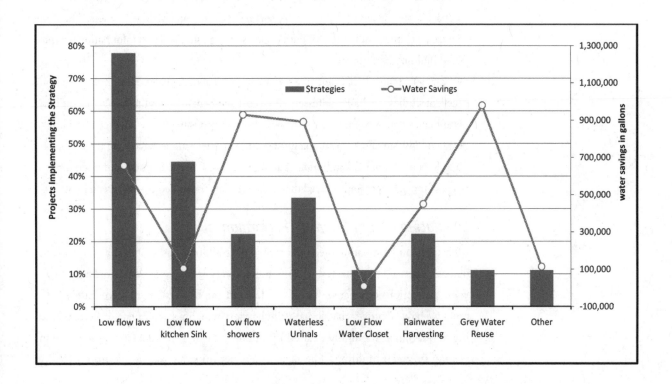

ment may reflect local conditions, such as code requirements or standard construction practice. In Seattle, stringent stormwater management codes meant that most projects achieved at least some of the related LEED credits (see figure 7.1). In addition, a fairly robust construction demolition recycling infrastructure and high tipping fees enabled local projects to consistently score well in these credit areas. Low adoption of some technologies could be addressed by introducing incentives or education programs to increase specific skill sets.

For each credit that was examined in the Paladino report, several issues were analyzed:

- Strategy benefits, or the expected benefits of meeting and achieving the credit requirements
- Achievement level, or the percentage of Seattle LEED-certified projects that achieved the credit, and the associated environmental savings
- Key strategies that were used to get the credit
- Tabulation of the total impact for the combined projects

Another question that is often asked relates to the cost benefit of green building. Once we understand what the benefits are, can we also speak to the initial cost to achieve the benefit, and the return on the benefit over time? Early in the evolution of its green building policy implementation, Seattle commissioned a cost benefit study with SBW Consulting Inc. The objectives of the study were to estimate costs and benefits for two city-owned buildings, the Seattle Justice Center and McCaw Hall, and to provide early feedback to the City as well as to private sector developers and building owners. The study showed a positive cost benefit for both projects, using estimated cost information and projected building performance.

Since that time, LEED and its adoption have expanded greatly. There have been some excellent studies that have addressed initial cost and benefit issues that use actual building performance data. Overall, the results have been very positive, showing green building to be a good investment. Some of the most comprehensive studies have been those done by Greg Kats of Capital E and by Davis Langdon. The Capital E study examined a broad range of project types and showed that there is little or no added cost for green building.[9]

Evaluating Actual Building Performance

Measuring and evaluating the impacts of green buildings based on actual performance data, as opposed to projected performance, is very important. Using foresight to develop projections of what we think will happen can be very informative, but at some point we have to prove what actually did happen, with hindsight. Data on actual building performance are highly desired by building owners and developers who are investing in green building. The facts about performance that result from building evaluations can be published in case studies to provide additional persuasion in the interest of market transformation.

Organizations that own and manage large portfolios of buildings have a unique opportunity to measure and assess their buildings for comparative evaluation. It may be beyond the reach of most individual organizations to do this alone, but partnership opportunities may be available by working with research, academic, nonprofit, or granting organizations. While this scientific work is very important, it tends to be underfunded.

Few clients or design firms can afford to pay the costs for post occupancy analysis. Most architectural resources are targeted for the design and construction phase of a project, and little or none for post occupancy. This is unfortunate because post occupancy analysis is the only way designers can learn from their designs in action. Things often turn out quite differently from what we visualize on paper, for many reasons. We need more lessons learned, more feedback loops, and more scientific inquiry, especially for aspects of the built environment that push the edge of standard practice. The biggest value of post occupancy evaluation is how the lessons may inform future projects for designers and their clients, so that they can repeat their successes and avoid repeating any failures.

Building evaluation also occurs less frequently because often people do not really want to know if there are problems. Such knowledge might mean increased liability for the design and construction team. For the building owner, admitting mistakes may create expectations that errors will be repaired. This might entail costly retrofits or disgruntled employees. There is also the risk of negative media, which most large organizations abhor. During a period of time when the media was writing unflattering stories about Seattle City Hall being an "energy hog," our post occupancy project was frozen by the mayor's office. They feared that the results of the study would confirm the allegation and that they would not be able to closely control and manage the release of its results. Luckily, the evaluation was eventually completed and the results showed the City Hall in a much better light. It is preferable to proactively track the performance of publicly owned green buildings, in order to be prepared with good information when public or press inquiries occur. Don't wait for negative allegations to find out how your buildings are performing.

The best way to uncover useful facts about how your buildings are working is by talking to their managers and operators. They are the unsung, behind-the-scenes heroes of the building industry. Without them, our workplaces, schools, and hospitals would come to a halt. They can tell you more than anyone else about which green building strategies work and which do not. Develop a relationship with your building operators. Take the time to get to know them, be on speaking terms, and even tell them "thank you" once in a while. Regular contact with building operators and janitorial staff can provide them needed moral support and can help identify problems, gaps, and lessons learned from the green buildings they manage.

City Hall and Justice Center Post Occupancy Evaluation

Over a three-year period, I led the development of a post occupancy study of two of our Seattle LEED buildings: the Seattle Justice Center and the Seattle City Hall. We had resources to study only a small sample of two of our buildings, but we hoped that once we established a methodology we could add more buildings to the study over time. We knew that two buildings would not yield a statistically significant study, but would provide more of a snapshot of green building performance. The goals of the study were as follows:

- Make the results comprehensible and useful for a broad audience. Interpret results so they can be easily understood by a lay audience.
- Select building types for analysis that will compare easily with buildings in the private sector. This will make the analysis more useful as a tool to serve private sector building developers and owners.
- Reflect performance across all three of the triple bottom line aspects of sustainability: environmental, social, and economic.

Once again, we hired Paladino and Company to help us develop the study and to gather and analyze data. We established an internal stakeholder team that included the staff from the department that owned and managed the buildings, an economist from the city's Department of Finance, utility analysts, and staff from the human resources department. The funders of the study were the City-owned utilities and the Northwest Energy Efficiency Alliance.

City Hall and the Justice Center were selected because of their office space functions, making them more similar to private sector buildings than projects such as our libraries or community centers. Their occupancy was not as variable as these other buildings, making it easier to analyze them. These were also public and highly visible buildings that were frequented by citizens and featured in green building tours, complementing our ability to tell a complete story about green building. The intended audience for the study was building managers, elected officials, visitors, and the green building industry.

The next step was to assemble the indicators against which we would be measuring building performance. We had to keep the number reasonable, both for cost and digestibility. We used the following criteria to select the indicators:

- Supports the mayor's Environmental Action Agenda goals
- Clear link to developing policies and incentives
- Accessible, measurable, and reliable data
- Available baseline
- Aligned with a LEED credit

Finding good baselines against which to measure performance was challenging. There were many pitfalls in this process. The negative article that had been published about the new LEED City Hall, calling it an "energy hog," had compared its energy use to the old City Hall. This comparison is not valid for several reasons. The buildings were built to different energy code standards, their occupancy was very different, and the square footage and functions contained within the buildings was not the same. Instead, a building's energy performance should be measured against the energy model that was used to design it and against the energy use intensity (EUI) of other similar buildings. The EUI is a very useful index for comparing energy use per building square foot and is used in the Energy Star Target Finder tool referenced by the 2030 Challenge.[10] Comparing green buildings to conventional buildings is valid only if the conventional building is similar in all regards except for green features. In addition, collecting data for building evaluation should commence only after an initial break-in period that gives building operators a chance to work out the kinks.

First, design and model the proposed building. Modeling may be related to energy, daylighting, water, or other building systems performance. Data available at this point are the design documents and the modeling results. Once the project is complete, its performance can be measured and evaluated. Building commissioning reports and utility bills or performance reports can be used at this stage. Commissioning is the process used after construction and before occupancy to ensure that all building systems are operating correctly. Surveys or other forms of data collection can also be used to account for some of the human elements of building performance and perception. Once the data are collected, they can be evaluated to reveal its performance characteristics. The findings can be compiled into a database, which can be maintained over time, adding data for additional buildings as the opportunity or funding becomes available. The resulting lessons learned and new knowledge can then be applied to future projects.

Table 7.4 shows the indicators, organized around the triple bottom line, that were finally selected to guide the project. Some indicators had to be eliminated due to challenges that arose during the building evaluation process, such as data anomalies and incomplete data sets.

The study was based on several different data sources. Historical records were used for utility meter readings, maintenance complaints, sick leave and turnover, and project data on recycling and materials specifications. Some physical measurements had to be done, including for air temperature, light, and air quality. Calculations were used for energy simulations and water savings. Some data, such as for green roof performance, were very difficult to collect. No direct metering or digital controls had been installed that allowed us to directly collect data from the green roofs, so in the end we had to use other research that had been done in Seattle and extrapolate possible results for our buildings. Plan ahead for building evaluation projects, and be sure to install measurement equipment as part of the design that can be utilized later. Digital building controls enable the

TABLE 7.4 CITY OF SEATTLE BUILDING POST-OCCUPANCY EVALUATION INDICATORS ————
Building evaluation can reflect all three areas of the triple bottom line: environmental, social, and economic. Results of this study will be posted at http://www.seattle.gov/dpd/GreenBuilding/.

City of Seattle Green Building Post Occupancy Evaluation Indicators	
Environmental	• Stormwater quality • Stormwater volume and peak flow • Potable water use • Energy use • Emissions associated with energy use • Construction demolition and land-clearing waste • Recycled content materials used • Indoor air quality
Social	• Comfort complaints • Absenteeism rates • Employee turnover rates • Access to daylight • Visual comfort conditions • Thermal comfort conditions • Perceived worker effectiveness • Workplace satisfaction
Economic	• Water cost • Energy cost • Staff-related overhead costs • Net present value of first cost increment and savings

Source: LEED Performance Evaluation Plan. City of Seattle and Paladino and Company. December 2003.

management and data collection of a building to be automated. A good set of digital controls is an important tool for the building operator and evaluator. However, digital controls installed must also be programmed to collect data, and someone must review and utilize the data in order to make it useful.

One of the most interesting areas that came out of the research was related to staff costs. Some research has been done in the area of productivity related to green building. However, government staff are usually knowledge workers, whose productivity is very hard to measure. Instead, we used occupant surveys to find out the perceptions of people about their productivity and their attitudes about the buildings they worked in. The Center for the Built Environment at Berkeley provides an online survey tool that we used as a pre-survey and post-survey for occupants in the old City Hall before they moved out and then at the new City Hall.[11] Judith Heerwagen managed the survey and data analysis process. One useful aspect of this research is that the results of our survey could be compared to a national database of survey data, which provided a comparable benchmark. Leveraging existing resources, such as the Berkeley survey tool, also serves to extend your evaluation dollars.

We held some very interesting discussions with our human resources staff. In fact, we discovered that the City employs a full-time person to respond to air quality issues and complaints. It was during these discussions that a lightbulb went on about building better-quality buildings via our green standards. If we built better buildings to begin with that offered better air quality, daylight, and thermal comfort, a lot of complaints might be prevented in the first place. To be sure, there will always be some building complaints no matter what. But these complaints could be greatly reduced, freeing up the staff member who responds to air quality issues to do other work. We had identified new stakeholders who were excited about working with us to help advance green building in the City.

REPORTING PERFORMANCE METRICS

Once you have done the hard work of developing performance measures and collecting data, you will want to share this information. Think about the audience when compiling data. How will the data be presented so that it is understandable to the target audience? What kind of results will be compelling to them? Information that will be released to elected officials and the general public will need to be crisp, concise, and devoid of jargon. Results that will be used only internally can be much less formal in presentation and may contain jargon or more technical language. Jargon may not be an issue if results are to be shared at conferences or in technical reports. For general audiences, if the data becomes excessively technical, use footnotes to explain, but avoid putting too much of this detail in the body of the report.

Develop a standard reporting format that will be used consistently so the readers will get used to how it is organized. This report can be developed so that it is automatically generated from spreadsheets or other tracking documents. Try to organize the performance metrics within a framework that relates to local environmental issues, the current political agenda, the program mission, or other desired program outcomes.

The frequency of reporting also affects the related overhead for this activity. Try to keep the reporting frequency to no more than twice a year. Each time a report is due, data must be updated, reviewed for accuracy, compiled into a report, cleared with management, and then delivered up the chain of command. This is all very time consuming.

In addition to our assessment goals, mayor Greg Nickels had publicly set a goal of making Seattle the "green building capital of America." Table 7.5 shows the annual performance measures for the program, organized around the mayor's political agenda and overarching program objectives.

TABLE 7.5 CITY OF SEATTLE ANNUAL GREEN BUILDING PERFORMANCE METRICS————————

Program metrics should be clearly stated and expressed in relationship to political priorities, if possible.

Mayor's Priority	Performance Metric	Measurable in 2007
Market transformation (*"Seattle, the Green Building Capital of America"*)	Number of projects assisted	103
	Number of new LEED commercial/institutional certifications and precertifications	10 (9 + 1)
	Number of LEED-certified single-family housing units	5
	Number of Built Green–certified multifamily and single-family housing units	410 (290sf +120mf)
	Number of affordable housing units completed within the Office of Housing SeaGreen program	258
Climate protection	Electricity savings*	670,000 KWh[1]
	Natural gas savings*	410,300 therms[2]
	GHG/CO_2 emissions reduction potential*	456.7 metric tons CO_2e[3]
Restore our waters	Potable water savings*	3,700,000 gals
	Stormwater removed from system*	250,000 gals
Zero waste	Commercial construction waste diverted from landfill*	32,354 tons[4]
	Number of of residential deconstruction projects and tons of waste diverted from landfill	8 ~ 320 tons[5]
	Number of residential building relocations and tons of waste diverted from landfill	7 ~ 280 tons[6]
	GHG/CO_2 emissions impact reduction from recycling/waste diversion	74,806 tons CO_2e

*Anticipated annual savings based on twenty-five LEED projects in Seattle rated prior to September 2007, as calculated based on LEED scorecards.

1. Projected annual energy savings as compared to ASHRAE 90.1, the national standard energy code and LEED referenced standard (not the Seattle energy code). Total annual energy savings for the twenty-five LEED buildings analyzed was 7,600,000 kWh and 84,000 therms.

2. Ibid.

3. Based on electric and natural gas savings reported above, assuming the building conserved power that would have been purchased on the grid at current power mix. Carbon dioxide equivalent conversion factors are 0.6 kg-CO2e per kWh of electricity and 5.306 kg-CO2e per therm of gas.

4. Waste diverted from landfill as one-time measure, calculated based on LEED scorecards.

5. Based on average single-family home size and an approximate weight of forty tons without foundation material.

6. Ibid.

Source: City of Seattle, City Green Building

Janet Stephenson, who served as Seattle's City Green Building communications staff member, developed a very attractive illustrative communication tool for program reporting.[12] It became an important tool that was visually compelling and imparted a great deal of information at a glance. This format was used for more detailed reporting on program activities, including technical assistance, educational programming, market activity, and status of LEED City capital projects. You may choose to develop several subreports that can be rolled up into a summary annual report.

The most important thing to remember when doing any kind of reporting is to try to tell a story. Seattle's program publishes a multiple-page report every five years that provides summarized program reporting and the state of green building in the City. This report also adds stories and case studies to give some flavor of what's happening out in the field. Make your stories compelling and visually interesting, and be sure to add human interest, if possible. It always helps to sprinkle images of actual projects and quotes or testimonials from stakeholders to make the information more "real." It's never a bad idea to inspire people. Intended to inspire, this is Seattle's program vision as stated in its annual reporting:

- We believe the Northwest is a special place, with people who value its unique natural beauty.
- We believe that we can live in balance—a balance that includes economic prosperity, environmental health, and quality of life.
- We believe there is a better way to build—greener, healthier, and more profitable.
- We are here to help make that dream a reality.
- Together, we can build great places for Seattle's citizens to live, work, and play.

TIPS

- Develop performance indicators for your program related to your stated goals and mission.
- Ensure that you spend an appropriate balance of your time and effort measuring programs as well as actually delivering them.
- Consider the intended audience and purpose behind each evaluation measure.
- Draw measurement data from a wide variety of sources, including surveys, independent observation, anecdotal data, and ongoing program tracking data.
- Be sure your performance indicators are relevant, easy to understand, and timely.
- Distinguish between program outputs and outcomes. Try using some of each measure in your evaluation package.
- Measure and track the green building activity in your local marketplace with green building project counts or tallies of total square footage or dollars invested.

- Develop tools to monitor and evaluate the performance and customer satisfaction with educational programming and technical assistance services.
- Track your program's numbers of projects assisted, people trained, publications distributed, or Web sessions.
- Attempt to determine the actual, as opposed to projected, performance of green buildings in your market.
- Assess which green building technologies local projects are using and why. Are there barriers to those they don't use that can be addressed?
- Measure the actual energy, water, solid waste, or other performance of green buildings. Partner with nonprofits or educational institutions to help fund such research.
- Work with your human resources department to track staff-related overhead costs, such as sick leave, turnover, and insurance costs.
- Stay in contact with, and learn from, building operators and managers.
- Develop a standardized, visually recognizable, and easy to understand reporting tool.

CHAPTER 8

The Road Ahead for Green Building Programs

In this book, I have shared with you lessons learned from my own and others' experiences in developing green building programs and policies. My story has spanned the past twenty years, but what about the next twenty and beyond? How will the shifting landscape of environmental, political, institutional, and technological changes affect the needs that green building programs must address as well as the support they will receive?

I see two recent events that will positively drive the future of green buildings in the United States, and the programs that support them, more than any other. These events are (1) the dramatic economic downturn and (2) the new Obama administration. It may seem odd to speak of the worst economic collapse since the Great Depression as a positive. However, a crisis situation, painful as it is, can also open up welcome opportunities for change. If the status quo is upset as the result of a human-made crisis, it will cause many to question the norms and "standard" practices that may have set up the fall. The question is, of course, what will we learn from the experience? How will we take the lessons and exhibit intelligent, mature, adaptive behavior? Paul Romer, Stanford economist, has often been quoted as saying "A crisis is a terrible thing to waste."[1] This takeoff on the United Negro College Fund slogan "A mind is a terrible thing to waste" has more recently become referred to as "Rahm's Doctrine," in reference to the White House chief of staff for Obama. Russ Linden, author of practical guides on producing better government, noted that during times of emergency, new opportunities emerge: "Resources become available, priorities are clear, rigid rules and regulations become pliable, leaders pay attention and are accessible, . . . (and) even far-reaching change is possible."[2]

The question in many people's minds might be whether the economic downturn will kill the momentum of the green building movement. The report Emerging Trends in Real Estate 2009, produced by the Urban Land Institute (ULI), includes as their best advice to go green and cut energy expenses.[3] It also identifies higher-density residential, infill, and condos near transit as the places to invest. This list clearly identifies sustainable development as the place to be. Even while the real estate market is slowing dramatically, it is unmistakable that green building will retain a clear leader position as the alpha dog. In biology, the alpha individual leads the pack while others follow. Green leaders will set the pace for several reasons. For one, green is clearly a market differentiator. The level of aware-ness of green building in consumer groups has never been higher. For those looking to find a competitive edge, green provides a way to brand and promote their buildings to buyers and tenants who now have increased consumer savvy about what their purchasing choices are and why choosing greener buildings will make a difference to their health and their budget. As mentioned earlier in this book, research analysis shows that green buildings lease more quickly, for a higher cost per square foot, and have higher real estate value.

In addition, with money becoming scarcer not only in real estate lending but for op-erating budgets, smart businesspeople will begin to realize that they are sitting on top of a veritable goldmine of opportunities to cost-effectively improve the buildings they own and operate. This forward thinking can help lower the bottom line for businesses indefi-nitely, at a low initial cost premium. An investment of that nature just makes sense. There are many aging buildings in this country that are in desperate need of renewal. For some, building efficiency upgrades can have almost immediate paybacks of less than a year. For others, the paybacks may take a few years, but this is still a very short period compared to many other investments. By saving money on building operating costs, organizations will have more capital dollars available to retain staff and focus on their business mission.

As our population ages, development for health care and assisted living facilities can be expected to remain stronger compared to commercial and retail projects. With the ad-vent of the *Green Guide for Healthcare*, followed by the new LEED for Healthcare tool, medical institutions have additional tools at their disposal to leverage their facilities toward green performance. Not only are the costs to operate hospitals high, but administrators have also embraced the evidence-based research that shows better quality environments can reduce hospital stays, increase patient satisfaction, and lower staff stress. They understand the relationship between health and green building, and health is their core mission.

There may be other ways that green building will play into the tough economic times. For those facing foreclosure, lower operating expenses can help them hold on to their prop-erties longer. The ULI report also predicts that the "main beneficiaries of the real estate downturn in the US are cash-rich offshore buyers" and that these will buy "trophy proper-ties in major 24-hour cities."[4] These cities include Seattle, San Francisco, and New York. These are some of the cities (and states) who have made a significant investment in green building already. I predict that some of their new green buildings will be considered "tro-phies" attractive to buyers who are well aware of the edge that greener buildings give them.

The backdrop of the real estate downturn provides a rich opportunity for President Barack Obama to create positive change. The psyche of the nation is one of renewed hope for the future, even in the face of recent losses as a nation and, for many, very personal losses. As discussed in chapter 2, strong leadership that offers a compelling and positive future vision is instrumental in creating broad organizational and cultural change. When strong leadership from the top is met with leadership from among the bottom ranks, virtually anything is possible. Among many others, locally based green building initiatives have provided inspiration for Obama and his vision. During his campaign, he visited the Seattle offices of McKinstry, a leading mechanical construction and engineering firm focused on building energy efficiency and carbon emissions reduction. Obama referred to McKinstry as "a model for the nation" for his intention to invest in wind, solar, biofuels, and green-collar jobs. Many have been inspired by Obama's message, and the message of green building has, in turn, inspired him.

The new administration will provide increased opportunities for collaboration across government sectors at the state, national, and international levels. A shared agenda around climate change, energy independence, and green buildings is needed. Lessons learned from what has been accomplished thus far should be leveraged, and new resources should be brought to bear to increase existing capacity for green building incentives and programs. I hope that Obama's hopeful "yes we can" message can further empower those in the green building industry, and in every sector of government, to reinvent their programs, policies, and local visions for the future. This spirit of entrepreneurial creativity, as well as our skill at reinventing ourselves, has helped to make our nation great in the past and can restore us to a renewed sense of empowerment and courage for the future. In Obama's words: "We should never forget that we are the heirs of that first band of patriots, ordinary men and women who refused to give up when it all seemed so improbable; and who somehow believed that they had the power to make the world anew. That is the spirit we must reclaim today."[5]

The $787 billion Economic Recovery and Reinvestment Act, approved early in 2009, bears direct relationship to multiple items on the following list of trends. Among the stated purposes of the bill are "to preserve and create jobs," and "to invest in transportation, environmental protection, and other infrastructure that will provide long-term economic benefits."[6]

TEN GREEN BUILDING TRENDS

From this backdrop of crisis, change, and hope, I see ten key trends and issues that should inform the road ahead for green building programs. Each of these is listed with brief reference to the implications that should be considered for those planning green building programs or policy development.

More Price Signals and Mandatory Requirements

As the shift to a carbon economy materializes, it will create significant price signals that will reinforce increased green building adoption. The first steps toward this are already being seen based on the Seattle and King County greenhouse gas disclosure requirements for significant development projects (discussed in chapter 6). Developers will see energy efficiency and carbon offset strategies as part of their overall investment strategy, which will make them financially competitive with other investment options. Carbon pricing in the form of either a cap-and-trade approach, such as that undertaken in Europe, or a direct tax on carbon emissions will further drive innovations and increased investment in green energy, lowering prices and increasing choices. We can expect to see additional mandatory requirements emerging from the regulatory environment. Ordinances to make green building a development requirement using LEED or other standards has already been implemented by some cities. Other jurisdictions can be expected to follow.

Since green building is no longer a new concept and the building industry has started to adapt to it voluntarily or based on incentives, regulatory requirements will not be far behind. Mandatory construction recycling has already been adopted by some cities and can be expected to increase as the space and cost for landfilling waste reach their limits. Mandatory energy audits of existing buildings have been adopted by the cities of Berkeley, San Francisco, and Sacramento and are under consideration in Portland, Austin, Denver, and Seattle. In Boulder and Santa Monica, excessively large homes are required to provide at least half of their energy needs on site.

Responding to Greenwashing

As the green building and green consumer market have expanded, so has the jockeying for position for a piece of the pie. Everywhere you look, "green" is a label added to a multitude of purchasing choices, whether it is buildings, cars, food, clothing, furniture, or vacations. With this explosion of sometimes conflicting information, options, and definitions, the marketplace has become confused. Some green claims are true; others less so. The false claims represent what is commonly referred to as greenwashing.

What standards or criteria are being used to make the claims, and can they be compared effectively? Simple, clear, recognizable, and credible labeling or certification programs can help to address marketplace confusion and inform consumer choice. However, some labels still conflict. In the case of green building, many claim their building materials or products to be "LEED Certified," which is not possible, and others may want to put a green label on their buildings purely as a marketing strategy without underlying substance. Recent debates between the public policy adoption of LEED versus Green Globes have been particularly intense. Behind the debate is the program used to certify lumber products using either the FSC (Forestry Stewardship Council) or SFI (Sustainable Forestry Initiative) label. These types of debates can be expected to continue and intensify as more competing tools and certifications emerge.

Clarity for consumers about exactly what it is they are buying or what the standard that government may sanction represents is paramount for the sake of clarity, transparency, and scrupulousness. The public sector is in a unique position to help address greenwashing and provide a perspective less biased by industry. Green building programs should address which standards and certifications they sanction and why. They can provide a credible source of information for those in the building industry striving to make sensible and informed choices.

Considering Urban Sustainability and Community Scale Impacts

Green building initiatives thus far have focused primarily on the parcel scale of development. With the development of LEED for Neighborhood Development (LEED ND) and the up-and-coming Star Community Index (discussed in chapter 7), new tools are available to help guide the design, and benchmark the performance, of entire neighborhoods and even cities. This focus on the monumental sustainability impacts at the larger community scale is much needed. Many acknowledge that the decision about where to develop may vastly outweigh the impacts associated with how the development is done, primarily because of transportation impacts. The Urban Land Institute's 2008 book *Growing Cooler* calculated that shifting 60 percent of new growth to compact development would save 79 million tons of carbon dioxide annually by 2030. Findings also showed that people living in compact green neighborhoods are contributing to fighting global climate change as much as those who buy efficient hybrid vehicles and live in car-dependent neighborhoods.[7]

Smart growth strategies advocate for more transit-oriented developments and "new urbanist" neighborhood patterns where people can walk to goods and services or commute via public transit. Richard Florida's March 2009 article in the *Atlantic* foresees that the economic downturn signals the end to life as we know it in this country, not only financially but regarding our patterns of urbanization and home ownership. Florida writes: "The housing bubble was the ultimate expression, and perhaps the last gasp, of an economic system some 80 years in the making. . . . [It] encouraged massive, unsustainable growth in places where land was cheap and the real estate economy dominant. It encouraged low-density sprawl . . . and created a workforce too often stuck in place, anchored by houses that cannot be profitably sold, at a time when flexibility and mobility are of great importance."[8] He posits that the age of suburbanization is resoundingly over and recommends that government policies should encourage renting versus buying, more housing choices, growth in existing mega-regions, and efforts to make attractive urban areas more affordable to all. He also recommends "liberal zoning and building codes within cities to allow more residential development, more mixed-use development in suburbs and cities alike, the in-filling of suburban cores near rail links, new investment in rail, and congestion pricing for travel on roads."[9]

Green building programs can build on their existing momentum to help leverage sensible changes in urban public policy and land use codes. The Federal Transit Administration changed its rules to allow transit agencies to retain profits from real estate sales or leases, removing a disincentive for such agencies to engage in urban infill development. In one instance, TriMet of Portland concluded that even if they gave away land to a developer, the cost of developing new rail lines would be ten to twenty-three times more cost effective.[10] With numbers like these, joint public/private developments make both financial and environmental sense.

Another area in which green building policy can support more sustainable communities is for communities in crisis and disaster preparedness and response. Displaced populations can be expected to increase as a result of violent conflicts, resource shortages, and natural disasters. Climate change may spur abandonment of the Sun Belt due to rising temperatures and diminishing water resources, and coastal communities may be displaced by rising sea levels. Refugee populations need easily accessible, affordable, healthy places to live. For disaster-prone regions, green building design can address what is referred to as "passive survivability," or the ability to maintain critical life support services in the event of power outages or other disruptions. Alex Wilson, executive editor of *Environmental Building News*, coined the term after attending several post-Katrina workshops, and I first heard it at a USGBC-sponsored design charrette focused on New Orleans recovery.[11] Green building strategies that can support passive survivability include natural ventilation, operable windows, solar-powered systems, on-site battery power storage, rainfall cisterns, and on-site water treatment. Increased building functionality during extreme conditions, such as heat waves combined with power outages, may also prevent unnecessary deaths, which affect elderly people and children disproportionately.

Renewing Existing Buildings

Given the fact that the economic downturn has pulled the rug out from under real estate development, fewer new construction projects will be occurring in the foreseeable future. This trend allows green building programs to focus more on existing buildings (see box 8.1). Much of the country's existing building stock is in need of upgrades to bring it in line with current standards of health and efficiency. With a suite of design tools, such as LEED for Existing Buildings, that can be exerted in this arena, more comprehensive building upgrades will occur than those that focus on energy or water alone.

Maintaining existing buildings, as opposed to tearing them down to make way for new ones, is one of the most fundamentally sustainable strategies we can employ. The embodied energy contained in buildings is vast. The National Trust for Historic Preservation has been pursuing an initiative to address the energy efficiency of historic structures. This is a challenging area of improvement because many energy upgrades, such as replacing windows, represent an aesthetic problem for landmarked structures. An emerging partnership between the City of Seattle and the National Trust is aimed at creating a center for preservation and energy efficiency of historic buildings.

BOX 8.1 NEW VISIONS FOR GREEN BUILDING

Don Horn, *Sustainability Program director, Office of Federal High-Performance Green Buildings, U.S. General Services Administration*

Our program within the U.S. General Services Administration (GSA) has shifted from being called "sustainable design" to "sustainability" to reflect the importance of the role of existing buildings. We have been building fewer new buildings each year for more than a decade, so the existing inventory of buildings needs to be renovated, operated, and maintained in a sustainable manner to meet our energy reduction mandates. We have learned basic green building concepts from LEED and new building projects, but applying sustainable building strategies to existing resources always seems more of a challenge.

Understanding how daylight can be enhanced in an existing building and how furniture layouts affect air flow patterns involves more than simple operations and maintenance. It involves creating a vision of how the building can be transformed into a functioning, sustainable part of the community and environment in which it is located.

In the case of many of GSA's historic buildings—nearly one quarter of our inventory—it is a matter of rediscovering or restoring the way the building was originally designed to operate. High ceilings, large windows, natural ventilation, and de-sign for disassembly are only a few of the sustainable characteristics of their original design. Just as we look to indigenous cultures for clues to design for local conditions, it also helps to look at the ways in which our turn-of-the-century buildings were designed with the climate and culture in mind. We seem to have lost this innate awareness of the natural world and our place in it.

The sustainability movement of today is bringing back that awareness and attempting to restore balance between economic and social concerns along with environmental. The question becomes, is stabilization possible or even adequate at this time? One thing is certain: we must move forward with a larger, longer-term vision. Our current knowledge of green building and sustainable design principles serves as a base, but our vision must move beyond sustainability to a restorative and even regenerative relationship with the environment. The market has taken an unprecedented shift toward green but still focuses narrowly on lessening our damage to the natural environment. A new vision of the interconnectivity of the built environment to living systems is needed to overcome the challenges that face the world today.

Tenant improvements are another area that will maintain an ongoing focus in spite of the downturn. With increased competition in a soft office market, new leases will be signed and others renegotiated. With these changes comes a myriad of tenant improvement projects that can have significant environmental impact. Some tenants or building owners will not want to go as far as LEED for Commercial Interiors, but they would benefit from green building education and outreach to help them understand how to make better choices. On the other hand, for those renting Class A office space, some believe that LEED is the new standard that defines that tier within the marketplace.

Increase in Programs Addressing Energy Efficiency and Climate Disruption

Never has our collective awareness of the impacts of our behavior on the global environment been more keen. Popular press and media, including Al Gore's film *An Inconvenient Truth*, have catapulted environmental awareness to the front of our national consciousness. Obama's appointment of an Oregon State University researcher focused on oceans and global warming as the head of the National Oceanic and Atmospheric Administration signals that he will take this topic, and science, quite seriously—a refreshing change. Our dependence on foreign oil is increasingly being recognized as having negative impacts on both our national security and our economic stability. Investments in energy efficiency were a big part of the Economic Recovery Act, with a variety of measures totaling over $42 billion.[12]

While energy efficiency is only one key aspect of green building, these funds can be leveraged to expand broader programs and to utilize green building as an umbrella that includes energy efficiency. With an infusion of resources available via grants to cities, counties, and states to increase energy efficiency, these funds could be applied to green building programs with an expanded focus on energy or carbon reduction. Funding to increase energy efficiency of housing (particularly affordable and subsidized housing) and federal buildings could also be attached to green building programs with a focus on the affordable housing market sector or for federal green building programs that have been underfunded.

Private developers will have new resources available in the form of tax credits for energy-efficiency improvements and renewable energy facilities including wind, tax credits for guaranteed energy loans, and tax cuts for businesses that use innovative strategies to transmit and distribute electricity or to sequester and capture carbon. Such additional resources make investment in green building more attractive from both an initial and a long-term cost standpoint. Green building programs should prepare to promote these new resources and programs to their customers. Finally, green building programs will have an increasing role in revising energy code requirements to reach increased levels of sustainability. Albuquerque, Santa Fe, and the State of Florida are pursuing performance-based energy codes that will meet the 2030 Challenge discussed in chapter 2.

Growing Opportunities for Green-collar Jobs

With the recent recognition that environmental benefit and economic development can be linked, the term *green-collar jobs* has become all the rage. New federal funding for green-collar job training was included in the Economic Recovery Act, with $500 million to train workers for careers in energy-efficiency and renewable energy fields; $2 billion for jobs related to science, engineering, and the environment; and $250 million for at-risk youth training for energy-efficiency jobs.[13] Putting people to work to repair aging buildings and infrastructure with a green focus holds great promise for rebuilding a greener, more resilient country. The term *green-collar job* has not yet been clearly defined, but it should also include manufacturing of green products and materials, research and development of the same, and green professional and trade skills related to the green economy.

One of the gaps that continues to exist in the green building industry is workforce development of skilled construction and maintenance workers to build and manage contemporary facilities. New skills are required for this. A building may be designed to be green, but if the contractor does not understand how to build it, progress can be stopped in its tracks. Green building programs can help fill this gap by partnering in green job skills training programs, providing referrals to graduates and participating companies, and supporting the market development of such jobs (this topic was mentioned briefly in chapter 5). Partnerships with economic development programs and organizations such as Green for All can expand the focus of green building, making it more holistic and inclusive of the entire complex web of skills and relationships within the building industry.

Rebuilding Failing Infrastructure

Green building programs must prepare to expand their expertise and advocacy for projects that do not include buildings. Most of the focus to date has been on buildings while using tools like LEED. However, many public works projects, such as parks and infrastructure, have not received much attention in the green building dialogue, and tools like LEED do not currently apply to them. This must change. Long an ignored problem, the challenge of repairing our country's ailing infrastructure is finally receiving focus. *Infrastructure* is a term that comprises a wide array of types, including transportation, energy and water, flood control, and communications. The failures that occur as the result of infrastructure collapse can be catastrophic, as evidenced by Hurricane Katrina's aftermath or the chaos and disruption to electric service and price stability triggered in the United States by the rolling blackouts of 2001.

The American Society of Civil Engineers estimates that $2.2 trillion is needed for infrastructure repairs.[14] Infrastructure failure can have many causes, including the simple fact that much of our infrastructure is so old it is falling apart. Many cities still have combined stormwater and wastewater sewers, which often results in extreme system overloading during storms, sending raw sewage into sensitive waterways. Climate change is projected to increase not only sea levels but also flooding as a result of extreme weather events. In Canada, a publicly funded initiative led by the National Round Table on Sustainable Infrastructure has developed a protocol to assess the vulnerability of infrastructure, such as bridges and dams, to climate change.[15] Green building programs should work aggressively with public works officials to ensure that green standards are being used in the process of rebuilding infrastructure. Less monolithic and more distributed approaches to infrastructure should also be pursued as a part of the rebuilding efforts. Many green infrastructure solutions occur at the site level or tie together benefits from multiple utility areas, defying the way we traditionally plan and design infrastructure systems. Andy Lipkis of the Los Angeles–based nonprofit Tree People has been extremely successful in redirecting flood control funding from traditional, centralized drainage structures to site-level tree planting, rainwater collection, and asphalt removal as a much greener way to handle the problem.[16] Luckily, the Economic Recovery Act has earmarked $100 billion for public works projects.[17] However, the amount of funding needed vastly exceeds what has been set aside at the federal level.

Investing in Water-saving Strategies

With the burgeoning focus on climate disruption, the global water crisis has recently received short shrift. While climate change is likely to intensify water problems by raising temperatures and decreasing snowpack, shortages of water are likely to become a much more pressing and catastrophic problem in the near term. Water shortages relate not only to drinking water but also to producing our food supply. The southwestern portion of the United States is rapidly drying up and is likely to experience a water crisis of epidemic proportions in the near future. The Economic Recovery Act provided water financing for wastewater treatment and drinking water at $6 billion, for rural water and waste facilities at $1.4 billion, and for water supply to rural areas and western areas affected by drought at $1 billion.[18] In Las Vegas, water supply is dependent on Lake Mead, which stores water from the Colorado River. The Southern Nevada Water Authority is currently in a race against the clock to lower the level of their intake pipes to match the dropping lake level. They hope to finish the massive reengineering project by 2012 but are looking for ways to accelerate the project and avert a possible water disaster.[19] Arizona, California, and Nevada are at risk for massive water supply losses, which some say would create an apocalypse.

Regionally customized green building programs and incentives will need to increasingly focus attention on water issues. Adaptive solutions, elimination of irrigation for purely ornamental landscapes, high-efficiency technologies, and, in particular, water reuse will be front and center. Green building programs have had stronger ties to energy utilities than to any other utility thus far. In the future, water utilities will increasingly see the value of investing in green building programs to help slow water demand and encourage innovative solutions.

Integrating Social and Food Issues

Thus far, green building has focused more of its attention on the environmental and, to a lesser degree, economic aspects of the triple bottom line of sustainability. The missing third piece has to do with social issues, sometimes called human factors, which are harder to quantify but no less important. Social sustainability may include human health and disaster preparedness, fair trade and wages, equity and diversity, affordable housing, environmental and social justice, wayfinding and universal access, arts and culture, and social capital development. In 2008, the USGBC added social equity to their guiding principles and strategic plan. Some of the new goals associated with this include partnering with social justice and quality-of-life initiatives and developing and advocating "a public policy agenda that ensures that the benefits of green buildings become available to currently underserved populations."[20]

The widespread lack of affordable and workforce housing (that is, built to green and healthy standards) is a key policy area where green building programs and policies can exert an influence. Another area that serves social, and also environmental, benefits of the triple bottom line is increasing urban agriculture. U.S. agricultural production has increased by more than 100 percent since 1950 but on only about three quarters of the acreage it occupied then. Land has been removed from agricultural use eight times as fast as it has been developed, and much of the land that has not been converted to suburbs has returned to forest.[21] We need to use developed parcels more creatively and efficiently in order to integrate agricultural uses rather than separate them. Growing and consuming food locally benefits human physical and mental health and lowers the transportation and climate footprint of transporting food long distances.

Many public entities and NGOs now talk about "food security" in relationship to risks to food safety and supply based on massive food importation. The Slow Food and "eat local" movements have huge followings and have managed to focus more people on eating healthy, seasonal foods produced without chemicals. Green building programs can partner with local food organizations, community garden programs, community-supported agriculture, and farmer's markets. Pushing for local food policies and encouraging integration of urban agriculture into new or infill development via a partial redirection of federal agricultural subsidies are two possible areas of action. LEED for Neighborhood Development has a credit for "local food production," a credit that should be added to the entire LEED tool suite. Andres Duany, a Miami architect who is the evangelist of new urbanism, has begun to broadly promote urban agriculture with the term *agricultural urbanism*. He notes that "agriculture is the new golf" and that "food is quite good-looking."[22] He is referring in part to a study in Loudoun County, Virginia, that found views of farmland added as much real estate value to views as golf courses. Duany has integrated an organic farm, which will be commercially operated, into a new urbanist residential development outside St. Louis, in St. Charles, Missouri. Producing food in existing dense urban areas is where a lot of the focus will occur. Small infill urban gardens, green roofs that produce food, and building-integrated vertical agriculture can improve the productivity of even very dense urban environments. Attention will also need to be paid to healthy production methods, addressing the possible impact of urban soil and air contaminants on food gardening.

Advancing Research and Innovation

Preparing for innovation may seem to require a crystal ball. What will the next innovation be, and from where will it arise? While we cannot know the answers to these questions with any surety, we can help to anticipate and guide the process. The USGBC launched a multimillion-dollar green building research funding initiative in 2008 in response to an in-house study that indicated applied research and development funding availability falls far short of what is needed. At the time, the national science budget just for renewable and energy efficiency was about $1 billion annually, compared to a budget of $29 billion for the National Institutes of Health.[23] The Economic Recovery Act provided $2 billion for science and research at the Department of Energy, $300 million for research in using renewable energy for defense and military bases, and $2.5 billion for energy-efficiency and renewable energy research grants.[24]

The public sector, NGOs, and research institutions are in a unique position to fill funding gaps toward serving the public good, even in a time of economic downturn. The key is that, "to get solutions at scale, we're going to have to find answers that are economic for all people everywhere. We've got to use policy to harness innovations to make sure that the right thing to do is a profitable thing to do."[25] However, the potential for business sources of innovation funding should not be underestimated, particularly in the area of venture capital. According to Josh Lerner of the Harvard Business School, one dollar of venture capital is roughly equivalent to three to four dollars of corporate research and development.[26]

We can expect some of the best innovations to come from unexpected areas or from young inventors who are unhampered by a "this is the way we do things" mentality. In the developing world, where self-sufficiency and off-grid technologies may be a matter of survival, innovations such as cell phone networks have flourished unfettered by the sometimes cumbersome regulatory environment and the previous investments in the status quo that often hamper innovation. Student researchers and the budding graduates of design programs are coming up with some of the best ideas, and we would do well to pay attention and create more public-private and government-academic partnerships to solve real-world problems. *Metropolis* magazine's Next Generation annual competition for young designers and students is just one of the treasure troves of emerging genius.[27]

In spite of, or perhaps because of, the tremendous challenges we face, the future still looks bright. Genius can be born of need. The pressing problems and crises that face us can be viewed with panic and despair, or they can be viewed more philosophically, as natural collapses that occur when the limits of a system are reached, opening up new opportunities for creativity and reinvention. In his fascinating book *The Upside of Down*, Thomas Homer-Dixon discusses how cycles of growth, collapse, reorganization, and rebirth characterize ecological systems, such as forests, in something called "the adaptive cycle." The forest is a highly efficient system with an extraordinary degree of connectedness. This also means that since redundancies have been eliminated through evolution of a highly ordered system, shocks travel extremely quickly through the entire system, causing collapse. The increasing interconnectedness of many of our modern systems, such as global material transportation and an interlinked world economy, has contributed to collapse.[28]

These systems seek equilibrium and stability within situations of fluctuation and change (as discussed in chapter 3). The recent upheaval and chaos within our political, environmental, and economic systems feel quite overwhelming, but it would serve us well to remember that inherent in this chaos lies opportunity for change and growth. In the forest model, collapse allows new niches within the system to open up, and the growth of new species and genetic diversity that may be extremely useful. We must take the long view, recognizing that as a species we are still in some ways children. We must remind ourselves that "cycles of breakdown and renewal are normal in modern capitalist economies."[29] Therefore, we can see it as normal that we are breaking down our old ways of building shelters, infrastructure, and neighborhoods and that we are reinventing ourselves and our cities. With a new vision of an Emerald City, renewal and resilience can become our new models for creating quality of life. This is what we can hope for with the newborn opportunities that lie ahead. I, for one, feel confident that we have enough imagination and ingenuity to use the tools already at hand and that we will find a way to create new ones that will take us where we want to go. The adventure continues in the world of green building and beyond. Travel well, and don't forget to write.

ACKNOWLEDGMENTS

A warm thank you to my husband, Bill, whose patience was limitless during the process of giving birth to this book. Thank you to Heather Boyer for her editorial guidance, to Thor Peterson for his expert review and opinions, and to Holly Zipp for help with images.

Thank you to all of the contributing authors: Doug Seiter, Dan Burgoyne, Stephen Hardy, Thor Peterson, Joan Kelsch, Clark Brockman, Lynne Barker, and Don Horn.

Thank you to so many people who have been a part of the City of Seattle green building program. A few I'd like to particularly thank: Tony Gale, Marya Castillano, Richard Conlin, Peter Dobrovolny, Lynne Barker, Thor Peterson, Janet Stephenson, Jayson Antonoff, Sandra Mallory, Sandy Howard, Joanne Quinn, Amanda Sturgeon, Diane Sugimura, and John Rahaim.

And, finally, thank you to the many people along my educational and career path who have helped to guide my way: Pliny Fisk III, Gail Vittori, Alan Stacell, Phil Pregill, Bob Muggerauer, Paolo Baruchieri, John Motloch, Larry Speck, Stephen Ross, Tom Paladino, Peter Templeton, Bob Berkebile, and David Eisenberg.

It is impossible to appropriately thank everyone who has been a part of the experiences shared in this book. Countless people, from all backgrounds and in a variety of roles, have been a part of the stories shared here. Some of you I know. Others I will never know. To all of you, thank you. I look forward to learning from our expansive community. I encourage you to share with me what you have learned as a result of this book or through your own adventures.

City of Seattle Public Projects Green Building Portfolio

This section provides portraits of some of the projects in the City of Seattle's extensive green building portfolio. The information is shared to give an idea of the range of projects that are possible with a public entity and to emphasize the importance of an organization walking the talk of green building. The diversity of Seattle's green building assets creates rich opportunity for research and learning.

SEATTLE CITY HALL: THE PEOPLE'S HALL

FIGURE A.1 Seattle City Hall, LEED NC Gold
Photo credit: Erik Stuhaug

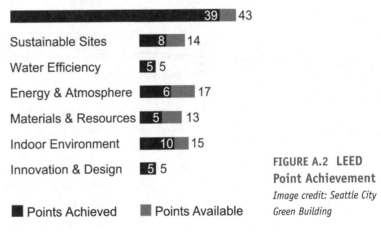

	39	43
Sustainable Sites	8	14
Water Efficiency	5	5
Energy & Atmosphere	6	17
Materials & Resources	5	13
Indoor Environment	10	15
Innovation & Design	5	5

■ Points Achieved   ■ Points Available

FIGURE A.2 LEED Point Achievement
Image credit: Seattle City Green Building

Fast Facts

LEED Certification: Gold, New Construction (NC)
Facility Type: Public assembly and office
Square Feet: 198,000; seven stories

Neighborhood: Downtown Seattle
Construction Cost: $363/square foot
Completed: July 2003

Benefits

- 24% reduction in energy use
- 100% less potable water used for irrigation
- 30% less potable water used indoors
- 27% reduction in rate of stormwater runoff
- 75% of waste generated by construction recycled

Project Highlights

No building is more symbolic of local government than the City Hall—a place that can embody our ideals regarding citizenship, governance, and civil life. Seattle's new City Hall was one of the earliest projects that gave form to the new green building policy. The building is the anchor within a three-block downtown civic campus redevelopment project. Functions include city council chambers, offices, and a public access television station. It was designed as a one-hundred-year facility, replacing one that saw only forty short years of life and which lacked a civic sense of place and earthquake safety.

The anchor of this project is an expansive social space that serves as public lobby, performance space, and the City's "front porch." This highly transparent space uses an abundance of glass in interior and exterior walls to symbolize democracy as a transparent process. Glass is also the theme of its considerable art in public places program. Seattle, like many cities, has a provision to fund art with a required 1 percent of the overall budget. A glass bridge, a picture wall, and hanging sculptures address social sustainability and also provide a nod to Seattle's importance as an international art glass capital.

Energy efficiency is addressed through customized facades utilizing vertical fins, sunshades, and fritted and low-e (low-emissivity) glass. A raised floor system places all electrical and communications systems in a fifteen-inch space above each floor slab, distributing air through adjustable floor diffusers. Modular floor panels and carpet tiles are intended to allow easy access for maintenance and flexibility to reconfigure interior spaces.

A planted green roof surrounds the council chamber portion of the building. While not publicly accessible, the green roof provides visual relief in a highly urban environment and can be seen from floors three through seven. High-efficiency plumbing fixtures provide demand-side conservation with waterless urinals and low-flow lavatories and toilets. All stormwater from the roof and outdoor plaza surfaces is collected in a 225,000-gallon tank and reused for toilet flushing and irrigation.

Lessons Learned

- Design sequencing and installation of underfloor air systems must be handled carefully. The layout of interior offices was finalized after the layout of floor vents. Vents in the wrong locations negatively affected occupant comfort and had to be moved later.

Carpet tile modules should be correlated with floor hatch modules to ease the steps in relocating vents. Incorrect installation of many floor vents also had to be corrected. Be sure that design decisions that are linked occur in the correct sequence. If change occurs in one area, be sure to go back and adjust the design in linked areas. Ensure that installers understand new systems.

- When designing innovative systems for the first time, get additional expert help if your team has never done them. When the rainwater harvest and green roof systems were designed, the technology was relatively new in this country. Several errors occurred that might have been avoided if green roof or cistern design specialists had been consulted. Rainwater harvest systems that collect water from vegetated surfaces, such as green roofs, can create increased discoloration of collected water due to organic matter. Organic matter should be limited to 2 to 3 percent in such cases, or rainwater should be collected only from hard surfaces. Size cisterns appropriately for the situation. Install water treatment systems that are carefully matched to the needs. Be sure there is good access and tool storage for roof maintenance. Signage should always be provided to help users and maintenance staff understand differences with unfamiliar technologies. Water rights issues also emerged during the design of the rainwater system, so be sure to determine if there are similar issues in your jurisdiction.

- Set design standards early in the project, and make it clear to the client that they apply to every occupant. Some tenants of City Hall refused to give up hard wall offices, which negatively affected the daylighting design. Daylighting strategies are dependent on good access to daylight not only at the perimeter but also deeper inside the building. Proper configuration and detailing of partitions, such as lower heights, will help to protect daylight access. Hard wall offices should not be allowed if they interfere with daylighting schemes.

- Design in flexibility for future facility adaptation. Solar photovoltaic collection was originally proposed for the roof of City Hall. This was never realized due to a lack of funding. However, the building was constructed to easily allow the addition of the solar panels in the future, when costs and benefits are more realizable.

The Team

Owner: Seattle Fleets and Facilities Department
Architect: Bassetti Architects/Bohlin Cywinski Jackson
Mechanical Engineer: Wood/Harbinger
Landscape Architect: Gustafson Partners with Swift & Co.
Civil and Structural Engineer: SvR Design Company
Electrical Engineer: Sparling
Lighting Designer: Fisher Marantz Stone (public areas); Candela (offices)
Daylighting Consultant: The Daylighting Lab
Contractor: Hoffman Construction
Commissioning Agent: Engineering Economics Incorporated

YESLER COMMUNITY CENTER: GREEN BUILDING ON A BUDGET

FIGURE A.3 Yesler Community Center, LEED NC Gold
Photo credit: ©Mithun, Juan Hernandez

	46	69
Sustainable Sites	11	14
Water Efficiency	3	5
Energy & Atmosphere	8	17
Materials & Resources	6	13
Indoor Environment	13	15
Innovation & Design	5	5

■ Points Achieved   ■ Points Available

FIGURE A.4 LEED Point Achievement
Image credit: Seattle City Green Building

Fast Facts

LEED Certification: Gold, New Construction (NC)
Facility Type: Public center
Square Feet: 22,800; two stories
Neighborhood: Residential, near downtown
Construction Cost: $158 /square foot
Completed: January 2005

Benefits

- 42% reduction in energy use
- 30% less water use
- 76% of construction waste diverted from landfills
- 95% of building is naturally ventilated and daylit
- 41% of products and materials from regional sources

Project Highlights

Yesler Community Center is an outstanding community model for green building on a budget. It serves as the social hub for a neighborhood that emphasizes affordable housing, with diverse residents that speak twenty-three different languages. The facility includes a gymnasium, a teen center, a childcare facility, a fitness center, and computer and meeting rooms. The brownfield site offers commanding views of the surrounding city and Mt. Rainier. Usability of the site area is enhanced by tucking parking below the gym, leaving space available for a children's outdoor play area.

Passive strategies and a southern exposure led the design team to divide the building into three major volumes to maximize daylight and cross-ventilation. The building has no mechanical cooling system, instead relying on passive cooling and natural ventilation. The cost offset was used to pay for operable windows and controls, with long-term operational savings. Daylighting with windows, skylights, and clerestories provides for all of the building's lighting needs during the day, including the gymnasium. The gym's ventilation system relies on cross-ventilation and a thermal stack effect to bring cool air in through low louvers and release it through clerestory openings. Thermal modeling, daylighting, and natural ventilation studies were performed to fine-tune design strategies. High-efficiency plumbing fixtures result in a 30 percent water reduction, while adding no capital cost and an annual operating savings of $1,700.

Resource-efficient materials strategies were a focus for the owner, who had minimal maintenance capabilities and the need for a fifty-year facility. High durability and minimal finish materials include brick and concrete facades, concrete floors, galvanized steel decks, and exposed ceiling structures as the exposed finish. Forestry Stewardship Council maple gymnasium and multipurpose room flooring was included at no additional cost.

Lessons Learned

- Designing to meet a limited budget can be complementary to green building, leading design teams to explore nonmechanical strategies that save on both first cost and operations budgets. Use of natural ventilation versus air-conditioning has long-term costs savings. Highly durable materials that double as finish materials, such as concrete and steel, can provide for economical construction cost and long-term low maintenance and long life.
- Design simulation and touring other projects can help to allay concerns regarding design departures. This client, initially fearful of glare issues experienced historically at other gyms, was convinced with simulation and modeling tools. The client also visited a 1950s gym that was daylit. The risk was a success, and the popular gym is functioning comfortably.
- Building an anchor project in a neighborhood in transition to green building standards can set a precedent for future community redevelopment. The anchor project can help to educate residents about green building, and raise the bar for future neighborhood projects. The Yesler Terrace neighborhood is slated for extensive redevelopment of its affordable housing units to create increased density and a highly sustainable community. The site design and street edge design will allow flexibility for increased pedestrian traffic and space for new right-of-way amenities that are anticipated in the future.
- Creating user-friendly places with good wayfinding is a part of green design. This project meets many needs of a highly diverse neighborhood of affordable housing residents that speak twenty-three different languages. Design with clearly visible entries and a generous common entry space oriented to the sidewalk help people to feel welcome. Staff monitoring needs are handled by placing the reception desk with high visibility to entries, active use areas, a teen room, and childcare entry.

The Team

Owner: Seattle Parks and Recreation

Architect and Landscape Architect: Mithun

Mechanical: Keen Engineers (now Stantec)

Civil and Structural: Coughlin Porter Lundeen Inc.

Electrical: Hultz BHU Cross Engineers

Lighting: Candela

Daylighting: Seattle Daylighting Lab

Contractor: Berschauer Phillips Construction Co.

Commissioning: Engineering Economics Inc.

AIRPORT WAY CENTER, BUILDING C: ADAPTIVE REUSE

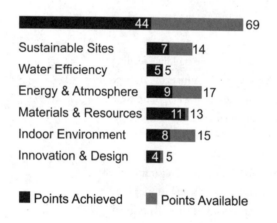

	44	69
Sustainable Sites	7	14
Water Efficiency	5	5
Energy & Atmosphere	9	17
Materials & Resources	11	13
Indoor Environment	8	15
Innovation & Design	4	5

■ Points Achieved   ▒ Points Available

FIGURE A.5 LEED Point Achievement
Image credit: Seattle City Green Building

Fast Facts

LEED Certification: Gold, New Construction (NC)

Facility Type: Police support

Neighborhood: Industrial brownfield

Square Feet: 163,241

Construction Cost: $95/square foot

Completed: August 2006

Benefits

- 18% energy savings—$32,425 in annual savings
- 31% water savings—$9,467 in annual savings
- 99% reuse of structural systems and building envelope
- 96% of construction waste recycled
- 57% of all wood Forest Stewardship Council certified

Project Highlights

This police support facility has twenty-four-hour occupancy and houses forensic labs, offices, classrooms, locker rooms, and extensive storage used to store evidence. (The latter sometimes even includes automobiles!) Adaptive reuse of the existing high-bay warehouse building preserved the entire shell and core. The tidal mudflat site has high watertable challenges, with three hundred gallons of groundwater per hour entering the site. Previously, this was pumped into the storm sewer. This water is now recaptured and stored in a nineteen-thousand-gallon vault, which provides reused water for toilet flushing, irrigation, and police vehicle washing.

Extensive reuse saved over 99 percent of the building's structure and shell. Office furniture purchased from the original owner was cleaned and refurbished. In addition, 14 percent of the building's interior materials was salvaged, including windows, doors, cabinets, and ceiling tiles. Including furnishing, this represented a savings of $513,530. Construction demolition waste recycling diverted 3,369 tons from the landfill, with a 96 percent diversion rate overall.

Energy efficiency is addressed with a heating and cooling system that is plenum based and features individual user control. Waste heat is discharged to heat the garage space. Typical warehouse lighting is rarely turned off. This warehouse lighting uses sensors triggered by people or forklifts.

Lessons Learned

- Problems can become opportunities when viewed through the lens of sustainability. The excessive groundwater had always been considered a headache, but with the project's new green approach and water demands, it became a resource asset.
- Adaptive reuse of old concrete tilt-up wall buildings can maintain their useful life and preserve the embodied energy inherent in existing buildings. Creativity can transform such facilities to meet new user requirements.
- The design team originally thought that the use of Forest Stewardship Council (FSC) lumber was cost prohibitive. Extra effort by the contractor added to the supplier pool and awareness of the potential size of the sale. More cost competitive bids resulted in 57 percent of all wood carrying the FSC label (a $133,000 purchase).
- The design process required extensive exploration of the programmatic needs of police staff who are not assigned to precincts. Simple design details such as ventilated lockers helped to provide for good air quality and created pleasant, odor-free locker rooms that are very popular with staff.
- Design for future flexibility to add new technology. An urban wind turbine was originally proposed for the project. Due to a lack of funding, this part of the project was never realized. It would have been useful to design in accommodation for this for a future time when it is more cost effective.

The Team

Owner: Seattle Fleets and Facilities Department
Architect: DKA Architecture
GCCM: Turner Construction
Civil: Haozous Engineering
Structural: Peterson Strehle Martinson
Mechanical and Electrical: Wood/Harbinger
Commissioning: Engineering Economics Inc.

CARKEEK PARK ENVIRONMENTAL LEARNING CENTER: MODEL FOR A GREENER LIFESTYLE

FIGURE A.6 Carkeek Park Environmental Learning Center, LEED NC Gold
Photo credit: Brad Miller

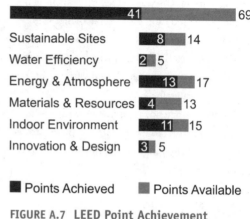

	41		69
Sustainable Sites	8	14	
Water Efficiency	2	5	
Energy & Atmosphere	13	17	
Materials & Resources	4	13	
Indoor Environment	11	15	
Innovation & Design	3	5	

■ Points Achieved   ■ Points Available

FIGURE A.7 LEED Point Achievement
Image credit: Seattle City Green Building

Fast Facts

LEED Certification: Gold, New Construction (NC)
Facility Type: Education/interpretive
Neighborhood: Suburban park
Square Feet: 1,756; one (plus) story
Construction Cost: $317/square foot
Completed: May 2003

Benefits

- 66% reduction in energy use
- 33% reduction in overall potable water uses
- 50% less potable water used for irrigation
- 8% decrease in impervious surface on site
- 80% demolition and construction waste recycled

Project Highlights

This project is nestled into one of the jewels in Seattle's park system: Carkeek Park. With active salmon runs within a wooded hillside, the neighbors are community and environmental activists. The building complements adjacent facilities as a multipurpose meeting and an event room with green building interpretive information. The small scale of the one-story building helps visitors relate it to the scale of a home. One key goal for the project was "to translate long term goals for the Pipers Creek watershed into a model for residential-scale development."[1]

The site design redeveloped a previously disturbed area, preserving existing habitat and tree snags, and manages stormwater through an infiltration trench. A 3,850-gallon rainwater collection system serves toilet flushing and seasonal irrigation, while a smaller rainbarrel provides home owner education.

The site includes a photovoltaic demonstration that produces 22 percent of the total building energy load, or about 3,100 kilowatt hours per year. The system was funded by Seattle City Light's Green Power program. Radiant panel heating provides for highly variable occupancy demand with quick start-up and provides heat close to users for short periods of time. Deep building overhangs, a daylighting clerestory, and low-e glazing minimize energy demands further.

Lessons Learned

- This project met and exceeded the City's green building policy, even though it was not required to. The small square footage was less than the five thousand square feet that triggers the policy. Tireless community activists were responsible for the project vision and the aggressive green design goals. Partnerships between the public sector and private citizens are a powerful tool for market adoption of green building.
- Residential neighborhoods need green building projects at a scale they can relate to. Workshops, interpretive signage, and community events help the community learn how to integrate green strategies into their own homes.
- Calculate water demands carefully, and design in flexibility in case calculations are not exact. Project challenges include miscalculation of the total water demands that needed to be met by the cistern, due to high summer use and a seasonal drought. A larger cistern would have been able to meet all of the annual water demands for both irrigation and toilets.

The Team

Owner: Seattle Parks and Recreation
Architect: Miller Hayashi Architects
Mechanical Engineer: Notkin Engineers Inc.
Landscape Architect: Herrera Environmental Consultants Inc.
Civil Engineer: Herrera Environmental Consultants Inc.
Electrical Engineer: Case Engineering
Contractor: Gemkow Construction
Commissioning: CHDS Commissioning and Engineering

CEDAR WATER TREATMENT FACILITY OPERATIONS BUILDING: LIGHT FOOTPRINT FOR A SENSITIVE WATERSHED

Photo credit: CH2M Hill

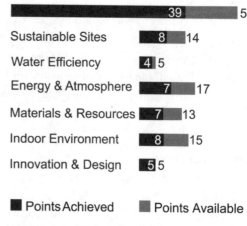

	39	51
Sustainable Sites	8	14
Water Efficiency	4	5
Energy & Atmosphere	7	17
Materials & Resources	7	13
Indoor Environment	8	15
Innovation & Design	5	5

■ Points Achieved   ■ Points Available

FIGURE A.9 LEED Point Achievement
Image credit: Seattle City Green Building

Fast Facts

LEED Certification: Gold, New Construction (NC)
Facility Type: Infrastructure
Neighborhood: Protected rural watershed, source of Seattle's drinking water
Square Feet: 5,480; one story
Construction Cost: $200/square foot (shell and core)

Benefits

- 61% reduction in energy use
- 33% less water use inside building and 42% including site
- 80% sediment removed from stormwater
- 90% of building naturally daylit, with views
- 75% of construction waste diverted from landfills
- 5,300 gallons of potable water
- 107,450,000 less BTUs of energy (gas and electric combined)

Project Highlights

This project is part of a large water treatment facility located in a pristine watershed where Seattle obtains 70 percent of its drinking water. The water treatment system features ozone and ultraviolet light primary disinfection. The operations building is within a 2,482-acre reserve containing old growth forest, no farm or parkland, and strictly limited public access to protect the drinking water supply. Due to the very sensitive nature of the site and its adjacency to wetland habitat, low-impact site design and construction techniques were paramount. Stormwater is treated on site with a system of three large constructed wetlands that are purposely oversized and designed to remove sediment and phosphorus. Turbidity and water quality are closely monitored to ensure pristine conditions.

Energy-efficient systems comprise a vast array of strategies, including passive ventilation, highly insulated building envelope, waste heat recapture with heat exchangers, clerestory daylighting and skylights, and thermal mass concrete floors. One of the more interesting mechanical system features is a water-source heat pump that is connected to an underground water supply pipe that is part of the treatment system. The presystem functions similarly to a ground-source heat pump.

Material resource efficiency emphasized recycled content and regional materials. Sixty-three percent of the materials have recycled or renewable content. Fifty percent of the materials were manufactured or harvested locally.

Lessons Learned

- Bring in contractors as partners through alternate contracting models. The project contract utilized a unique design-build-operate model. This contracting method gave the design and operations team a vested interest in the project outcome, quality of design, durability, and operational efficiency.
- Consider creating special project incentives. A reward of $50,000 was offered by the city if the team could deliver a LEED Gold project, above the Silver requirements of the contract. This incentive was successful in driving the team to higher levels of achievement. The project did attain the Gold certification.
- The LEED design standard was applied only to the small operations building. The vast water treatment part of the facility was not designed to green standards. The LEED tool currently does not fit such projects. The Sustainable Site Initiative has created a tool that might be applied better, but there are still no energy or other green performance standards for facilities such as water treatment plants.

The Team

Owner: Seattle Public Utilities
Architect: CH2M HILL
Landscape Architect: Susan Black & Associates
Mechanical Engineer: University Mechanical Contractors
Sustainability Consultant: Paladino & Company

FIGURE A.10 Northgate Civic Center Campus, LEED NC Gold

Photo credit: Nic Lehoux

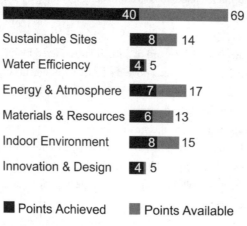

	40	69
Sustainable Sites	8	14
Water Efficiency	4	5
Energy & Atmosphere	7	17
Materials & Resources	6	13
Indoor Environment	8	15
Innovation & Design	4	5

■ Points Achieved   ■ Points Available

FIGURE A.11 LEED Point Achievement

Image credit: Seattle City Green Building

Fast Facts

Project Type: Public library and community center
Neighborhood: Suburban
LEED Rating: Gold, New Construction (NC)
Square Feet: 10,000 library; 20,000 community center
Construction Cost: $295/square foot, library; $228/square foot, community center
Completed: July 2006

Benefits

- 46% reduction in energy use—$34,500 in annual savings
- 77% reduction in potable water use—$2,500 in annual savings

- 94% construction waste diverted from landfills through recycling
- 30% decrease in the rate of stormwater runoff
- 19.5% decrease in impervious surface area

Project Highlights

The Northgate Civic Center integrates two neighborhood facilities—a branch library and a community center—into a single campus-style setting with abundant open space. The suburban site is within a neighborhood struggling to transform its identity from an automobile-dependent area centered around a shopping mall and strip centers to a more pedestrian zone with a civic identity. The two buildings emphasize energy conservation via daylighting, deep overhangs, an air-to-air heat recovery system, and natural ventilation.

The project's most unique innovations appear in the stormwater management system, which cascades through a series of collection and treatment functions. Runoff from roof and paved surfaces, plus from a one-acre off-site area, is collected in a vault that also includes treatment to remove suspended solids. The vault serves a dual function, as it is also the source for landscape irrigation. Extensive native plantings complement a natural stormwater swale, which exposes drainage to daylight, a high priority for Thornton Creek neighbors and community activists. The project received an innovation credit for its maintenance as a pesticide-free park.

Lessons Learned

- Combine capital projects whenever possible. The project allowed two separate city agencies to collaborate on a single development project, which allowed for a more efficient planning, design, and construction process and a single LEED submittal. If developed separately, the end result would have had far less positive community impact, especially from a site-amenity perspective.
- Set LEED goals early. The project was far along in design when the LEED Gold goal was set, which would have been more efficient had it been set earlier.
- Expand thinking about what constitutes the site boundaries. The ability to provide upstream and downstream community benefits can expand the range of design options by addressing adjacent sites, rights-of-way, and other neighborhood needs. Teams may tend to think of their project sites fairly narrowly unless encouraged to do otherwise.

The Team

Owner: Seattle Parks and Recreation; Seattle Public Library
Architect and Landscape Architect: Miller|Hull
Mechanical and Electrical Engineer: PAE Consulting Engineers
Landscape Architect: Site Workshop
Civil and Structural Engineer: AHBL
Lighting Designer: Luma Lighting Design
General Contractor: Absher Construction

SEATTLE JUSTICE CENTER: SUSTAINABILITY FOR ALL

	33	69
Sustainable Sites	9	14
Water Efficiency	2	5
Energy & Atmosphere	7	17
Materials & Resources	4	13
Indoor Environment	8	15
Innovation & Design	3	5

■ Points Achieved   ■ Points Available

FIGURE A.13 LEED Point Achievement
Image credit: Seattle City Green Building

Fast Facts

LEED Certification: Silver, New Construction (NC)
Square Feet: 300,000; thirteen stories
Neighborhood: Downtown Seattle
Construction Cost: $307/square foot
Completed: August 2002

Benefits

- 19.35% reduction in energy use
- 100% less potable water used for irrigation
- 7% reduction in water use inside building

Project Description

This building is within the three-block downtown civic campus that also includes City Hall. It houses the Seattle Police Department headquarters and the City's municipal courts. One of the biggest problems this project faced was that the site had outstanding views of Puget Sound to the West but this exposure also has the highest heat and solar gain problems of any other exposure. The problem was solved using a thermal-glazed buffer wall, or a double-wall system that traps air between an outer and an inner facade. In hot months, the air is vented out the nine-story thermal stack via actuated louvers at the top. In cold months, the heat buildup insulates the interior from winter outdoor temperatures. While simple in concept, this had never been done in the Pacific Northwest previously. Views and energy efficiency were achieved simultaneously.

An accessible green roof system was included on the top floor, adjacent to pleasant jury waiting rooms with ample daylight. The outdoor deck, with its planted roof, seating, and panoramic views to the West, is a pleasant space. Citizens serving on jury duty have expressed their pleasant surprise that the spaces they occupy are aesthetically pleasing, helping participants in the process to feel valued.

Lessons Learned

- Design for maximum flexibility in case design predictions contain errors. The building's mechanical shade system was not designed with flexibility in mind. The shades do not come down far enough to block out sun glare at certain times of day. The western exposure and increased perimeter floor-to-ceiling glazing create a problem. Build in room for error when sizing such systems. They are much cheaper to oversize slightly today than to replace tomorrow.
- Research design precedents and tour other projects with the design features sought in order to gain comfort in trying out new solutions. The double-skin wall technology was not familiar to the design team or the client at the outset of the project. The strategy has been used extensively in Europe, but only about a dozen projects in North America have included it.
- Be sure to gain expert assistance when designing green roofs, and designate accessible green roofs as nonsmoking areas. As the first green roof in the City, the design team struggled to detail the soil mix and plant selections correctly. The plants had to be replaced several times due to excessive organic content. In addition, some occupants used the outdoor deck near the green roof as a smoking area, and discarded cigarette butts actually started a fire on the roof once.
- Consider how required design features can serve more than one purpose. This can also lower the cost for some green design alternatives. The required stormwater detention vault was designed to serve a dual purpose as a rainwater cistern to store irrigation water. The water is collected from roof and paved surfaces in the stormwater detention vault, which added four feet of dead storage to provide a dual purpose as a cistern. The vault also improves water quality via sediment removal.

The Team

Owner: Seattle Fleets and Facilities Department
Architect: NBBJ Architects
Mechanical Engineer: CDI Inc.
Landscape Architect: Gustafson Guthrie Nichol Ltd.
Civil Engineer: SvR Design Company
Structural Engineer: Magnusson Klemencic Associates
Electrical Engineer: TAC
Lighting Designer: J. Miller & Associates
Daylighting Consultant: Seattle Daylighting Lab
Contractor: Hoffman Construction Co.
Commissioning Agent: Engineering Economics Inc.

SEATTLE CENTRAL LIBRARY: GREEN AT THE EDGE OF INNOVATION

**FIGURE A.14
Seattle
Central
Library,
LEED
NC Silver**
*Photo credit:
Courtesy of
Seattle Public
Library*

	37	69
Sustainable Sites	7	14
Water Efficiency	3	5
Energy & Atmosphere	9	17
Materials & Resources	6	13
Indoor Environment	5	15
Innovation & Design	4	5

■ Points Achieved   ■ Points Available

**FIGURE A.15 LEED Point
Achievement**
Image credit: NancyEllen Regier

Fast Facts

LEED Certification: Silver, New Construction (NC)

Facility Type: Library Headquarters

Neighborhood: Downtown

Square Feet: 362,987; eleven floors (does not include parking garage)

Construction Cost: $267 square foot (does not include parking garage)

Completed: May 2004

Benefits

- 50% energy savings (data from Cascadia Region GBC study)
- 20% indoor water savings
- 100% irrigation water savings
- 75% recycling construction demolition waste
- 20% local/regional materials, manufactured and harvested

Project Highlights

This highly unusual facility in terms of both form and function has inspired criticism and praise from critics. Herbert Muschamp, former architectural critic for the *New York Times*, called it "a chandelier to swing your dreams on."[2] An extra three months was taken prior to schematic design to conduct research regarding the future of libraries, resulting in a library that still contains books but that also has a large focus on digital technology. Instead of separating the physical collection in different locations, books and materials are laid out in a continuous spiral on levels 6 through 9, maximizing space and research flexibility. Dubbed the "book spiral," this system also improves wayfinding in the stacks.

About half of the exterior glass is a triple-glazed system with an expanded aluminum metal mesh sandwiched between the two outer panes of glass. This mesh serves as a shading device, reduces heat buildup, and softens the light coming in. The cavity between the two inner layers of glass contains Krypton gas, which further increases insulation. Finally, the outer layer of glass has low-e coating, which filters nonvisible light energy. The total shading effect of the glass is better than most tinted glass buildings, without the undesirable darkening.

The library design focuses on resource efficiency with a number of strategies that minimize material use, which lowers both cost and resource use. These include:

- minimal finish materials, such as (a) exposed structural concrete as finish, (b) galvanized aluminum railings, (c) spray-on fireproofing as ceiling finish, and (d) Plexiglas panels that serve triple function as bottom of return air plenum, finish ceiling, and light fixture lens for the fluorescent tubes hidden above
- minimization of structural elements, such as (a) vertical columns, almost completely eliminated by using perimeter platform trusses and sloping columns that do not require girders and that provide counterbalancing;[3] (b) specially detailed diamond-patterned steel grid exterior framework that provides glass curtain wall support, seismic and lateral bracing, and interior finish. The steel diamond system was designed with special connections that allow for stabilization of interior floors without carrying any gravity loads, which also allowed the elimination of fireproofing according to Seattle code.[4]

Lessons Learned

- Additional time spent in the predesign phase of a project may greatly benefit the eventual solution. Gain insight into the challenges faced by similar facilities by going on tours. After seeing how many libraries had lost their social space over time, these spaces were carefully handled at Central Library to ensure their long-term function as social space. Book storage was addressed with maximum flexibility in order to minimize the disruption by growing collections to other space uses.
- Creating new building systems to solve challenging problems may require research funding. This is not the case for most green building projects, only those on the furthest edge of innovation. The designers invented the state-of-the-art triple glazing system, which underwent extensive research and development before its use was approved. Additional research funds were raised to assist with this process.
- Actual user testing is sometimes the best way to determine if new solutions will work. For the innovative book spiral design, the library design team worked closely with two accessibility consultants, both in wheelchairs themselves, and with a group of disabled citizens in order to get expert input. Two successive design concepts were built as full-scale warehouse mock-ups and tested with wheelchairs, bookcarts, and strollers. The original concept was for a single continuous spiral ramp at a 1:30 gradient. In the end, a better solution for wheelchairs was arrived at: an alternating system of one-foot ramps at 1:12 and a five-foot flatter section at 1:50.
- Efficient design solutions sometimes require additional approval time. The large central atrium design maximizes daylight and utilizes a displacement ventilation system. Considerable additional time was spent with fire code officials doing simulations to prove that the building could meet fire code with the atrium.

The Team

Owner: Seattle Public Library

Architect: Office for Metropolitan Architecture (OMA, Netherlands), partners in charge Rem Koolhaas and Joshua Ramus; joint venture with LMN Architects (Seattle), partner in charge John Nesholm, project director for LEED, Sam Miller

Landscape Architect: Inside/Outside with Jones and Jones

Mechanical and Electrical, IT Engineer: Arup

Structural and Civil Engineer: Magnusson Klemencic Associates (MKA) with Arup

Facades: Dewhurst Macfarlane & Partners

Interiors: OMA/LMN, Inside/Outside

Lighting: Kugler Tillotson Associates

Acoustical Engineer: Michael Yantis Associates

Environmental Graphics: Bruce Mau Design

ADA: McGuire Associates, Karen Braitmeyer

General Contractor: Hoffman Construction Company

SEATTLE FIRE STATION 10: A GREEN MODEL FOR DISASTER PREPAREDNESS

FIGURE A.16 Seattle Fire Station 10, LEED NC Silver
Photo credit: Chloe Collyer

FIGURE A.17 LEED Point Achievement
Image credit: Seattle City Green Building

	Points Achieved	Points Available
	33	69
Sustainable Sites	8	24
Water Efficiency	4	5
Energy & Atmosphere	2	17
Materials & Resources	5	13
Indoor Environment	9	15
Innovation & Design	5	5

Fast Facts

LEED Certification: Silver, New Construction (NC)

Square Feet: 69,497; five stories

Neighborhood: Chinatown-International District

Construction Cost: $403/square foot
Completed: January 2008

Benefits

- 18% reduction in energy
- 33% less potable water inside building
- 40% less potable water used
- 25% decrease in impervious surface on site
- 25% reduction in rate of stormwater runoff through green roof and planting area

Project Highlights

This facility serves three functions: a fire station, fire alarm center, and emergency operations center for the City. It houses forty-eight personnel working around-the-clock shifts, living quarters for the fire crew, offices for the 911 dispatch center, a training room, and communication equipment/server rooms. The emergency operations center includes an executive policy room, breakout rooms, a radio communications center, and media production and briefing rooms.

The brownfield site, which previously contained a gas station and surface parking, transformed a previously nearly 100 percent impervious site. It now has over seven thousand square feet of open space, much of it planted, and a fifteen-thousand-square-foot green roof. Publicly visible art is included as part of the 1% for Art program.

Lessons Learned

- Facilities with special uses or specific characteristics, such as high water demand, may be ripe for customized solutions that do not fit other building types. The facility has high water demand for fire drills and washing of emergency response vehicles, estimated at 13 million gallons annually. Site runoff from roofs and nondrivable hardscape is collected and combined with spillover water from fire drills and vehicle washing. The reused water is used both for irrigation and vehicle wash water.
- There is little need to "sell" green building to emergency preparedness and critical support staff such as police or fire officials. The need to maintain functionality off grid and to supply more needs on the site is a natural fit for a disaster-preparedness mind-set. This facility's unique needs require it to stay functional in the event of a seismic or other emergency.
- Construction projects may present special opportunities to conduct additional research or explore solutions to specific sustainability challenges. Special research, funded by the Seattle Public Utilities solid waste fund, was commissioned as a part of the project to analyze alternatives for materials containing persistent bioaccumulative toxins (PBTs). These include mercury, dioxins, and polybrominated diphenyl ethers. The result was substitution of portions of the electrical conduit as rigid metal versus polyvinyl chloride and irrigation piping manufactured of polypropylene. Since materials that contain PBTs are particularly hazardous to humans during fires, the client representatives who were firefighters easily saw the benefit of extra effort in this area.

The Team

Owner: Seattle Fleets and Facilities Department

Architect: Architect, Weinstein A|U; associate architect, RossDrulis Cusenbery; consulting architect, TCA Architecture-Planning Inc.

Mechanical Engineer: Notkin Engineers Inc.

Landscape Architect: Gustafson Guthrie Nichol

Civil and Structural Engineer: Magnusson Klemencic Associates

Electrical Engineer: Sparling

Lighting Designer: Candela

Contractor: Hoffman Construction Company

Owner's Representative: Sheils Obletz Johnsen

Sustainability Consultant: Paladino & Company

NORTH CASCADES ENVIRONMENTAL LEARNING INSTITUTE: INSPIRATION WITHIN NATURE

FIGURE A.18 North Cascades Environmental Learning Center, LEED NC Silver

Photo credit: David Hall

	Points Achieved	Points Available
	37	69
Sustainable Sites	10	14
Water Efficiency	2	5
Energy & Atmosphere	5	17
Materials & Resources	7	13
Indoor Environment	9	15
Innovation & Design	4	5

■ Points Achieved   ■ Points Available

FIGURE A.19 LEED Point Achievement

Image credit: Seattle City Green Building

Image note: Since this table was created, the project has achieved LEED NC Silver certification with a total of 37 credits as follows:
Sustainable Sites, 10;
Water Efficiency, 2;
Energy and Atmosphere, 5;
Materials and Resources, 7;
Indoor Environmental Quality, 9;
Innovation in Design, 4.

Fast Facts

LEED Rating: Silver, New Construction (NC)

Square Feet: 38,582; one story

Neighborhood: North Cascades National Park

Construction Cost: $295/square foot

Completed: January 2006

Benefits

- Zero water used for irrigation and zero stormwater runoff
- 20% reduction in energy use—$5,784 in annual savings
- 84% of wood is Forestry Stewardship Council (FSC) certified from well-managed forests
- 52% of products and materials from regional sources
- 100% of occupied areas have outdoor views

Project Highlights

This unique project was made possible through a partnership among the North Cascades Institute, the National Park Service, and the City of Seattle. The breathtaking site is located within the upper Skagit River watershed and near one of three dams that provide hydroelectric power for 25 percent of Seattle's total electric demand. The park is part of a large protected area that extends north into Canada. The Center and the Institute serve to "inspire a closer relationship with nature through direct experiences in the natural world."[5] Retreats, seminars, school programs, and wilderness discovery events are hosted here amid the classroom, teaching labs, and three lodges with overnight accommodations for sixty-nine people.

The complex includes fifteen buildings, which are located on the footprints of older buildings. The campus is car and pavement free. The multiple-building approach reduced site disturbance by minimizing grading and setting small buildings into the rocky mountain hillside. Landscaping plants were grown from seed collected on the site or propagated locally.

The surrounding forest is expressed on the site with vertical concrete and wood treelike columns. Wood is used extensively throughout the design, including cedar siding, flooring, decking, doors, casework, glue-laminated beams and columns, and rough framing. Eighty-four percent by cost of the wood was from Forestry Stewardship Council forests, further reinforcing the stewardship mission of the Center. Natural drainage features on the site appear as rockeries, swales, and drywells, protecting site water quality. Salvaged wood materials were also used extensively.

Lessons Learned

- Development of remote and pristine greenfield sites poses many challenges. The wilderness site and low-bid contracting added to the challenges of developing this project. Contractors not familiar with LEED had to be educated. Transportation costs to the site were high, and accessibility was limited by seasonal snow closures and a landslide that closed the road accessing the site.

- Contractor communication and education are key in handling sensitive sites. Tree and site protection were accomplished with extensive on-site measures. Fencing protected existing trees, some of which are very close to the finished buildings. Concrete had to be mixed in small batches to minimize site impact, and storage of materials had to be handled carefully to prevent additional site disturbance.
- Areas with limited infrastructure may not allow some construction practices that are standard for more urban areas. Be sure to know your end markets for recyclables before proceeding with construction demolition recycling. The contractor source-separated recyclables into separate bins, only to find out that county recycling centers did not provide such separate recycling services. Separated loads had to be recombined.

The Team

Owner: Seattle City Light
Architect: HKP
Landscape Architect: Richard Haag Associates
Mechanical Engineer: Berona Engineers
Civil Engineer: SvR Design Company
Structural Engineer: Martens/Chan Inc.
Electrical: Path Engineers/Travis, Fitzmaurice & Associates
Lighting: Radiance Lighting & Design
Landscape Restoration: Springwood Associates
General Contractor: Dawson Construction

Thanks to Seattle's City Green Building Program and Clair Enlow for compiling and writing the case studies from which much of the preceding information was gathered. For access to the full case studies, see http://www.seattle.gov/dpd/greenbuilding/.

APPENDIX B

Green Building Certification Tools

Note: This listing of green building certification tools does not include all of the programs being created internationally. For a comparison of several of the major green building certification programs, see the report published by the American Institute of Architects: *Quantifying Sustainability: A Study of Three Sustainable Building Rating Systems and the AIA Position Statement.*[1]

A NOTE ON LEED

In the interest of full disclosure, the reader should know that I helped to develop LEED 2.0 as chair of the site and water technical advisory committee and that I previously served on the USGBC board of directors. I am likely to be biased toward LEED. However, I think there are good reasons for its preferred use. This book and many of the green building programs it profiles refer primarily to LEED. There are several reasons why LEED has become, and continues to be, the dominant green building benchmark tool in the marketplace, and the tool of choice for this author. Foremost is the requirement for third-party verification, which lends credibility to the system and serves to remove bias from claims that may plague self-certification programs. Green Globes offers a self-assessment pathway, with an optional third-party review, while such a review is mandatory for LEED. There are some necessary downsides to third-party verification, such as associated costs and the unpredictability that accompanies lack of user control, but these are far outweighed by the benefits provided.

In addition, a transparent process of vetting tools with a broad range of industry stakeholders helps to remove bias. While both Green Globes and LEED offer a participatory process for creation of their tools, the USGBC takes this one step further with member balloting for final approval and modification of the LEED tool suite. The USGBC strives to lend scientific credibility and a level of rigor to their tool with the use of a Technical Scientific Advisory Committee for additional stringent review of credits and credit interpretation.

A diversity of tools in the marketplace with varying point-of-entry stringency may be healthy in that the net benefits of wider adoption of less rigorous standards may still be positive. While the level of stringency varies somewhat among different tools, overall LEED is the most robust tool in the marketplace today in terms of the level of green performance it commands. In an American Institute of Architects analysis of green building ratings systems, the report notes in regard to Green Globes that "more stringent and specific requirements in the areas of energy reduction and operational performance are needed, as these are two areas that most influence carbon production."[2] LEED includes mandatory energy-efficiency performance as well as some documentation of actual energy performance via building commissioning. On the other hand, LEED could benefit from the addition of Life Cycle Assessment tools, which the Green Globes system provides.

Finally, easy public access to information helps speed the adoption of green building. The LEED tools are freely available via the USGBC Web site, while information on Green Globes is limited for those who are not members of the parent organization, the Green Building Initiative (GBI). I find this obscuring of information self-limiting and counter to the spirit of inclusivity needed to achieve market transformation. Of course, the costs for LEED certification are also a barrier to market adoption.

BREEAM

The BREEAM tool (British Research Establishment Environmental Assessment Tool) predates LEED. As a market transformation tool, it has not gained the broad appeal of LEED in the United States. It is used primarily in the United Kingdom, Canada, and Asia. An international BREAM tool is available worldwide. A subtool (BRE Global) has been created specifically for the United Arab Emirates. BREEAM's tool suite includes components for doing life cycle assessment, specifications, and special assessment programs for homes, multifamily, offices, schools, industrial, prison, courthouse, and retail projects. This tool has a somewhat more scientific basis than LEED because of its inclusion of life cycle assessment. Like LEED, BREEAM requires an independent certification process. The BRE Global tool has ISO 9001 certification for its tools, training, and licensing processes. See http://www.breeam.org/.

ENERGY STAR

The Energy Star program originated as a voluntary labeling program for identifying energy-efficient products, such as computer monitors, office equipment, major appliances, and heating and cooling equipment, and was extended to include new homes and commercial and industrial buildings. The program includes tools to increase the efficiency of both new and existing buildings and to address building management. The program has specialized tools for homes, retail, industrial, health care, hospitality, education, and other project types. Included is an energy Target Finder index of the average energy intensity for various building types, adjusted for climate. This provides a useful baseline for efficiency goal setting, and is also the index being used by the Architecture 2030 program. The EPA has since added the WaterSense program, which provides product certification of plumbing and irrigation products. Thus far, the program has not provided a building-scale certification program for water use. See http://www.energystar.gov/ and http://www.epa.gov/WaterSense/.

GREEN COMMUNITIES FOR AFFORDABLE HOUSING

This tool was created specifically for affordable housing by the nonprofit Enterprise Community Partners and other key partners. Its scope includes both new and remodeled projects, and multifamily and single-family housing. It is based on the LEED framework. Projects must comply with all requirements in eight categories and must also earn thirty points in an "Optional" category. Meeting the requirements can be used to help qualify for affordable housing funding. See http://www.greencommunitiesonline.org/.

GREEN GLOBES AND GO GREEN PLUS

The Green Globes tool emerged after LEED as a competitor. It seems to have reached broader market acceptance in Canada than it has in the United States. Some see it as preferable to LEED for its relative simplicity and lower cost. It offers the option of self-certification or third-party certification. The self-certification option makes it more attractive from a cost standpoint to some, while it is considered by many to be less stringent than LEED due to different performance requirements. To its credit, the Green Building Initiative (GBI), which initiated and administers Green Globes, became the first green building organization to be accredited as a standards developer by the American National Standards Institute, and USGBC quickly followed suit. In addition, the GBI has created a companion tool called Go Green Plus, which is geared toward existing buildings. See http://www.greenglobes.com/.

GREEN GUIDE FOR HEALTH CARE

The Green Guide for Health Care (GGHC) is a toolkit of best practices that is voluntary and self-certifying. The guide uses LEED as its framework and also focuses on building operations and maintenance. The tool—the result of a partnership between the Center for Maximum Potential Building Systems and Health Care Without Harm—applies to new construction, renovations, and existing facilities. The evolution of the program began with the Green Healthcare Construction Guidance Statement, a 2002 project of the American Society for Healthcare Engineering. The USGBC and the Green Guide for Health Care have agreed to work jointly on developing resource materials, education programs, and a research agenda. The GGHC will continue to develop tools while the USGBC administers LEED for Healthcare. See http://www.gghc.org/.

GREEN HOME SCORING TOOL

The National Association of Homebuilders has created a green building rating tool for the mainstream builder and for novices to green building. A Certified Green Professional designation is also offered. The tool is divided into seven sections, including "Lot Design" and "Operations, Maintenance, and Homeowner Education." Three award levels are based on points earned. See http://www.nahbgreen.org/ScoringTool.aspx.

LABS21

Laboratories for the 21st Century (Labs21) is a voluntary partnership program dedicated to improving the environmental performance of U.S. laboratories. The rationale for this special tool is that the typical laboratory uses far more energy and water per square foot than the typical office building due to intensive ventilation requirements and other health and safety concerns. Laboratory facilities have unique design parameters, which makes a customized tool useful. Labs21 is designed to meet the needs of laboratory and high-performance facility designers, engineers, owners, and facility managers. Labs21 was developed and cosponsored by the U.S. Environmental Protection Agency and the U.S. Department of Energy. The Labs21

Toolkit includes a checklist based on LEED but with different performance standards and additional areas of focus. Because the requirements of laboratories and related high-performance facilities differ so dramatically from those of other buildings, this tool was developed. See http://www.labs21century.gov/.

LEED™

The Leadership in Energy and Environmental Design benchmarking system developed by the U.S. Green Building Council offers tiered levels of performance based on a menu of options. While there are some tools competing with LEED in the marketplace, such as Green Globes, LEED leads the pack in the United States and is the most widely recognized standard in North America. LEED provides a suite of nested tools that are customized to various project types, including LEED for Neighborhood Development. There are also special tools for health care and building interiors. A LEED Accredited Professional designation is also offered. See http://www.usgbc.org/ and http://www.gbci.org/.

LIVING BUILDING CHALLENGE

Jason McLennan, chief executive officers of the Cascadia Region Green Building Council, is the originator of the Living Building Challenge. The International Living Building Institute was formed to oversee the ongoing evolution of this amazing tool. The Challenge is conceived of with the metaphor of a flower, with six petals comprising six mandatory performance areas: Site, Energy, Materials, Water, Indoor Quality, and Beauty and Inspiration. Unlike LEED, there are no optional credits—only mandatory performance requirements. Projects may satisfy individual petal designations in addition to satisfying all of the requirements to be designated a Living Building. While the program is attractive in its ambitiousness, its downsides include its lack of a participatory process to develop the tool and the requirement to pay a membership fee to have access to a user's guide and other resources. See http://ilbi.org/.

LOCAL HOMEBUILDER PROGRAMS

Many local governments and trade associations, such as local HomeBuilder Associations (HBA) or Masterbuilder Associations (MBA), have created their own homegrown residential green building certification tools. One program, called Earth Advantage, transitioned from a utility-based program to operation as a stand-alone nonprofit organization (see http://www.earthadvantage.org/.)

These programs vary widely by jurisdiction in terms of the structure, deployment, and stringency of the programs. There are over seventy such localized residential green building programs. These programs have commanded significant market share and have led the USGBC to create the LEED for Homes tool as a competitor. The HBA-led programs are often appealing for members of the MBAs that sponsor them, partly due to their ability to directly influence the tool and for the marketing edge it provides. The entry point to certification in many HBA programs tends to be lower than LEED, but part of the benefit of this has been the initial participation by a broader range of people. Once builders try the program, the initial barrier is removed and in subsequent projects they often achieve higher levels of green performance. For a listing, see http://www.greenhomeguide.org/green_home_programs/index.html.

ONE PLANET LIVING

One Planet Living is not a certification program but, rather, a broad framework of ten guiding principles that can be used as a framework to highlight sustainability challenges. One Planet originated in the United Kingdom and has projects worldwide. It was developed by the Bioregional Development Group and the World Wildlife Fund, who pose the question, what constitutes a sustainable community or lifestyle? The program can be applied at many scales, including individual buildings, neighborhoods, and cities. Principles include zero energy, zero waste, zero water, sustainable transport, local/sustainable food, and equity/fair trade. The program is based on the concept of living within the resource base of the one planet we have rather than needing multiple planets to support unsustainable lifestyles; it also follows the practice of measuring ecological footprints. See http://www.oneplanetliving.org/.

SBTOOL 07

The International Initiative for a Sustainable Built Environment (iiSBE) provides a generic toolkit for development of localized rating systems that can be tied to regional climate zones and the specific regulatory environment. This program evolved from the Green Building Challenge initiative, which attempted to measure and compare the green performance of projects around the world. The result is a fairly complex software program that can be downloaded at no cost and used to conduct detailed building analysis with the user option to weigh and adjust various parameters, including building type. Results of using the framework are compared to benchmark values, which can be adjusted regionally. See http://www.greenbuilding.ca/.

STAR COMMUNITY INDEX

This emerging tool is based on the LEED program and is applied to sustainability performance at the city and county scale. The partners behind STAR are Local Governments for Sustainability, the USGBC, and the Center for American Progress. The tool will provide a benchmarking standard for local governments attempting to implement a broad sustainability agenda and will allow for a shared set of standards created by a broad group of experts and approved via a consensus process. See http://www.starcommunityindex.org/.

SUSTAINABLE SITE INITIATIVE

The Sustainable Site Initiative focuses specifically on landscape sustainability. The initiative has created standards and guidelines and an associated rating tool. The initiative has many partners, but the primary ones are the American Society of Landscape Architects, the National Wildflower Research Center, and the U.S. Botanic Garden. The tools can be used for (1) open spaces, such as local, state, and national parks, conservation easements and buffer zones, and transportation rights-of-way, and (2) sites with buildings, including industrial, retail, and office parks, military complexes, airports, botanical gardens, streetscapes and plazas, residential and commercial developments, and public and private campuses. The tool is divided into five sections: hydrology, soils, vegetation, materials, and human well-being. The USGBC is participating in the project and anticipates that the standards and guidelines will be integrated into LEED eventually. See http://www.sustainablesites.org/.

NOTES

Preface

1. The acronym *LEED*™ stands for Leadership in Energy and Environmental Design. It represents a third-party green building rating and certification system developed by the U.S. Green Building Council. Different levels of performance—Certified, Silver, Gold, and Platinum—are awarded based on the total credits earned in each of several categories.

2. Susan Gilmore, "Fertile Ground for Optimism," *Seattle Times*, May 21, 2000.

3. University of Washington Libraries Digital Collection online database, Seattle, November 31, 2005.

1. Introduction: The Promise of Green Building

1. U.S. Conference of Mayors Climate Protection Agreement (n.d.), http://usmayors.org/climateprotection/.

2. U.S. Conference of Mayors Climate Protection Agreement.

3. Visit the Mayors' Climate Protection Center (http://usmayors.org/climateprotection/) or the Architecture 2030 Web site (http://www.architecture2030.org/) to see if your city has signed on.

4. D. Suzuki, Greenbuild Conference (November 2002).

5. Build Green Northwest, "Build Green Everyone Profits" (July 29, 2004), http://www.buildgreennw.com/.

6. Build Green Northwest, "Build Green Everyone Profits."

7. Cedar River Group, *Report to City of Seattle* (n.d.).

8. U.S. Green Building Council (n.d.), http://www.usgbc.org/.

Chapter 2. Building Support for Green Building Initiatives

1. See http://www.sustainlane.com/us-city-rankings/.

2. Seattle Office of Sustainability and Environment, *City of Seattle Environmental Management Program Manual*, version 99-01 (1998), sec. 1.2, http://www.seattle.gov/environment/Agenda_EMP.htm.

3. Seattle Office of Sustainability and Environment, *City of Seattle Environmental Management Program Manual*, version 99-01, sec. 1.1.

4. See the resources section of the USGBC Web site (http://www.usgbc.org/) for access to download-able presentations that explain the benefits of green building.

5. Commission for Environmental Cooperation, "Secretariat Report to Council under Article 13 of the North American Agreement on Environmental Cooperation," in *Green Building in North America: Opportunities and Challenges* (2008), http://www.cec.org/files/PDF//GB_Report_EN.pdf.

6. Interview with Ray Anderson, in *Journal of Business & Design* (published by the Corporate Design Foundation) 13, no. 1 (Spring 2008), http://www.cdf.org/.

7. See http://www.usgbc.org/.

8. S. Bennett, "City Turns towards Greener Building," *Seattle Daily Journal of Commerce*, online edition (January 31, 2000).

9. Letter from Mayor Merino (2003), Green Building Task Force Web site, http://www.bostonredevelopmentauthority.org/gbtf/GBTFhome.asp.

10. C. D. Plessis, "A South African Perspective on Decision-making for Urban Sustainability," in *Sustainable Building 2000* (Maastricht, Netherlands: Aeneas Technical Publishers, 2000), 304.

11. Database of State Incentives for Renewables and Efficiency, http://www.dsireusa.org/.

12. "Playbook for Green Buildings + Neighborhoods" (n.d.), http://www.greenplaybook.org/.

13. "Playbook for Green Buildings + Neighborhoods."

Chapter 3. Change and Innovation in Markets and Organizations

1. Seattle Department of Planning and Development, "City Green Building: Green Home Guides," http://www.seattle.gov/dpd/GreenBuilding/SingleFamilyResidential/Resources/RemodelingGuides/default.asp.

2. Draper L. Kauffman Jr., *Systems One: An Introduction to Systems Thinking* (Minneapolis: Carlton, 1980).

3. Bob Doppelt, *Leading Change towards Sustainability: A Change Management Guide for Business, Government and Civil Society* (Sheffield: Greenleaf, 2003).

4. Doppelt, *Leading Change towards Sustainability*, 231.

5. McGraw-Hill Construction, *Green Building Smart Market Report* (McGraw-Hill Research and Analytics, 2006).

6. To download the ads, see http://www.buildgreennw.com/.

7. "Fostering Sustainable Behavior: Community-based Social Marketing" (June 6, 2009), http://www.cbsm.com/.

4. Developing and Implementing Policy for Publicly Funded Green Building

1. U.S. Green Building Council Web site (May 30, 2009), http://www.usgbc.org/.

2. See http://www.usgbc.org/. Much of the policy-related data in this chapter comes from this site. A useful searchable database can be found here, with links to many of the specific programs and policy language.

3. U.S. Green Building Council, "LEED Initiatives in Governments and Schools," http://www.usgbc.org/DisplayPage.aspx?CMSPageID=1852.

4. For more information, see "Harvard's Sustainability Principles," http://www.green.harvard.edu/sustainability-principles/.

5. These cities and counties include Alameda County (CA), Albuquerque (NM), Anchorage (AK), Atlanta (GA), Chapel Hill (NC), El Paso (TX), Gainesville (FL), Nashville (TN), New Albany (OH), Normal (IL), San Francisco (CA), St. Louis (MO), Syracuse (NY), and Tampa (FL).

6. New Mexico Energy, Minerals, and Natural Resources Department, Energy Conservation & Management Division, *Executive Order 2006-001 High Performance Schools Task Force Final Report*, January 8, 2007, http://www.emnrd.state.nm.us/ecmd/GovernmentLeadByExample/documents/HIPTFRecommendation.pdf.

7. For more on the Chicago Standard, see http://egov.cityofchicago.org/webportal/COCWebPortal/COC_ATTACH/ChicagoStandard.pdf. For more on the Florida Green Coalition Building standards, see http://www.floridagreenbuilding.org/db/.

8. U.S. Green Building Council, "LEED Initiatives in Governments and Schools."

9. Excellent resources on costs and benefits of green building are available in the Green Building Research section of the USGBC Web site, http://www.usgbc.org/DisplayPage.aspx?CMSPageID=1718.

10. Many of these can be accessed in the Resources section of the USGBC Web site, http://www.usgbc.org/DisplayPage.aspx?CategoryID=20.

11. Davis Langdon, "Cost of Green Revisited: Reexamining the Feasibility and Cost Impact of Sustainable Design in the Light of Increased Market Adoption" (July 2007), 3.

12. Norm Miller, Jay Spivey, and Andy Florance, "Does Green Pay Off?" CoStar Group Study (July 2008), http://www.costar.com/josre/.

13. For more on Greensburg, Kansas, see http://www.greensburgks.org/recovery-planning.

14. Green Building Playbook, http://www.greenplaybook.org/.

15. Capital Division, Treasury Board Staff, Ministry of Finance and Corporate Relations, "British Columbia Value Analysis Guidelines: Provincially Funded Facilities" (December 2000), http://www.bced.gov.bc.ca/capitalplanning/projectmanagement/documents/va_guidelines2001.pdf.

16. Capital Division, Treasury Board Staff, Ministry of Finance and Corporate Relations, "Green Buildings Checklist" (December 2000), http://www.bced.gov.bc.ca/capitalplanning/projectmanagement/documents/green_buildings_checklist2001.pdf.

17. For more on the Portfolio Manager, see http://www.energystar.gov/index.cfm?c=evaluate_performance.bus_portfoliomanager.

18. USGBC Portfolio Program FAQs, http://www.usgbc.org/ShowFile.aspx?DocumentID=3387. For more on the Portfolio Program in general, see http://www.usgbc.org/portfolioprogram/.

5. Developing Green Building Program Services

1. See http://www.greenplaybook.org/.

2. A. W. Webber, *Institutional Efforts for Green Building: Institutional Approaches to Foster Green Building in North America* (Commission for Environmental Cooperation, 2008).

3. See http://betterbricksresources.com/book/.

4. See http://www.southface.org/.

5. See http://www.seattle.gov/dpd/Publications/Client_Assistance_Memos_(CAMs)/default.asp.

6. See http://www.dsireusa.org/.

7. See http://ecobuilding.org/green_pages/.

8. See http://sconnect.org/greenbuilding/.

9. For more information, see http://www.cascadiagbc.org/education/programs/.

10. For more information, see http://www.gbci.org/.

11. See http://www.nasbap.org/.

12. For more information, see http://www.nahb.org/category.aspx?sectionID=1174.

13. V. Jones, *The Green Collar Economy: How One Solution Can Fix Our Two Biggest Problems* (New York: Harper Collins, 2008).

14. R. R. Ortega, "Newark Dons a 'Green Collar' with a Construction Training Program," *New Jersey Star-Ledger*, January 13, 2009.

15. R. Pollin, *Green Recovery: A Program to Create Good Jobs and Start Building a Low-carbon Economy* (Amherst: Political Research Institute at the University of Massachusetts–Amherst, 2008).

16. 7group and Bill Reed, *The Integrative Design Guide to Green Building* (Hoboken, NJ: Wiley, 2009).

6. Green Building Incentives and Codes

1. The Opus Group, "2007 Green Building Survey: A Special Report from National Real Estate Investor and Retail Traffic" (November 2007), http://nreionline.com/images/GreenBuildings.pdf.

2. See http://www.dsireusa.org/gbi/.

3. See http://www.usgbc.org/ShowFile.aspx?DocumentID=2021.

4. City of Portland, press release (December 1, 2007). For more information on the Green Investment Fund, see http://www.PortlandOnline.com/osd/greenbuilding/.

5. For more information, see http://www.homedepotfoundation.org/ and http://www.kresge.org/.

6. See also http://www.metrokc.gov/dnrp/swd/greenbuilding/.

7. For more information, see http://www.ci.el-paso.tx.us/downtown_plan.asp.

8. See also http://www.metrokc.gov/dnrp/swd/greenbuilding/.

9. For more information, see http://www.savingwater.org/.

10. For more information, see http://www.ci.pasadena.ca.us/waterandpower/program_highperfbldg.asp.

11. For more information, see http://www.portlandonline.com/BES/index.cfm?c=43444&.

12. See http://www.firemansfund.com/green/.

13. Shore Bank (n.d.), http://www.shorebankcorp.com/.

14. For more information, see http://www.ci.berkeley.ca.us/ContentDisplay.aspx?id=26580.

15. For more information, see http://www.dec.ny.gov/energy/1540.html.

16. For more information, see http://www.oregon.gov/ENERGY/LOANS/selphm.shtml.

17. U.S. Department of Energy, "Tax Breaks for Businesses, Utilities, and Governments" (n.d.), http://www.energy.gov/additionaltaxbreaks.htm.

18. For more information, see http://www.energy.gov/additionaltaxbreaks.htm.

19. For more information, see http://www.architecture2030.org/.

20. A. W. Webber, Council for Environmental Cooperation, *Green Building in North America: Opportunities and Challenges. Secretariat Report to Council under Article 13 of the North American Agreement on Environmental Cooperation. Institutional Efforts for Green Building* (2008),

http://www.cec.org/files/PDF//GB_Report_EN.pdf.

21. Erik Olsen, "City of Chicago Green Permit Program," PowerPoint presentation (n.d.), http://www.illinoisashrae.org/HealthySchool/ASHRAE%20Green%20Permit%20Program.pdf.

22. For more information, see http://www.cob.org/services/environment/lid/green-building.aspx.

23. For more information, see http://www.cascadiagbc.org/news/city-of-vancouver-clark-county -code-study.

24. Some concerns about this may be valid. The early 2009 fire that significantly damaged the unfinished Beijing Mandarin Oriental Hotel, designed by Rem Koolhaas and Arup, was caused by fireworks that spread a massive fire through a huge internal atrium. For more information, see http://www.skyscrapernews.com/news.php?ref=1982.

25. For more information, see http://www.seattle.gov/util/About_SPU/Drainage_&_Sewer_System/ Natural_Drainage_Systems/index.asp.

26. Playbook for Green Buildings + Neighborhoods Web site, http://www.greenplaybook.org/.

27. Playbook for Green Buildings + Neighborhoods Web site, http://www.greenplaybook.org/.

28. A. Webb, "Chicago's Green Permit Program Exceeds Expectations," *Architectural Record* (July 20, 2006), 34.

29. City of Santa Cruz, "City Council Agenda Report" (October 25, 2005), http://www.ci.santa-cruz .ca.us/pl/gbwg/PL296rpt-GreenBldgOrd.pdf.

30. For more information, see http://www.bouldercolorado.gov/index.php?option=com_content&task =view&id=208&Itemid=489.

31. For more information, see http://www.ashrae.org/pressroom/detail/16309.

32. For more information, see http://www.aspencore.org/sitepages/pid45.php.

33. For more information, see http://apps.leg.wa.gov/billinfo/Summary.aspx?bill=5854&year=2009.

34. For more information, see http://www.coolroofs.org/codes_and_programs.html.

35. For more information, see http://egov.cityofchicago.org/webportal/COCWebPortal/COC _EDITORIAL/City_of_Chicago_Sustainable_Development_Policy_Matrix_1.pdf.

36. For more information, see http://www.smartcodecentral.org/module.html.

37. For more information, see http://www.kingcounty.gov/property/permits/codes/legislation/detail/ FormBasedCodeProject.aspx.

38. "City of Portland Proposed High Performance Green Building Policy" (December 4, 2008), http://www.portlandonline.com/osd/index.cfm?c=45879&.

39. For more information, see http://www.portlandonline.com/osd/index.cfm?c=45879&.

40. For more information, see http://www.chicagoclimateaction.org/.

41. J. W. Kandel, *Transformation and Multiple Equilibria* (report, California Energy Commission, 2002), 6.

42. S. J. Dubner and S. D. Levitt, "Unintended Consequences: The Case of the Red-cockaded Woodpecker," *New York Times Magazine*, January 20, 2008.

43. The Precautionary Principle was established in 1998 by a gathering of scientists, lawyers, environmental activists, and philosophers. The perspective emerges from the fact that most regulations focus on controlling damage rather than prevention and that policies do not sufficiently protect human and ecological health. For more information, see http://www.sehn.org/ppfaqs.html.

7. Measuring Program Impacts

1. J. Bagby, "What Is Performance Evaluation?" Seattle Public Utiliies training handout (2005).

2. Bagby, "What Is Performance Evaluation?"

3. Retrieved from Sustainable Measures, http://www.sustainablemeasures.com/.

4. For more information, see http://www.usgbc.org/LEED/Project/CertifiedProjectList.aspx.

5. "Kirkpatrick's Four Levels of Evaluation," *Encyclopedia of Educational Technology* (n.d.), http://coe.sdsu.edu/eet/articles/k4levels/index.htm.

6. For more information, see http://www.surveymonkey.com/.

7. D. L. Kirkpatrick *Evaluating Training Programs: The Four Levels* (San Francisco: Berrett-Koehler, 2006).

8. Paladino and Company, *LEED Certified Buildings in Seattle: Analysis and Projections* (Seattle: City of Seattle, 2006). To view the entire report, go to http://www.seattle.gov/dpd/GreenBuilding/

OurProgram/Resources/Specialreportspresentations/default.asp.

9. To access these as well as other cost benefit reports, see http://www.usgbc.org/DisplayPage.aspx
?CMSPageID=77#economic_analysis.

10. For more information, see http://www.energystar.gov/index.cfm?c=new_bldg_design
.bus_target_finder.

11. To access the online survey tool, see http://www.cbe.berkeley.edu/research/survey.htm.

12. For examples, see the appendices of the 2007 Annual Report at http://www.seattle.gov/dpd
/GreenBuilding/OurProgram/Resources/Specialreportspresentations/default.asp.

8. The Road Ahead for Green Building Programs

1. T. L. Friedman, "Kicking over the Chessboard," *New York Times Magazine*, April 18, 2004 .

2. R. Linden, "A Crisis Is a Terrible Thing to Waste," *Governing Magazine*, May 23, 2007. Russ Linden is also the author of *Seamless Government: A Practical Guide to Re-engineering in the Public Sector* (San Francisco: Jossey-Bass, 1994).

3. Urban Land Institute (ULI) and Pricewaterhouse Cooper, *Emerging Trends in Real Estate 2009* (report, ULI, 2009), http://www.uli.org/.

4. ULI and Pricewaterhouse Cooper, *Emerging Trends*.

5. J. Zeleny, "Evoking Lincoln, Obama Approaches His Inauguration by Train Ride," *New York Times*, January 18, 2009, A19.

6. For reference to the adopted legislation, and updates on related bills, see http://www.washingtonwatch.com/bills.

7. R. Ewing et al., *Growing Cooler: The Evidence on Urban Development and Climate Change* (Washington, DC: Urban Land Institute, 2008).

8. R. Florida, "How the Crash Will Reshape America," *Atlantic Monthly*, March 2009, http://www.theatlantic.com/doc/200903/meltdown-geography.

9. Florida, "How the Crash Will Reshape America."

10. U.S. General Accounting Office, *Physical Infrastructure: Crosscutting Issues Planning Conference Report* (2001), http://www.uli.org/ResearchandPublications.

11. See "Sustainability Guidelines for Gulf Coast Reconstruction" and "The New Orleans Principles" at http://green-reconstruction.buildinggreen.com/.

12. U.S. House of Representatives Committee on Appropriations, press release (February 13, 2009), http://appropriations.house.gov/pdf/PressSummary02-13-09.pdf.

13. U.S. House of Representatives Committee on Appropriations, press release.

14. U.S. House of Representatives Committee on Appropriations, press release.

15. For more information, see http://www.nrtsi.ca/.

16. See http://www.treepeople.org/.

17. M. Cooper, "Big Ideas, Grand Plans, Modest Budgets," *New York Times*, February 15, 2009, Week in Review, 6.

18. U.S. House of Representatives Committee on Appropriations, press release.

19. J. Gertner, "The Future Is Drying Up," *New York Times Magazine*, October 21, 2007.

20. *U.S. Green Building Council Strategic Plan 2009–2013* (Washington, DC: U.S. Green Building Council, 2009).

21. M. Lind, "The New Continental Divide," *Atlantic Monthly*, January/February 2003.

22. "Agriculture Is the New Golf," *New Urban News* 13, no. 8 (December 2008): 1, http://montgomeryfarm.com/index.php?option=com_content&task=view&id=127&Itemid=38.

23. J. Gertner, "Capitalism to the Rescue," *New York Times Magazine*, October 5, 2008, 61.

24. U.S. House of Representatives Committee on Appropriations, press release.

25. Gertner, "Capitalism to the Rescue," 83, quoting John Doerr, partner at Kleiner Perkins Caufield & Byers (http://www.kpcb.com/), which has backed Google, Amazon, Intuit, and other successful ventures that have created over 150,000 new jobs.

26. Gertner, "Capitalism to the Rescue," 57.

27. A sampling of the winning projects and runners-up can be found at http://www.metropolismag.com/nextgen.

28. T. Homer-Dixon, *The Upside of Down: Catastrophe, Creativity, and the Renewal of Civilization*

(Washington, DC: Island Press, 2006).

29. Homer-Dixon, *The Upside of Down*, 289.

Appendix A: Public Projects Green Building Portfolio

1. City Green Building Case Study, Carkeek Park Environmental Learning Center (2009).

2. H. Muschamp, "The Library That Puts on Fishnets and Hits the Disco," *New York Times*, May 16, 2004, Arts and Leisure, 1.

3. N. Post, "Seattle's Eccentric 'Book Behemoth' Shatters Stereotypes," *Engineering News Record*, November 3, 2003, 24.

4. Seattle Library press release (January 21, 2005), http://www.spl.org/lfa/LFApr/central/ACECaward.html.

5. North Cascades Institute mission statement (n.d.), http://www.ncascades.org/.

Appendix B: Green Building Certification Tools

1. American Institute of Architects, *Quantifying Sustainability: A Study of Three Sustainable Building Rating Systems and the AIA Position Statement* (AIA Sustainability Discussion Group, 2008), http://www.aia.org/aiaucmp/groups/aia/documents/pdf/aias076586.pdf.

2. American Institute of Architects, *Quantifying Sustainability*.

INDEX